A Long Journey

A LONG JOURNEY

The Autobiography of

PITIRIM A. SOROKIN

COLLEGE AND UNIVERSITY PRESS • New Haven, Conn.

Library of Congress Catalog Card Number: 63-17365

MANUFACTURED IN THE UNITED STATES OF AMERICA BY
UNITED PRINTING SERVICES, INC.
NEW HAVEN, CONN.

Contents

Chapter

Prologue

The Earliest Remembrance

A winter night. The room in a peasant house is poorly lighted by burning dry birch splinters* that fill the room with smoke and elusive shadows. I am in charge of replacing each burnt splinter in the forked iron holder that hangs from the ceiling.

A snowstorm howls outside. Inside, my mother lies on the floor of the room. She is motionless and strangely silent. Nearby, my older brother and a peasant woman are busily occupied. Father is away, looking for work in other villages. I do not understand exactly what has happened but I sense it is something catastrophic and irreparable. I am no longer as cold and hungry as I was a short time ago; yet I suddenly feel crushed, lonely, and lost. Howling storm, fugitive shadows, and the words "died" and "death," uttered by my brother, and "poor, poor orphans," mumbled by the peasant woman, deepen my sorrow. I wish father were here, but he is not, and we don't know when he will return.

Next I recall the funeral service in the village church. My mother lies in a coffin as my father, brother, and the villagers silently stand with candles in their hands, and the priest, the deacon, and the reader intone funeral prayers and perform the last rites. I do not understand the words, but the "dust to dust" and the gesture of the priest throwing a handful of earth into the coffin are impressed on my memory.

With the funeral service over, the coffin is placed upon a sleigh to be driven to the cemetery. My brother and I are

* The ordinary source of light for peasants of northern Russia at that time was thin dry birch splinters about three feet long. They were pressed into a forked iron holder. Each splinter burned about two or three minutes and then had to be replaced by another. Kerosene, oil, and electricity came into use much later.

seated upon the coffin. Father, priest, and villagers walk behind the sleigh. The snow glistens brilliantly under the cold, blue, and sunny sky. After some time—I do not remember why—my brother and I leap down from the coffin and walk home. Arriving there, we climb up and lie down upon the "polati" (a sleeping loft in peasant houses of northern Russia). We are silent and subdued. . . .

* * *

This is my earliest memory. I was then about three years old. Of my life before this death scene, I remember nothing.

PART ONE

PART ONE

CHAPTER ONE

Background and Early Childhood

My mother's death marks the beginning of my conscious recollection. The scene is still vividly etched in my memory but, like a solitary monument on a vast prairie, it stands apart from all subsequent events. Although I do not remember the events immediately following this tragic prologue to the drama of my life, the subsequent years, remain quite clear.

The drama begins in northern Russia, in Yarensky County of Vologda Province, among the Komi or Syrian people—one of the Ugro-Finnish branches of the family of man. There, in Turya village I was born on January 21, 1889. There, in Kokvitzy village my mother died, probably in 1892 or 1893. And there, in this vast region I lived the first ten years of my life.

The area consisted mainly of a primeval forest stretching for hundreds of miles in all directions. As yet it was unspoiled by "civilization." Like small islands in a sea, the villages and hamlets of the Komi people were lost in its vast spaces. Two great rivers, Vychegda and Pechora, with their tributaries, ran their crystal-clear waters through the forest realm. Their effervescent flow was bounded by fine sandy beaches, steep hills, fragrant meadows, and trees and bushes growing down to the very edge of their banks. Widely scattered streams playfully raced their capricious course among the trees; and placid lakes, ponds, and swamps lay in the recesses of this green kingdom.

A variety of trees and bushes, but primarily pine and spruce, grew in the forest. Especially magnificent were its tall, slender pines. On earth covered by beautiful white moss (*yagel*), thousands of these pines rose like the most wondrous spires ascending to the sky in columns, now silent and mysterious as though lost in prayer, now roaring and agitated as though fighting their raging enemies. Many and many an hour I spent in these cathedrals of nature, fascinated by their majesty, their mystery, and their God-given beauty. They fired my imagination, infected me with their changing moods, and conveyed to me their mysterious messages.

The forest abounded with a variety of animals, from prosaic squirrels, rabbits, and foxes to graceful deer and meditative bears. A rich variety of birds filled it with enchanting music. The rivers, streams, and ponds were enlivened with fish of different sorts, including *sterliad* (the finest variety of sturgeon) and trout. No snakes, however, lived in this vast region. (This fact perhaps explains my strong aversion to poisonous and non-poisonous snakes when, later on, I happened to live in places marred by their presence.)

The forest was inexhaustibly rich in its ever-changing appearance and moods. On windless days, all was serenity, mystery, and motionless silence. And in stormy weather all was thundering and furious motion. It was an endless, colorful, fragrant ocean in the summer and a boundless, sparkling whiteness in the sunny days of the winter. Cheerful and serene in the daytime, its "face" would turn somber and terrifying at night.

I am glad I lived my early life in this virgin land. Even now, if I were given a choice, I would not trade it for the most civilized environment in the finest residential district of the finest city in the world. I feel lucky to have had an opportunity to live and to grow in this elemental realm of nature before it was blighted by industrialization and urbanization.

The Komi comprised my social and cultural environment. They numbered about 180,000 at that time.* Physically they were a tall, strong, and healthy people; racially, a mixture of the Alpine, the Nordic, and some Asiatic racial types; lin-

* A detailed anthropological, ethnographic, and sociological study of the Komi people can be found in a series of my articles: "Sovremennuie Syriane" (Contemporary Syrians), "Evolutzia semiy i braka u syrian" (Evolution of the Family and Marriage of Syrians), "Perejitki animisma

guistically, they had their own language, related to the Ugro-Finnish, and almost all the Komi spoke Russian as their second language. In literacy they occupied third place among the numerous peoples of Russia (the Russian Germans and Jews occupying first and second places). They subsisted chiefly by farming, supplemented by hunting, trapping, lumbering, and fishing. Their standard of living was higher than that of the rest of the Russian population. Industrialization and urbanization had not as yet invaded their way of life. In the entire region of the Komi, there was hardly a single factory or mill or city. Only Ust Sysolsk, a town of some two thousand people, functioned as the administrative, commercial, and cultural center.

The villages and hamlets of the Komi were situated for the most part on the banks of the rivers. In the summertime these rivers were used as channels for travel and transportation from settlement to settlement. Besides the waterways there were, of course, a few dirt roads and paths connecting village to village. The houses of the Komi were strung along both sides of the roads, stretching in large villages for a few miles, in small ones for shorter distances. Fields, meadows, and pastures were adjacent to the houses. Beyond these clearings the vast forest surrounded each settlement.

Peasant houses were large and built with very heavy logs. The houses usually consisted of two spacious rooms (one for summer, the other for winter living), a cellar, two storerooms, storage space for hay and grain, and a barn for cattle. Separate from the house were a bath or steam-house and an ice-house for keeping meat, fish, milk, and preserves. The houses of village intelligentsia and dignitaries—the clergyman, teacher, medical practitioner, storekeeper, village policemen (*uriadnik* and *pristav*), village-chairman (*starshina*) and clerk—were more comfortable and "modern."

u zyrian" (Survivals of Animism among Syrians), and others, published in the *Isvestia Arkhangelskago Obschestva po Izucheniu Russkago Severa* (Journal of the Archangels Society for a Study of the Russian North), 1910, 1911, 1912.

In each village a church dominated all the other buildings. Its spire and blue cupolas soared far above the settlement, and its whitewashed brick edifice with green roofs was visible from a distance of several miles. In the vicinity of the church were grouped public buildings, school, village-hall, and library.

The Komi were Russian Orthodox but along with their Christian faith they still maintained many beliefs, legends, and rituals of their pre-Christian, pagan religion. Each religion assimilated certain beliefs and practices of the other, resulting in a "paganized Christianity" or "Christianized paganism." However, there was no conflict or "cold war" between the elements of the two religions nor between the few sectarian believers in evangelical simplicity, peace, and non-violent resistance to evil. The basis of this "peaceful coexistence" was a commonly held conviction that the whole world is one living unity and that "Truth is one, but men call it by different names." Throughout all the years of my life among the Komi people, I do not remember a single case of religious intolerance or individual persecution.

The morality and mores of the Komi communities were rooted in the precepts of the Golden Rule, the Ten Commandments, and mutual aid. These moral principles were regarded as God-given, unconditionally binding upon all. As such they were not only preached but widely practiced. The same applied to the common law of peasants. The norms of this law were not so much recorded in the court-books as they were in the hearts and actions of my neighbors. They were obeyed not through fear of punishment but as deeply internalized "categorical imperatives." The houses of peasants did not have locks because there were no thieves. Serious crimes occurred rarely, if at all; even misdemeanors were few. Mutual aid was a daily routine which permeated the life of the community.

Politically and socially the Komi people never knew slavery or serfdom. They were always free and managed their local affairs autonomously through a direct self-government similar to the German *Gemeinschaft* or to the Russian *mir* and *obschina*. The village communities held their land in common possession; it was equitably distributed and redistributed among the individual families according to their size and their increase or decrease in the course of time. A *Gemeinschaft* spirit of mutual aid was still vigorous in my time, manifesting itself in many forms of collective activities within the whole village community. These conditions prevented the development of discernible inequities and sharp economic, political, and social stratification. There were neither notably rich, privileged, and "superior" nor particularly poor, "inferior," and disfranchised strata. Even the status of the sexes was essentially equal. As a result there was no "class-struggle" and no crystallized political parties of vested interests. The function of the county elective authorities (*semstvo*) consisted mainly in building schools, medical centers, and cultural institutions. The control of the central Czarist government was also limited.

Living and growing up in this type of community, I naturally absorbed its beliefs, moral precepts, and mores—its spirit of equalitarian independence, self-reliance, and mutual aid.

As for the esthetic climate of the Komi people, their world of beauty consisted, first, of the beautiful world of nature: huge rivers and lakes uncontaminated, as yet, by industrial and urban pollutions; endless forests, flowering meadows and fields surrounding each village in the summer; vast expanses of pure snow in the winter; and almost always a blue and cloudless sky with brilliant stars at night.

The realm of wild animals provided another aspect of this esthetic world. Swimming and fishing in clear rivers and lakes, hunting and observing animal life and the ever-changing natural scenery, and living and working amidst this natural splendor were a constant source of recreation and esthetic enjoyment to Komi peasants.

Their esthetic life was enhanced by a man-made world of fairy-tales, legends, myths, folksongs, pageants, village festivals, dances, and colorful rites attending birth, death, marriage, and other events of human life. Though the Komi had at that time only the beginnings of a written literature, their folk-literature of fairy-tales, legends, and stories was rich and very fascinating. This also applied to their folksongs and folk music, which were as yet unspoiled by the later invasion of vulgar, urban pseudo-music and "songless songs" (*chastushki*). The old folksongs and folk-literature of the Ugro-Finnish peoples were still alive in this region and adjacent areas whence they were collected by eminent Russian scholars and composers such as Rimski-Korsakov, Mussorgski, Tchaikovsky, Kastalski, and others. This explains why, when I later heard for the first time the music of these composers and also of Bach, Handel, Haydn, Mozart, and Beethoven, some of their tunes sounded familiar to me. I had heard them from the Komi peasants. They sang these melodies during their collective fishing and harvesting tasks or at their communal festivities and gatherings on winter evenings.

The Russian Orthodox religion, with its impressive rituals, sacred music, colorful processions, and profound mysteries, was an important aspect of the peasants' esthetic life. The village church served as their theater and concert hall. Here they actively participated in staging the immortal liturgical tragedy of the *agnus Dei qui tollis peccata mundi,* or the drama of a solemn funeral service, or the cheerful consecration of baptism and marriage, or the mysteries of confession and communion, redemption and resurrection. In church they enjoyed the deeply moving sacred music, listened to recitals of the sublime poetry of prayers, and took part in other religious pageants. In these and other ways, religion and church played an important role in their lives—one no less significant than any great theater plays in the lives of its urban devotees.

The Komi had a vigorous esthetic culture which ennobled and enriched the soul of these people. It also beautified my own existence and perceptibly shaped my esthetic tastes for the rest of my life.

Such, in brief, was the social and cultural milieu of my early years.

Except for her death, I do not remember anything about my mother. Later, from my father, relatives, and neighbors I learned that she had been a handsome and fine person. She was a Komi peasant girl. Her beauty and integrity possibly explain why my father married her; why, after her death, he never remarried and remained faithful to her to the end of his life; and why, after her death, he began to drown his sorrow in vodka, eventually to become a chronic alcoholic. "Her death turned me into a lonely, broken reed," he used to complain in his semi-drunken state.

A love that transcends the death of the beloved and endures to the end of the lover's life is a rarity today. Many modern sophisticates regard it as something primitive, antiquated, and irrational. Yet transcendent love has been, and still is, the finest, the holiest and most beautiful ideal in human life—truly immortal and sublime. My elder brother and I instinctively felt that this faithful love excused our father's alcoholism and somehow edified our own lives by its ineffable grace. (In this fact possibly lies the germ of my subsequent dislike of all forms of *unjustified* disloyalty in marriage or in other personal relationships.)

My father was a Russian, born and trained in Veliki Ustyug. This ancient city played an important cultural, religious, and political role in the history of this part of Russia. Among other things it was a center of several arts and crafts. My father served his apprenticeship in one of these artisan guilds. His guild diploma and his signboard, blue with gold letters, solemnly certified that "Alexander Prokopievitch Sorokin is a master of golden, silver and ikon ornamental works (*solotyikh, serebriannyikh i chekannyikh del master*)."

I do not know how and why he moved from Ustyug to settle in the Komi region. Perhaps a scarcity of his type of artisan and therefore less competition in the Komi territory prompted his migration; perhaps he was attracted by the natural environment and the characteristics of the Komi people. Whatever the reasons, he never returned to Veliki Ustyug.

I know little about my father's life before the death of my mother. From my aunts, clergy, and peasants I heard that he was a real master of his craft, reliable and honest, reasonably successful in his business, respected as a good and intelligent person, happy in his family life, and that he showed no signs of alcoholic addiction. After the death of my mother, I lived with my father until I was eleven years old. In the course of these seven years of a *conscious, remembered* life, I had two conflicting images of father as a sober parent and as a drunken souse. The sober father was a wonderful person, affectionate and protective, friendly to all neighbors, industrious and honest in his work, and diligent in instructing us in the skill of his craft, in the moral precepts, and in the three *R*'s. His habitual greeting, rather than the usual "How do you do," was "Christ is risen." "Good Lord, I try to do my best; the rest is up to You" was his maxim in regard to his work and his dictum in regard to any constructive activity. "Even the good Lord cannot demand more than that from you or anyone else." "One son is no son; two sons are a half-son; three sons are a son," he would say to those who asked him about the number of his children. He accepted the principal dogmas and myths of the Russian Orthodox religion but did not regularly attend religious services.

"Why should I? I am in the house of God most of my working time. By my honest work there I do my praying and conversing with the Lord. By my good deeds I do His will. The mere presence of a priest and deacon does not make my prayers or deeds holier or purer."

For similar reasons he did not insist upon our regular attendance at church services if we did not want to go. On the other hand if we perpetrated some mischief which violated traditional moral precepts, he strongly reprimanded us and persuasively showed us the stupidity and harmfulness of our misbehavior.

He had great pride in his craftsmanship and he felt disappointed when his work did not come up to his expected high standards. "Monkey's craftsmanship" he derisively called it.

"Don't you ever do this in any important work of yours." Whenever my brother or I accomplished our assignments well, he rejoiced with us at a task well done; and whenever we did the work poorly, he upbraided us for our negligence. This image of sober father still lives in my memory as a warm and fine recollection.

Unfortunately the stretches of sobriety, lasting for weeks and even months, were followed by periods of drunkenness. Sometimes his drunkenness resulted in *delirium tremens*. I well remember a typical incident. Both of us were lying on the floor, I in a high fever from some illness (medical help was rarely available for us), my father in his *delirium tremens*. He suddenly sat up on his straw mat, pointed at the big brick stove, and began to scream about horrible devils coming out of it, dancing around him and making faces at him. "Christ is risen, Christ is risen," he muttered repeatedly, his incoherent utterances accompanied by jerky and convulsive motions. I do not remember how long this convulsion continued nor how it ended because I also succumbed to delirium of a non-alcoholic nature from my high fever.

In his drunken periods he became depressed, irritable, tearful, and self-pitying over his lonely life of "a broken reed." Infrequently, he became violent during a fit of irritation. In one such outburst, enraged at us for some reason or other, he snatched a nearby hammer and with it struck my brother's arm and my upper lip. Fortunately the blows were light. Nevertheless, they benumbed my brother's arm for several days and slightly misshaped my upper lip for many years. This attack occurred when I was ten and Vassiliy (my older brother) was fourteen years old. Deeply offended by this unusual violence, we left father the next day and started our independent careers as itinerant artisans. We moved from village to village in one region, while father shifted about in another. We never met again. About one year later, he died in a village quite distant from the village where we were. Due to the poor means of communication we didn't learn of his death until several weeks later. Blessed be his soul! He died a very lonely man just as he had lived, after mother's death, a very lonesome life. Despite his alcoholism, his image as a sober, good father overwhelmingly prevailed while we were living together, and it still prevails in my memory up to the present time. Even in his drunken state he had nothing in common with the Freudian "father-tyrant" who is insensitive and cruel to his children. With the exception of his alcoholic interludes, which fortunately were shorter than his sober periods, our family—father, elder brother, and myself (my younger brother, Prokopiy, lived with our aunt and her husband)—was a good and harmonious team bound together by warm mutual love, common joys and sorrows, and modestly creative work. All in all, I remember these years of my life as being happy and adventurous despite the starvation and other physical hardships which occasionally fell upon us during father's alcoholic periods. After all, man lives not by bread alone, and life is infinitely richer than its temporary physical comforts or discomforts.

My elder brother, Vassiliy, was older than I by some four years. During our years of living together, he proved himself a man of energy, resourcefulness, and initiative. In painting ikons and sculpturing their metallic covers as well as in "scholastic intelligence" I soon surpassed him. But he certainly was the leader in other lines of activity, especially in acquiring and conducting our work, in performing household chores, and in providing some means of subsistence during father's alcoholic spells. As a business-leader he was pre-eminently successful during some two years of our independent work after we left father. Although only fourteen years old, he somehow managed to obtain commissions for painting and decorating churches—even a big cathedral in the town of Yarensk—for gilding and silvering ikons, candelabras, and other church objects, for making copper, silver, or gold ikon covers (*riza*), not to mention his finding some jobs in school buildings or private houses of village intelligentsia and peasants. He must have had some special talent to be able to entice the heads of these institutions to entrust this sort of work to a teen-age boy. And yet he succeeded in these tasks about as well as father had. Without his leadership I would not have ventured to leave father and certainly could not have earned a living as an itinerant artisan. With Vassiliy's business acumen, we made a good team, each of us acting as his brother's keeper and doing his work according to his ability.

After nearly two years of living and working together, we parted because of my entrance into "normal" school and, after graduation, into a teachers' school. For some time Vassiliy, alone, continued our work among the Komi people. Unfortunately our separation made him a lonely man. Chronic shifting from village to village gave him neither an opportunity to establish close friendships with the village neighbors nor a settled way of life. Because of this, he began to find solace in vodka and in the somewhat erratic life of a village "beatnik." With this deterioration, his work and earnings began to dwindle. Eventually, disgusted with this sort of life, he decided to leave the Komi region and to move to St. Petersburg. For several years he lived there and earned his living as a factory hand, craftsman, salesman, and clerk. After my arrival in St. Petersburg, we used to meet frequently and to share our scanty resources. This arrangement lasted for a year or more. These meetings, unfortunately, were abruptly ended by his arrest and banishment to Siberia for his revolutionary activities. In St. Petersburg during the years of 1905-7, he, like myself and many others, became "infected" with revolutionary ideas and aspirations. His subversiveness was soon detected by the Czarist secret police. Eventually they arrested him, and in "an administrative way," without due process of law, he was banished to Siberia for many years. Like all political prisoners, at the beginning of the Revolution of 1917 he was liberated by the Kerensky government.

After the establishment of the Communist government, he participated in anti-Communist activities. In the fall of 1918, on the Arkhangelsk-Ustyug front during the civil war, he was captured and shot by Communist executioners. Thus his adventurous and eventful—although not too happy—life was ended. *Lux perpetua luceat ei.*

My younger brother Prokopiy did not live with us. After mother's death, he was taken by her elder sister Anissya and her husband, Vassiliy Ivanovitch Rymskikh. They lived in a small hamlet, Rymia, on the shore of the Vychegda River.

Having no children of their own, they raised Prokopiy and treated the three of us as their own sons. In times of emergency, especially during father's alcoholic periods, Vassiliy and I quite frequently would seek refuge and always find shelter, food, and loving care in their peasant house. We often stayed with them for several weeks at a time. They heartily shared their simple means with us. On our part, we helped them in their daily work, and we felt and behaved toward them as did the sons of Rymia peasants toward their parents. In our nomadic life with father, this hamlet, Rymia, became "our little Fatherland"; the house of Anissya and her husband was our real "home," and our aunt and uncle "our family." We stayed more frequently and longer in Rymia than in any other village of the Komi region. Instead of being just "migrants and strangers," as we were in many villages, in Rymia we were regular members of the community, fully sharing the life of its children and feeling and being treated as "Rymia boys." This explains why Rymia occupies such a prominent place in my life and memory.

Despite their illiteracy, both Aunt Anissya and Uncle Vassiliy were friendly, intelligent, honest, and industrious people, at peace with the world, their neighbors, and themselves. In modern terms, they would be considered well-integrated individuals free from envy, resentment, depressive moods, and other psychoneuroses. Uncle was a red-haired, wide-shouldered, strongly built man. At the end of the agricultural season, he spent the greater part of each fall and winter away from home in the vast forest, hunting, trapping, and fishing in order to increase his income. This outdoor life stamped him with the robustness of "a forest man." He intimately knew vast areas of the forest, the habits, behavior, and tracks of animals, the streams and ponds rich with fish, and the secret life of the forest kingdom. He considered himself a living part of the tremendous kingdom inhabited not only by ordinary creatures but also by fantastic beings like "the master-spirit of forests" (*leschiy*), and by a legion of other "spirits" of the skies, swamps, lakes, winds, snow, night, and so on. For him they were almost as real as actual living beings. He told us many stories about his encounters and experiences with these spirits. At heart a poet of nature, he loved this mysterious kingdom and admired its inscrutable beauty.

In Rymia and surrounding villages he was called "*tun*" or "*koldun*" (wise man, medicine man, or shaman). This reputation was probably due to his uncanny ability to fix all sorts of dislocated joints. Knowing nothing about human anatomy, he somehow manipulated the dislocated parts and invariably succeeded in putting them back in their proper place. He never charged any of his numerous patients for this service and never boasted about his "God-given" talent. As a real artist he enjoyed this osteopathic activity for its own sake.

He was a taciturn man. When he spoke, his speech was laconic and direct. Once I became enbroiled in a fight with my brother Vassiliy. Sitting on the front steps, Uncle imperturbably watched our fight. Dear Aunt Anissya became quite agitated and tried to stop us. "Woman, never interfere with the fight of two crazy dogs," was his only reaction to the whole incident. His somewhat stern appearance concealed a stout heart and sensitive nature. When once I became sick with pneumonia, he and Anissya tirelessly nursed me for many days and nights.

I spent many a day and night with him in his hunting and trapping treks through the vast forest, accompanied him in his fishing trips for *sterliad* and trout, and helped him in his farming. Not only did he teach me the techniques of agricultural and forest work, but he also initiated me into the secret lore of the forest: everything from the intricacies of fishing for *sterliad* to the kinds and properties of the fantastic spirits of the woods, lakes, rivers, and even houses.

I still vividly remember the last moments of his life. Together with other peasants of Rymia, during the spring-flood of the Vychegda, he used to take the temporary job of floating big rafts made of heavy timber cut in the forest down the Vychegda and Dwina rivers to Arkhangelsk. Each crew guided its raft down the rivers to prevent it from being broken by storms and from becoming grounded in shallow places or on the shores. It usually took three or four weeks to float a raft from Rymia to Arkhangelsk. That spring when he returned, he had contracted dysentery somewhere on the journey. For a few days his sickness turned from bad to worse. Finally, he was "told" by one of "the spirits" that his death was imminent. On one sunny afternoon he dragged himself from his bed to the front entrance of the house. There he stood silently for a few moments and then quietly said: "Want to have a last look at the blue sky, silvery river, and the trees and meadows. And to say my last goodby to the world and to all of you. Farewell!"

The next morning he died. Though illiterate, this "*tun*" and "forest man" was a natural philosopher, poet of nature, and a truly good man. *Requiem eternam* to him!

Dynamic and energetic in her household duties and agricultural work, Aunt Anissya took an active role in the Rymia community life in addition to concerning herself untiringly with our needs. She clothed and fed us and always had time to rejoice with us in our pleasures, console us in our sorrows, admonish us for our misdeeds, and encourage us in our worthy achievements. She was indeed a tender, loving, and beloved mother to us. Without her love and care, the world would probably have been a much colder and less friendly place to live, and our character development would undoubtedly have proceeded along coarser, more aggressive lines.

For many years after Uncle's death, and only with Prokopiy's help, she had to do all the agricultural and other chores of a small peasant farm and household. And she valiantly did this until her death at the age of eighty-nine or ninety. I continued to visit her and stay with her for many years after the death of her husband. Her modest log cabin continued to be my "home" even in the later years of my student days at the Teachers' School, the Psycho-Neurological Institute, and the University of St. Petersburg. During many a summer vacation I used to spend a month or more with her. During such "vacations" in Rymia, I naturally assisted her in agricultural and other labors. Fortunately for me, during these later years I was able to help her in a modest financial way—thus "repaying" an infinitesimal fraction of the unbounded love she showered upon me and my brothers. Deprived of our real mother at an early age, we had found a wonderful mother in dear Aunt Anissya.

For this reason I cannot say that my childhood was without the ineffable grace of warm motherly love.

As mentioned previously, after mother's death, at the age of one year or so, Prokopiy was taken by and lived with our aunt and uncle. They reared him as all Rymia peasant children were reared. Somehow he learned reading, writing, and arithmetic. During our frequent stays in Rymia, all three of us learned to know each other well and became real brothers. In his appearance and character Prokopiy was more a peasant and less "sophisticated" than his itinerant brothers. From us, however, he learned much of the people, mores, and life of the wider world beyond the boundaries of Rymia and its adjacent regions. Honest, friendly, and reliable, he lived the life and performed the tasks of a Rymia peasant youth under the guidance of our uncle and aunt. He continued to live such a life after Uncle's death until he was drafted into the Russian army and sent to a Russian city for his military service. There he came into contact with "the civilized world" and, among other things, learned the skills of a bookkeeper, clerk, and salesman. After termination of his service, and with the full approval of Anissya, he took a salesman-bookkeeper position with a merchant firm in Veliki Ustyug. There he lived with another aunt, Anna, a sister of our father, and her husband Mikhail Drankovsky. They even formally adopted him as their son. There also he eventually married and had two children. His life continued in the orderly and satisfactory fashion of a regular bookkeeper-salesman until the Communist

Revolution. When the Communist regime was established in Veliki Ustyug, he was arrested—partly for some of his "subversive" activities, but mainly for "guilt by association," being a brother of "Communist Enemy No. 1," as I was then declared by the local Communist authorities. Prokopiy's health, not too good at that time, was rapidly destroyed by the truly inhuman conditions of Ustyug's Communist prison (in which I was also imprisoned and condemned to death). A few months after his arrest he died in prison.

Thus both my brothers perished in the Russian Revolution. I do not know where they are buried, just as I do not know where the unmarked graves of my father and mother are. To deepen my sorrow, on many a Memorial Day I desired to but could not visit their graves prayerfully to thank them for the full and joyful life they gave to me during our years together. My only consolation is that they still live vividly in my memory and are still cherished and blessed not only on Memorial Day but on many days in the late afternoon of my long life-journey. *Requiem eternam* to their immortal souls!

Such in brief were the natural, the social, and the family circumstances of my early years.

CHAPTER TWO

Early Itinerant Life

Arrivals and Departures

Our life with father was nomadic. As soon as our work in one village was finished we had to move on to another. If, during our stay in a village, father secured an engagement in another village, we migrated there. If such an engagement could not be arranged, we moved to a settlement where we hoped to find employment. Sometimes our expectations were realized, sometimes they were not. In the latter case, with a heavy heart, we had to drift from village to village until some job was found. Most of our moves were made in hired peasant carts. Our scanty belongings and working tools were packed into one cart while we climbed into the other. Sometimes, when we moved to a hamlet for a "small job" or when father did not have money to hire horses, we walked, carrying with us a minimum of tools and a few clothes.

During the years of our itinerancy we visited and worked in many villages and hamlets. We crossed and recrossed the entire Komi region several times. Despite some rewards, this nomadic existence had its physical and psychological hardships. Often, when the distance from village to village was considerable, we had to spend the night on the road without any (or sufficient) food. Since villages had no public eating places, we frequently could not even buy food from the peasants. In the winter we often were half-frozen in our inadequate clothing.

Perhaps even more trying was the psychological pain involved in these "departures" and "arrivals." Most of the departures took place when, after staying weeks in a village, we had just established good, friendly relationships with its children and adults, when we had begun to feel "at home" in the village and had graduated from the position of "passing strangers" to that of regular members of the community. Each departure meant an abrupt separation from all our newly acquired friends and a shocking break of all warm and affectionate ties. It signified a return to the homeless and rootless existence of nomadic wanderers. These pains of departure were intensified by those of our arrivals, by our feelings of insecurity and our apprehensions at coming into a new village. How would they treat us? Would they be friendly or hostile? Would we find work there? Would we secure lodging and food? This sort of anxiety, combined with our sense of psycho-social isolation in not belonging to the community, was trying indeed. Later, as a sociologist, I learned that such conditions lead to so-called "anomic" suicide and other mental disorders. I well remember how depressing these departures and arrivals were, and how, on several occasions, while alone, I unashamedly wept, lamenting these sudden separations from friends and the regression to the life of a rootless stranger.

Along with these pains, however, our itinerancy did have its happy moments. In our travels we fully enjoyed ever-changing beautiful scenery, observed animal life, breathed the fragrance of forest and meadows, swam and fished in clear streams, and spent nights around a campfire. Under the starry sky we lived the exciting life of outdoorsmen at its roughest and best. In this life of chronic mobility, there was no boredom from a day-in, day-out monotonous routine.

Our life was a continuous stream of meeting and dealing with new people, new situations, and new mores. In this sense it was the best school for mental and moral development; its lessons of direct experience were more effective and instructive than all lessons taught in formal schools. From this school of direct life-experience I acquired more basic knowledge of the psycho-social world than from all the books I read and all the lectures I attended, and it disciplined my character more efficaciously than all the training later received in various schools. Despite its hardships, our nomadic life had its joys, variety, and thrills. Like the life of Huckleberry Finn, it was richer than the lives of many urban children who are confined to a narrow experience in their passage from nursery school to college, and especially than the lives of children in the slums of our heartless cities.

After arriving in a new village, father first used to go to the priest to find out whether or not there was work to be done in the village church. If he was lucky enough to contract a substantial job, we settled down in the village for several weeks, even for a few months, depending upon the extent of the work.

We usually lodged in a rented "half" of a peasant house. Our simple fare was prepared mostly by ourselves, sometimes by a peasant woman. In more affluent times we had enough food to keep body and soul together. During periods of unemployment we starved. I must have suffered from malnutrition, as evidenced by my "rickety legs" which have remained slightly deformed from those days.

Our work was done mainly for village churches. A large portion of our time was spent in, around, and upon church buildings, painting their interiors and exteriors, silvering and gilding their cult-objects, painting and making *rizas*—metallic relief covers for ikons. As most work, these jobs had their pleasures, drudgery, and dangers. I disliked whitewashing and painting high and spacious church ceilings. To accomplish these tasks I had to remain in various strained positions for hours, with whitewash or paint dripping onto my face and falling into my eyes and ears. In addition I had to be on guard against falling from the narrow boards of primitive scaffolding or from a rickety, high ladder. Later, when I read how Michelangelo painted his immortal frescoes on the ceiling of the Sistine Chapel, I sympathized with the extraordinary physical exertions he had to endure to accomplish this gigantic task.

However, I liked to paint or gild spires, domes, and roofs of the churches on the sunny summer days when such work was usually undertaken. Perched on top of the building (and most of the Komi churches were some 100 to 250 feet high), caressed by the gentle wind, I had the boundless blue sky above me and a beautiful view of the countryside, with its villages, fields, streams, and lakes surrounded by the endless, colorful forest! Working under these conditions was not tedious. Such labor served as a splendid recreation.

Of all the varieties of our jobs I particularly enjoyed painting ikons and making *rizas.* The *riza,* made of copper or silver plates, reproduced in relief a painted picture on an ikon, with the exception of the face, hands, and feet of its divine or saintly images. Designing and painting ikons and making *rizas* required great skill and creativity. Especially complex was the process of fashioning an artistic relief of the ikon-picture out of a thin copper or silver plate. First, the plate was plastered to the surface of a special wooden frame with a warmed, softened, and evenly spread mixture of tar and pitch. Then an outline of the figure of the ikon-saint and background was made upon the plate. Then a rough "negative" form of the picture was indented upon the metallic sheet by expertly hammering it with many small spikes containing different head-shapes (*tchekans*). When the "negative" of the *riza* was done, the plate was turned over on the tar framework for a fine elaboration of its "positive" relief. At this stage, every detail of the saints' images—their posture, the position of their arms, their vestments with all their folds and pleats, and every detail of the background—had to be "sculptured" into their finished polished and natural forms. This was accomplished by a skillful use of the *tchekans* and hammers. When the relief of the *riza* was finished, it was washed, silvered or gilded, then polished, and, finally, carefully nailed to the ikon.

From this description one can see that the art of making a fine *riza* required the combined skills of an expert designer, engraver, embosser, and sculptor. The creative nature of this art explains my particular satisfaction in making *rizas* and possibly my rapid progress in this difficult craft. After a few years of working with father and Vassiliy I became the best ikon designer, painter, and *riza* maker of our family team. When a more eminent craftsman in this field saw samples of my work, he offered me an apprenticeship for the further development of my talent. This offer was gratefully declined; nevertheless, this craftmanship at an early age developed my sense of line, color, and form, and evidently inspired my lifelong interest in painting, sculpture, and architecture.

As a matter of curiosity, I now have a great desire to see some of my *rizas* and ikon-paintings to appraise them with the tired eyes of a septegenarian. I doubt, however, that they survived the holocaust of the Russian Revolution, and to this day, since my banishment, I have not had the opportunity to return to the Komi region. Perhaps it is better that this curiosity of mine remain unsatisfied: its satisfaction may have only sentimental value, and in this heartless atomic age sentimental values, we are told, have no value at all.

Together with these joys our labor had its drudgery and perils. Once, painting the steep iron roof of a church, I carelessly painted it around myself. As I walked toward the unpainted part, I began to slide down to the edge of the roof some hundred feet above ground. I shouted for help and, with all the strength in my fingers, gripped the slightly protruding joints of the roof's iron sheets. This desperate grip braked my slide and gave Vassiliy a chance to throw me a rope. I grabbed it and was pulled out of the painted circle. If Vassiliy and the rope had not happened to be nearby and if he had hesitated momentarily in throwing the rope, my life would probably have ended then and there.

On another occasion Vassiliy and I, with two helpers, were lifting and tying heavy, long ladders to the spire of a cathedral in Yarensk. This operation generally was one of the most dangerous phases of our work, especially in a church with a narrow, steep roof at the base of a steeple or dome, on which a ladder had to be placed and then safely tied to the tapering cone. Engrossed in this difficult task, we failed to notice a storm gathering until its violent blasts, thunder, and lightning suddenly burst upon us. Fierce squalls felled our ladders, not yet securely fastened, and stranded us on a narrow ledge open to all the assaults of nature's fury. We desperately clutched a strong rope previously tied around the spire's foundation and clung to the structure as closely as possible. This saved us from being swept down. When the storm was over, with the help of the townspeople we were safely freed from our precarious perch.

These and other occupational hazards, however, were well compensated for by the aforementioned joys and beneficial habits acquired from our work. To this day, at the age of seventy-four, I can still easily climb a ladder to the tops of tall trees in my garden and without dizziness or discomfort perform the various ministrations of "tree surgeon" and gardener.

Like our work, our other activities in the villages were absorbing and eventful. After a few days of settling in a village we would become acquainted with the peasants and the village intelligentsia—the clergy, teacher, medical practitioner, storekeeper, village chief, clerk, and constable. In a short time Vassiliy and I became friendly with the village children and as their regular companions took an active part in their games and activities.

At the moment of writing these lines, the images of these playmates suddenly arise and silently pass in my memory. What a motley crowd these fugitive visions make! Here is Vaska, "the judge," good-natured and fair referee of our games and conflicts. . . . And here is Grishka, "the simpleton." Dressed only in a long burlap shirt, this giant is the strongest and at the same time the most gentle boy in our company. Despite his undeveloped mind and his physical strength, he hardly ever quarrels with anybody and even avoids killing bothersome flies and mosquitoes. He is a prototype of the Simpleton in the last scene of Moussorgsky's *Boris Godunov*. I wish there were many more simpleton-Grishkas in this murderous world of ours! Perhaps they are better fit to establish a lasting peace than the supposedly sane leaders of the great nuclear empires! . . . Here comes Petka, "the singer." Graced with a good voice, he likes to indulge in singing at every available moment. Then here is Vanka, "the bully" a quarrelsome and overbearing son of a village official. Well I remember him. Once when I was returning home from my work in the village church he taunted me with insulting remarks. I answered his insults by pushing him from my path and then, in the ensuing fight, gave him a good thrashing. Crying, he retreated and fled. Next day, while I was going to work, his mother—the "village lady" —stopped me and threatened to have me arrested for attacking her dear boy. Then and there, for the first time, I suddenly felt myself a "proletarian" unjustly oppressed by the privileged class. I revolted and, instead of offering an apology, I indignantly told the lady that if her "dear boy" insulted me again I would thrash him even more thoroughly, arrest or no arrest. There were no punitive consequences to my encounter with Vanka, but after this incident he never tried to bully me again.

With the other boys and girls of the village intelligentsia I got along quite well. Since I kept pace with their mental and social interests, being alert and informed as they were, and often even excelling them in several ways, I had no difficulty in becoming a regular companion and sometimes even a leader of this set of village children.

As for the young girls, their upbringing and way of life in the Komi villages were fairly similar to those of the boys. With a few exceptions, there was no separation of the sexes in most of the activities and games of the village children. Since sex in a physiological sense was not important to us at that age, boys and girls worked and played together without particular problems of a sexual nature. I liked and admired some of the girls, to others I felt indifferent. Despite diverse feelings toward each other, the boys and girls in each village lived together as chums and pals. Among them, as among the villagers, there were neither "lonely crowds," nor "lonely souls." In gangs we swam, fished, played ball and "gorodki" games, went on berry-picking expeditions in the forest, did our haying and harvesting, and raided the turnip fields of neighbors, in the summer; skied, skated, and sledded, sang, listened, and told stories at the evening gatherings of peasants, in the winter; and at all seasons on important holidays, we attended church services and processions in groups, participated in village dances, and took an active part in the impressive ceremonies that accompanied such occasions as birth, death, or marriage. Bubbling vitality and excitement pervaded our activities. There was much laughter and harmless mischief in our games, a spirit of solemnity in the religious processions, and a sincere sympathy at funerals.

And how very dramatic and elaborate were most of these ceremonies! For instance, the whole cycle of marriage festivities from beginning to end usually lasted for a few weeks. It began with sending "ambassadors" (go-betweens) from the bridegroom's family to that of the prospective bride to determine whether or not the girl and her parents were willing to accept the marriage offer. This mission was transacted by both parties with traditional hospitality and intricate diplomacy. If the marriage offer was accepted, then, with the same tact, the parties agreed upon the mutual presents, dowry (or the price for the bride to be paid by the bridegroom's family), the place and date of marriage, and other important conditions. Usually this mission required two or three ceremonial meetings. Then, by means of a special ceremony in the village and in church, the agreed marriage was announced to the public.

The next ritual consisted of the bride's "weeping" for several days. Covered by a big shawl, seated on a bench in the center of a room, and led in her weeping by a special "lamenter-woman," she lamented first to her parents, siblings, and relatives, thanking them for their goodness and love and bewailing her separation from them and her departure to "the foreign, unknown, and unloved" family. Each person to whom she lamented was seated at her side and covered by her shawl. While lamenting, the bride dramatically and frequently slapped her thighs. After the family and relatives, she lamented to each of her friends and neighbors. Some of her tears might be genuine, others were merely conventional. However, after several days of crying and slapping, the bride grew hoarse and her thighs somewhat bruised, despite a pillow surreptitiously hidden beneath her skirt to absorb the blows. While the bride was lamenting, her merrymaking relatives, friends, and neighbors sang, gossiped, danced, and consumed vodka, beer, tea, berry-juices, and food in the "open house" of her parents.

On the eve of the church wedding the weeping ceased and was followed by the colorful ceremonies of washing the bride in a bathhouse, of sprinkling the public with the bride's water, and of a sham battle between her defenders and her kidnappers. Then followed other dramatic performances participated in actively by many neighbors and passively by the whole village. No less elaborate was the church wedding and the public ceremonies preceding and following it. After the church ritual, the married couple was led to the house of the bridegroom. There, amidst feasts and merrymaking which continued for two or more days, the final ceremonies were performed. In the evening of the wedding day, the newly married pair were ceremoniously led to their bridal chamber amidst laughter, jokes, blessings, and songs of the guests; the next morning they were elaborately greeted and welcomed by the community.

Just as painstaking and dramatic were the ceremonies on the occasion of a birth or death in a village family. Here again the whole village took part in the event. The community shared the elaborate character of these festivities, which indicates the Komi attitude toward birth, death, and marriage as significant landmarks not only for the individuals involved in them but also for the whole community. They demonstrate also that village life was neither monotonous nor poor in enriching experiences as many urbanites believe, but was in fact a colorful and exciting life free from mechanical routine governed by time-tables. For the most part free from such tyranny, Komi village life represented an ever-changing succession of diverse activities with its daily, weekly, and seasonal rhythms. On rainy days this life was quite different from its character on sunny days; in July its course was dissimilar from that in any other month; in the spring the activities, interests, and frame of mind of the villagers were unlike those in the winter or any other season. In its unhurried flow this country life was ever varied in its form, attitudes, and behavior. If anything, it was richer, less monotonous, and more meaningful than the life of a factory worker or a city clerk doing the same simple operations, and leading the same kind of existence day in and day out.

Early Formal Education

I do not remember exactly how, when, and where I learned the three *R*'s. Our nomadic life precluded my regular attendance at, and graduation from elementary school. Moving from village to village I could attend only a few days or weeks the schools of the villages where we were staying. The elements of reading, writing, and arithmetic I probably picked up from my father and brother. The earliest of my teachers was a single peasant woman in Rymia who taught the three *R*'s in her house to a few boys and girls of the hamlet. I remember this "school" because it was there I received my first and most cherished prize for excellence in learning. The prize was a wrapping from a piece of hard candy. I can still clearly visualize the yellow-green picture of a pear on the wrapping and vividly relive the joyful pride with which I accepted it from the teacher; I showed it to my aunt and uncle and, finally, carefully fixed it on the wall of their house, next to the ikons. None of the diplomas, prizes, and honors granted to me at a later period of my life by great institutions of learning, has elated me as much as this simple prize.

Somehow or other in this erratic way I acquired elementary school knowledge which I greatly increased by my voracious reading of all sorts of books obtainable in the Komi villages. This rapacious reading acquainted me at an early age with the classics of Russian literature. I read Pushkin, Gogol, Turgenev, Tolstoi, Dostoevski, and a few translated classics like Mark Twain's *The Prince and the Pauper* and some of Charles

Dickens' novels, fairy-tales and epics, lives of the saints and religious scripture, and the elements of history and natural science. Besides reading, my mental development was notably assisted by talks and discussions with the village intelligentsia and peasants, and especially by direct experience in challenging life situations and by continuous contact with new people and conditions in different villages. This real school of life greatly expanded my horizons and deepened my total knowledge.

Several teachers, clergymen, and peasants took an active interest in my mental development and helped by lending me their books, giving their advice, and, during the periods of poverty in our family, by offering me food and warm clothes in the winter season. I have never forgotten how one of these teachers, who was suffering from tuberculosis himself, brought me a pair of felt boots one severe winter to replace my worn-out shoes.

"Though the boots are old, still they may save you from pneumonia which, sure thing, you will catch in those good-for-nothing shoes of yours."

His gift probably saved me from pneumonia that winter. Three years later, however, I did encounter this illness. At that time I was enrolled in an advanced grade school in Gam village. For Christmas vacation I decided to visit my aunt and uncle in Rymia. On an early afternoon I started to walk to Rymia, some twenty-five miles from the school. The day was very cold and my jacket afforded little protection against the sub-zero temperature. Nevertheless, walking briskly I safely reached the village of Dsheshart, some five miles from Rymia. It was already dark and a severe snowstorm had started when I entered Dsheshart.

After some hesitation I decided to go on to Rymia that night despite the adverse weather conditions. Having walked for some time in the deep snow, I finally became lost in the darkness of the blinding and piercing storm. Without any sense of direction, I continued to walk in panic and desperation until I was completely exhausted and fell down on the snow which began to pile higher and higher around me. As

I started to lose consciousness, I was awakened by the clanging of church bells. (The main bells in the Russian churches are large and their ringing can be heard from a distance of a few miles.) This bell-ringing saved me from freezing to death. It indicated to me the direction of Dsheshart village toward which, with revived hope, I immediately began to walk. Guided by the bell-ringing, I eventually reached this village and spent the night there in the house of another aunt. The next clear morning I resumed my journey to Rymia and, after several hours of "wading" through snow, finally reached my destination. The next day, however, a high fever from pneumonia seized my "brother-body" (to use St. Francis' expression) and forced me to spend my vacation in bed instead of enjoying it in the convivial company of Rymia friends.

Other illnesses and "accidents" of various kinds happened to me during my early boyhood. In some cases they were due to a lack of the necessities of life; in others, like this case of pneumonia, they were caused by my own rash and adventurous spirit. Whatever their causes, their harsh consequences taught me many unforgettable lessons and thereby contributed to my mental and cultural development.

As a result of this erratic but many-sided education I had no difficulty in being admitted to an advanced grade school which was being opened at Gam village while my brother and I were working there. The day of the entrance examination in the new school was an important event in the life of the village. Many of the peasants, including the boys aspiring to become pupils, attended the public "show" of the entrance examinations. As one of the curious onlookers I attended also, without any plan of taking a part in the tests. After listening to the questions and finding them easy, I spontaneously volunteered to be examined too. I passed the tests with flying colors, was enrolled in the school, and was given a scholarship of five rubles ($2.50) which paid for room and board in the school's dormitory for the whole academic year. (How fantastic this sounds in comparison to present prices and scholarships!)

In this incidental way my irregular school education was

continued in advanced grade school. This step started me along an educational path that eventually led me to a career as a university professor. Five teachers in the school, headed by the local priest, were good men and excellent educators. Its library and other modest facilities were notably better than those of the elementary schools. Most of the students were capable boys, sound in body, mind, and moral conduct. The total atmosphere of the school was mentally stimulating, emotionally happy, and philosophically idealistic. As I happened to be the best student, I was given a scholarship of five rubles each for three years of the school curriculum. These five rubles paid for my room and board during nine months of each year. During the remaining three months I earned my living by performing my previous occupational work with my brother and by helping my aunt and uncle with their farm work. Three years in that school notably increased my knowledge, enriched my cultural awareness, awakened my creative propensities, and integrated my *Weltanschauung*.

Early Cultural Education

Since the Komi and my family were bilingual and spoke two languages, Komi and Russian, these languages naturally became my native tongues. To my regret, having had no practice in the Komi language for some fifty years, I have now largely forgotten it. And because the religion of the Komi and of my family was Russian Orthodox mixed with vestiges of the pre-Christian, pagan beliefs, both sets of beliefs and rituals naturally became my own religion and ritual practice. Their imprint upon my mind was greatly reinforced through our occupational work in, around, and for churches. In my work for churches I naturally met, talked, and interacted with many priests, deacons, and readers. Some of them were quite intelligent and learned persons. They greatly influenced the early formation of my personality and values. The total impact of those religious influences upon me was so strong that, after reading old quarto volumes on the lives of the saints, I wanted to become an ascetic hermit, and often retired into the solitude of the nearby forest to fast and pray.

This religious climate also served as a stimulus and outlet for the development of my creative propensities. Participation in church singing satisfied and stimulated my love of music, made me a popular singer at church services, and, later, a conductor of church and school choirs. Serving as an acolyte in religious ceremonies, I learned verbatim, prayers, psalms, and scriptural texts as well as the details of religious services. This intimate knowledge of religious texts and rituals gave me a deeper understanding of their wisdom and an appreciation of their splendor.

This knowledge was also partly responsible for my becoming a teacher-preacher at the neighborhood gatherings of peasants during the long winter evenings. In a room lighted by burning birch-splinters, with a big shawl over my shoulders—an imitation of the priests' ceremonial vestiment (*riza*)—I often talked with the peasants about various spiritual and human problems and answered their questions. In Rymia and in other villages where we stayed for any length of time, I became a sort of a popular teacher and preacher. There must have been something valuable in this activity of a boy of some nine to twelve years old; otherwise, my peasant audiences would not have sought, tolerated, and appreciated it. For my part I fully enjoyed it. Now I wish I knew the secret of the popularity of my early "lectures and sermons." Frankly, I do not know. Perhaps they were an early "syndrome" of my teaching-preaching "residue," or a "prepotent reflex," or just a "proclivity" which later fully manifested itself in my becoming a university professor and educator.

The work of painting ikons and making *rizas* had developed my sense of line, design, and color. The mysteries of the *Agnus Dei,* of Creation, Incarnation, Crucifixion, Resurrection, and Redemption as they are so dramatically unfolded in the Russian Orthodox Mass, opened to me the mysteries and enigmatic dimensions of reality and of the tragic aspects of life. They planted the seeds of my lifelong aversion to a philistine perception of life as being merely "fine and dandy fun" and toward a superficial conception of reality as being purely sensory and material. If there are elements of mysticism in my theories, as several scholars assert, such mystic and tragic strains were set therein at an early age by the tragic mysteries of the Mass and by the trying experiences of my life.

The moral precepts of Christianity, especially of the Sermon on the Mount and the Beatitudes, decisively conditioned my moral values not only in youth but for the rest of my life. The roots of the Harvard Research Center in Creative Altruism, established by me in 1949, go all the way back to these precepts of Jesus learned in my boyhood. Combined with my itinerant way of life and the social life of the Komi people, the religious climate of my early age played an important part in the formation of my personality, the integration of my system of values, and the crystallization of my early philosophy. All in all mine was an idealistic world-view in which God and nature, truth, goodness, and beauty, religion, science, art, and ethics were all united into one harmonious system. No sharp conflict and no inner contradiction between these values as yet marred my peace of mind. Despite material hardships and the sorrows and trials of human life, the world appeared to me a marvelous place in which to live and to strive for life's great values.

I did not then foresee that in the near future this peaceful and orderly world and my harmonious *Weltanschauung* would be violently shattered by my contact with urbanized "civilization" and by the explosion of the Russo-Japanese War and the Revolution of 1905.

CHAPTER THREE

First Crisis and Revolt

From Teachers' Seminary to Prison

In 1903, at the age of fourteen, I graduated from the Gam advanced school. Impressed by my work, my teachers and the higher educational authorities of the province strongly advised me to continue my studies and promptly secured a modest scholarship for me at Khrenovo Teachers' Seminary in Kostroma Province. I eagerly accepted and in August, 1903, started my long journey to the school. For the first time in my life, I traveled by train and steamer, had glimpses of big cities and industrial regions, and shyly observed various types of urban people. All this excited, confused, and depressed me. I felt strange to this unfamiliar bustle and environment.

The feeling of being a stranger persisted for a short while after my arrival at the Khrenovo school. Although the students and personnel there were in no way "stuffed shirts," nevertheless in my homespun clothes, with my manners devoid of urban polish, I looked and felt like a yokel and was treated as such by some of the Khrenovo people. Fortunately, this feeling and treatment soon disappeared for the most part; I rapidly acquired some urban manners, bought a new suit, and finally, through conversation and the first exams, I seem to have demonstrated that I was not the naive bumpkin I had appeared to be. I soon "adjusted" to the new conditions and felt quite at home at the seminary. (Later in my life I had to prove again and again that appearances may be misleading, and that I was to be taken more seriously than some people, judging superficially, seemed to think.)

The seminary was a denominational school under the jurisdiction of the Holy Synod of the Russian Orthodox Church.

It trained teachers for the Synod's elementary schools. The campus, located in Khrenovo village, was adjacent to several textile factories and was near sizable urban and industrial centers. The three-year curriculum of the school was much more advanced, the students and teachers were more qualified, the library and other school facilities better than those of the elementary and grade schools I had attended up to that time. I was quite happy during the two years of my studies there. With few exceptions, the courses and texts were interesting and informative; my studies proceeded successfully, and within a few months I had earned a reputation as the best student in my class and was a leader in literary, scientific, and political activities. My relations with both students and teachers were excellent, and life in and out of the school was exhilarating, meaningful, and promising. Among other things, my lifelong friendship with a younger student, N. D. Kondratieff, began. Subsequently he became an eminet economist and international authority in the field of business cycles. Eventually he perished in exile under Stalin's regime.

Besides students and teachers I met a wide variety of people: peasants, factory hands, clerks, clergy, government officials, doctors, writers, journalists, businessmen, leaders of local co-operatives, and representatives of different political parties—Social-Revolutionaries, Social-Democrats (Bolsheviks and Menshevicks), Monarchists, Anarchists, Liberals, and Conservatives of all shades. Through contact with these people I acquired many new ideas and values and became aware of social conditions. This new milieu, new acquaintances, and particularly my intensive reading of hitherto unknown books, journals, and newspapers rapidly broadened and deepened my outlook. My newly formed ideas were reinforced by the Russo-Japanese War of 1904 and particularly by the brewing storm which resulted in the Revolution of 1905.

The combined impact of all these forces was so powerful that within two years after my enrollment at the school most of my previous religious, philosophical, political, economic, and social ideologies had collapsed. My previous religiosity was supplanted by a semi-atheistic rejection of the theologies and rituals of the Russian Orthodox Church. Compulsory attendance at church services, imposed by the school, notably stimulated this revolt. My previous *Weltanschauung* and values were replaced by "scientific theories of evolution" and "natural science philosophy." My former acceptance of the Czarist monarchical regime and its "capitalist" economy was replaced by republican, democratic, and socialist views. Previous political indifference gave way to revolutionary zeal. I became an enthusiastic missionary for the anti-Czarist revolution and the leader of the Social-Revolutionary Party in the school and adjacent regions. In contrast to Social Democrats, the Social-Revolutionary Party claimed to be the party of all labor classes —peasant, worker, and intellectual. Unlike Marxist materialism and the economic interpretation of man and history, the philosophy and sociology of the Social-Revolutionary Party were much more idealistic or integralistic. They emphasized strongly the role of creative ideas, voluntary efforts, the "struggle for individuality" versus the "struggle for existence," and the importance of non-economic factors in determining social processes and human conduct. My previous *Weltanschauung* was more congenial to this kind of ideology than to the "proletarian," "materialistic," "economic" ideology of Marxian social-democracy. This congeniality explains why I chose the Social-Revolutionary over the Social-Democratic Party and why throughout my subsequent life I have never been "infected" by most Marxian ideologies.

Having become an ardent Social-Revolutionary, I began to spread the gospel of the Revolution among students, factory workers, and peasants of nearby villages.

In the evening of the first day of my Christmas vacation, 1906, I started for a scheduled meeting with one of my worker-peasant groups. As I approached the meeting-house I noticed that it was dark and silent. Despite some apprehension, I steathily opened the door. I was immediately ambushed and arrested by several policemen. Though I had expected to be arrested sooner or later because of my revolutionary activities, nevertheless this first arrest shocked me inordinately. While the police escorted me to a horse and sleigh which would carry me to the prison at Kineshma city, the consequences of this event rapidly flashed through my mind: inevitable expulsion from school, indefinitely long imprisonment, possible banishment to Siberia, the uncertainty of my future, and other not too cheerful prospects.

I was thrown into a dirty cell whose wooden bunk was crawling with bedbugs. However, with youthful optimism and vitality I took this discomfiture in stride. I wheedled a big kettle of boiling water from the guard and disinfected the bunk, swept my cell, and tried to adjust myself to the new conditions as well as I could. Next day I was cheered by several pleasant surprises: the warden of the prison moved me into a better cell and offered me the use of his office and telephone; political prisoners who had been jailed previously welcomed me into their company and arranged for the door of my cell to be kept open in the daytime so we could talk and stay together; my fellow students from the school arrived to visit me and brought books, food, and cigarettes to ease my existence. (These cigarettes introduced me to the habit of tobacco smoking, a frailty from which I had previously been free.)

In brief, political imprisonment turned out to be much less painful and frightening than I had imagined. During its last years the collapsing Czarist regime became quite humane. As a matter of fact, we political prisoners made the prison a safe place to store revolutionary literature and employed prison guards as liaisons with outside revolutionaries, freely visited one another, and, unhindered, met daily to discuss political, social, and philosophic problems. (When a political regime begins to crumble, the "viruses of disintegration" rapidly spread throughout its whole body, "infect" most of its antibodies, and penetrate into its deepest recesses. Its downfall is usually due not so much to the efforts of revolutionary leaders as to its senility, impotency, and uncreativity. In the case of our prison, we had a typical illustration of this principle.

If revolutions cannot be artificially started and exported, no more can they be artificially stopped. Nor do they necessarily need mighty leaders for their full development: in their natural course they create such leaders out of ordinary persons. Let this be remembered by all politicians, and particularly by the defenders of obsolescent regimes! They can neither revive the dead shell of a previously creative body nor activate a revolution where explosive material is lacking.)

Daily discussions and an intensive reading of the works of Mikhailovsky, Lavrov, Marx, Engels, Bakunin, Kropotkin, Tolstoi, Plekhanov, Tchernoff, Lenin, and other revolutionary classics acquainted me with various revolutionary theories, ideologies, and problems. Reading the works of Charles Darwin, Herbert Spencer, and other "evolutionists," as well as scientific texts and philosophical treatises, contributed to my knowledge of science, evolution, and philosophy. During the four months of my imprisonment I probably learned a great deal more than I possibly could have during the semester at the Teachers' Seminary. This extends also to my subsequent imprisonments under the Czarist (but not the Communist) regime as well as to the imprisonments of many Russian scholars and thinkers. Some of their best works were conceived and drafted in the Czarist prisons. In the academic circles of Czarist Russia, this fact was stated in a fairly common expression: "One takes a leave of absence in prison to do some reading, thinking, and writing." My own experience confirms this saying.

In prison I met and conversed daily with many ordinary criminals—murderers, burglars, thiefs, rapists, and other unfortunate "deviants," thus acquainting myself with the world of crime and criminals. This experience provided the topic for my first book, *Crime and Punishment, Service and Reward,* published in 1913, and led to my choice of criminology and penology as the field of my first specialization at the University of St. Petersburg.

After four months of imprisonment I was released and placed under "open supervision of the police" to whom I had to report regularly my domicile, my activities, and any change of address. From prison I went directly to the seminary to say goodbye to students, teachers, and neighborhood friends. Despite my "automatic" discharge from school, I was heartily welcomed and received as a hero rather than as a criminal, because most of the faculty and student body were in sympathy with the Revolution and its propagandists. After a few days in Khrenovo I decided to depart. But where to go? This question plagued me constantly. My position was difficult indeed. There was no school or business establishment willing to admit me as a student or employee because admission or employment of revolutionaries was prohibited by the government. Moreover, in my revolutionary zeal I was no longer eager to become a "loyal" student or a diligent clerk.

After due consideration of my situation, I took the only course which could fulfill my revolutionary aspirations. I decided to become an itinerant missionary for the Revolution, going from factory to factory, village to village, to spread the Social-Revolutionary gospel and to organize revolutionary "cells" and groups.

One early afternoon I departed from school without informing the police or anyone except a few close friends and co-revolutionaries. My destination was Ivanovo-Voznesensk, a big industrial center some twenty miles from the seminary. If my arrival at school had been joyful, my departure from it was gloomy. The sky was overcast, matching my somber mood. Soon it began to snow. Downcast and lonely, I walked along back roads, brooding over the dangers and hardships of my new "vocation," and over the ironic reversion, after some five years of an orderly, rooted life in two schools, to my previous condition of itinerant stranger with its painfully familiar "arrivals and departures." Expelled from the school, I felt derailed again from my previously secure educational life-track.

The road became more and more obliterated by the falling snow and less and less discernible in the approaching darkness of night. It seemingly led nowhere—certainly not to a long-sought destination of success and comfort. In this state of melancholia I finally reached Ivanovo-Voznesensk and located the apartment of a comrade-teacher, a local member of the Social-Revolutionary Party. Thus an orderly phase in my life ended and a new facet of dangers and trials opened.

* * *

Itinerant Missionary of the Revolution

In contrast to the missionaries of well-established religions, underground propagandists of the Revolution at that time and in that region had neither a rigid set of dogmas, nor funds, nor a hierarchy, nor even a closely knit organization. Instead, in the cities and villages there was a coterie of "avowed" Social-Revolutionaries who knew each other slightly and maintained a loose communication among themselves. Then there was a much larger circle of "fellow travelers" and, finally, large groups of sympathizing workers and peasants. To address large political meetings and big demonstrations, to promote the organization of the party's "cells," debate with the representatives of other parties, and, finally, to counsel the local members of the party, "itinerant professional revolutionaries" visited the region from time to time. They were invited by the local members or sent by the central and provincial committees of the Social-Revolutionary Party. With the exception of a few principal leaders, most of these revolutionaries did not receive any remuneration and had to depend entirely upon the hospitality of local members of the party or fellow travelers for shelter, food, and other necessities. During their stay in a given place they remained with one of these members or sympathizers, ready to move at a moment's notice if there was a danger of arrest or of their being followed by government agents. Their life was similar to that of the first missionaries of a new, unorganized religious denomination regarded as "subversive" and persecuted by the well-established spiritual and secular powers. Continuously hunted by police, now and then having no shelter or food or other necessities, risking being fired upon at meetings they addressed, they lived a life as full of danger, hardship, and martyrdom as that of the first apostles of Christianity or of any new "subversive" religion.

On the following day, after my arrival at Ivanovo-Voznesensk, my missionary activities began. For the world at large, especially for government agents, Sorokin disappeared; in his stead an anonymous "Comrade Ivan" emerged as a speaker at revolutionary meetings, as organizer and instructor for the "cells" of the party among intelligentsia, factory workers, and villagers; as a participant in political debates with the propagandists for other parties; and as a source of mimeographed and printed political leaflets distributed among the population. Being illegal and punishable, these activities had to be conducted under conditions of secrecy from the police and other government agents. Most of the important revolutionary meetings took place on the outskirts of cities, in wooded areas, with trusted observers serving as lookouts for the approaching police or Cossacks. As soon as they signaled such danger, the meeting was abruptly adjourned and its participants hurriedly dispersed, vanishing into the surrounding woods.

Most of the meetings addressed by Comrade Ivan were not disrupted by police or Cossacks; only a few were abruptly adjourned because of an imminent attack by the police. However, one of the larger meetings ended tragically, with two workers and one policeman killed, and several workers, Cossacks, and policemen wounded. It took place on a sunny spring afternoon, by a wooded bank of the Volga River near the city of Kineshma. The crowd was large, consisting of a thousand workers from nearby factories. Most of these workers passionately hated the Czarist regime, especially its police and Cossacks who were the regime's worst "pharaohs," "oppressors," and "executioners of the people." Standing above the crowd on a big stump, Comrade Ivan addressed the responsive audience in a fiery denunciation of the Czarist regime and a glorification of the coming order in which the government would belong to the people, the land to its cultivators the peasants, factories to their workers, and there would be freedom with justice to all.

Unfortunately neither the lookout men nor anyone in the crowd noticed a detachment of mounted police and Cossacks concealed in a nearby gully. At the climax of Ivan's talk they suddenly emerged and surrounded the meeting. "All are under arrest until your leaders surrender to us," was the ultimatum of the commanding officer. An ominous silence ensued for a few moments. It was broken by Ivan's indignant denunciation of the attackers as the worst enemies of the people. A shot from a policeman's rifle abruptly interrupted his speech. Whether it was only a warning shot or was aimed at Ivan, the most conspicuous target, remains unknown, but with the shot he was immediately pulled from the stump by the guardian-revolutionaries, then screened by, and "lost" among them.

Simultaneously the "pharaohs" charged the crowd with whips and sabers. Part of the audience started to run in panic and collided with the attackers, while another, more courageous part counterattacked with stones, knives, and clubs, yanked the Cossacks from their horses, beat, kicked, and fiercely fought with all the primitive means at their disposal. Overwhelmed by the sheer number of fighters, the "pharaohs" began to retreat in confusion. In the ensuing melée, whether in self-defense or anger, some of the Cossacks fired sporadically into the crowd. In revenge the infuriated workers redoubled their efforts and soon forced the "pharaohs" to run for their lives. . . .

An hour or so later, a long mourning procession began to move slowly from the battlefield toward the factories. The killed and wounded comrades were solemnly carried on hurriedly made stretchers. Black and red flags indicated the nature of the *cortège*. In the oblique rays of the late afternoon sun the sadness of the procession contrasted strongly with the spring flowering of the countryside and the glittering undulation of the river. A song, *Requiem of a Revolution,* sung by a thousand voices, rose powerfully in protest and sorrow to the blue sky.

Inspired by your boundless love for the people,
you fallen martyrs in the fateful struggle,
You sacrificed everything you had for the people's life,
honor, and freedom

. . . .

The time will come when the awakened people
will rise—great, mighty, and free. . . .

. . . .

Farewell, dear brothers. You honestly walked
the heroic and noble path of your life. . . .
Legions of fresh warriors, ready for battle and death,
are marching in your footsteps.
Farewell, dear comrades.

In a later period of his life Ivan would often hear the great Requiems of Mozart, Cherubini, Berlioz, Brahms, Verdi, and Fauré, and the magnificent funeral marches of Beethoven, Chopin, and Wagner. But none of these masterpieces could fill his soul with such deep sorrow, pure sympathy, and a quest for justice as this simple and unpretentious *Requiem of a Revolution*. Incidentally, the theme of this Requiem with the composer's variations is found in the third movement of Shostakovich's eleventh symphony.

After a few weeks of missionary activities, the name of anonymous "Comrade Ivan" became quite popular among the region's workers, peasants, and intelligentsia and was equally familiar to the police and security agents of the government. They had intensified their efforts to discover his identity and to arrest this "elusive comrade." Several times he barely escaped their traps. In all such cases he was saved not so much by his own alertness as by the helping hands of sympathetic workers, peasants, and intelligentsia. They informed him of all suspicious persons, spies, and ambushes, hid him in their rooms or apartments, concealed him during dangerous situations, served as guides in coming to and leaving meetings, transported him from place to place along unfrequented roads, and abruptly pushed, pulled, or jerked him into hiding at critical moments, as they had done at the meeting near

Kineshma. Only through their friendly intervention did Ivan remain free and out of jail for the approximately three months spent in the Volga region.

Toward the end of this period the effects of the continuous danger, strain, and hardship of this way of living began to show upon Ivan. His health became impaired, his energy weakened, and his peace of mind shattered. Moreover, a greatly intensified police hunt made his arrest practically imminent if he were to stay in the area any longer. Under the pressure of these circumstances and upon the urgent advice of his comrades, he reluctantly left the dangerous area and with some difficulty safely reached Aunt Anyssia's home in Rymia where his revolutionary activities were as yet unknown.

In Rymia life continued to flow in its traditional, orderly way, little disturbed by the revolutionary storm brewing over the urban-industrial centers of Russia. There, amidst my friends, I stayed for about two months, helping my aunt and Prokopiy with the harvesting and other farm work, visiting my teachers in Gam school, and rapidly regaining my vitality and peace of mind. Since I had no prospects either for attractive employment or for a continuation of my education in the Komi region, in the fall of 1907 I decided to move to St. Petersburg.

PART TWO

CHAPTER FOUR

Pre-University Years in St. Petersburg

"Rabbit" on a Train

It was easy to decide to move to St. Petersburg, but it was much more difficult to get there. The cheapest fare, including the steamer from Rymia to Vologda and the train from Vologda to St. Petersburg cost at least sixteen rubles. At that time my total capital amounted to only one mere ruble. I did some painting in two peasant homes and thereby increased my funds to some ten rubles. This sum was still insufficient for my trip but since gainful work was unavailable at that time, with youthful optimism, on a brisk September morning in 1907, I bade goodbye to Anyssia, Prokopiy, and my friends, boarded "Kupchik"—a little primitive steamer—and thus started my pilgrimage to the Russian metropolis. With the cheapest ticket in my pocket and with a food-basket supplied by Anyssia and replenished by Uncle Mikhail and Aunt Anna in Veliki Ustyug, I enjoyed, during six days of travel by steamer, the slowly changing view of rivers and countryside, and the simple company of my fellow travelers. These pleasures were increased by my thoughts and dreams. Though third-class accommodations on the steamer were poor and the ever-dwindling supply in my food-basket forced me to decrease my daily "rations," still these details did not matter much to a vigorous lad in a state of inner peace, quiet contentment, and bright hope.

Unfortunately this state of mind was disrupted in Vologda by a very prosaic financial problem. The cheapest train-fare from that city to St. Petersburg was some eight rubles while my "unexpended balance" had by then been reduced to some three rubles. Having no alternative, I bought a ticket to one of the stations not far from Vologda and boarded the train in the hope of traveling the rest of the way to the city in the "rabbit" class, as the ticketless passengers were called in Russia. With my ticket I passed the first inspection of passengers by the train conductors unnoticed and, hiding myself on the steps of one of the train cars, I remained undetected by the next few inspections. But on one of the subsequent inspections "the rabbit-passenger" was discovered, ordered back into the car, and questioned. I told the conductor quite frankly that I was going to St. Petersburg to find a job and gain an education, that with my money I could afford a ticket only to the station which we had already passed, and that I had hoped to ride the rest of the way as a "rabbit." Whether the conductor happened to be a particularly kind man or my frank explanation impressed him favorably, he told me that I could continue my trip to St. Petersburg under the condition that I earn my fare by cleaning the cars, particularly the lavatories, and by helping the train-stoker in his work. Gladly accepting his decision to earn my fare by this sort of labor, I safely reached the city. When I stepped onto the platform of Nikolaievsky station in St. Petersburg, I still had in my pocket an "unexpended balance" of fifty kopecks (the equivalent of twenty-five cents at the current rate of exchange).

Lucky Beginnings in the Metropolis

The only person I knew in St. Petersburg was Pavel Kokovkin, one of my friends from Rymia, who two years before had migrated to the capital of Russia. Having his address, I walked from Nikolaievsky station to his place and found him at home. This "home" was a room in an old apartment house of which he, his bed, and a few possessions occupied one of the corners. Three other corners were rented by an elderly woman, a young girl, and by a friend of Pavel who worked in the same factory. Despite its obvious poverty the room was clean and in good order. So also were the neighbors' friendly relationships with each other, as I found out later. They all received me cordially and invited me to supper. During the meal Pavel told me that I could stay with him for a few days until I found a job, and the whole company took part in a discussion of where and what kind of work I could get. They promised to sound out their bosses and friends about this matter.

Among other suggestions, Pavel advised me to post a sign at the main entrance of the apartment house offering my tutorial and secretarial services at a very low price. This suggestion, followed the same evening, turned out to be lucky; for the next afternoon a clerical employee of the central electric station came to the room and, after an interview, hired me as tutor to his two sons in the first grades of gymnasium (high school). In return for my tutoring I was to live in a room with the pupils and to have a breakfast and dinner free. We agreed that I was to move to their apartment the next day. In the evening when my friends returned from work I cheerfully informed them of my luck. With part of a room to live in and two sure meals a day, I felt my immediate problem was satisfactorily settled. Tutoring duties claimed only a minor portion of my time, leaving plenty of free time for my education as well as for earning additional money to meet my modest needs.

The next morning, before moving to the family's apartment, I decided to tackle the problem of my education. My objective was to become a university student. Since I had been expelled from the Teachers' Seminary, and had not attended any grade of gymnasium, there was only one way for me to be admitted to the university as a student, namely by passing a stiff "examination of maturity" for all eight grades of gymnasium, including some additional knowledge required from the "externs" who had not graduated from gymnasium. At that time I was not prepared for such an examination, particularly in the required fields of Latin or Greek, French or German, and mathematics. To acquire such preparation I wished to enter one of the night schools that, among other things, offered such training to capable students. As I did not have any money to pay the fairly high tuition, I decided to explore my chances of being admitted free to Tscherniayevskye Kursy, one of the best schools of the kind. I had learned previously that the founder of this school, Mr. Tscherniaeff, was from Vologda Province and was in sympathy with the Social-Revolutionary Party, and that one of the teachers at the Kursy, a close friend of Tscherniaeff, was professor K. F. Jakov, the first Komi man to achieve the distinction of university professor.

So that morning I walked some seven miles to the professor's apartment. He was not at home, but Mrs. Jakov, herself a teacher in a private high school, received me kindly and in a most friendly way asked me about my errand and my affairs. Several years later, when I became a well-known professor, she used to humorously describe my first visit with her to our friends. Her story went something like this: "I opened the door and there was a country lad, in a Russian shirt, with a small bundle in his hand. To my question whom did he want to see, he answered that he just arrived from the Komi people and would like to see the Komi professor. When I asked where he had left his luggage, the boy pointed to his bundle and said, 'It is here.' Asked whether he had money for his living expenses, he cheerfully answered, Yes, I still have fifty kopecks and I already have a place to live and two daily meals. I am not worried about money. If I need more I can earn it." While Mrs. Jakov explored my background through the technique of "directed interview" (as my sociologist colleagues call it), Professor Jakov arrived and, after being briefed about the visitor, joined our conversation.

He was a remarkable man in many ways. His background was somewhat similar to mine in his difficult "climb" from the position of a Komi peasant boy to that of a professor of philosophy and of a famous writer of novels and epics of Komi life in a style reminiscent of Longfellow's *Hiawatha* and the Finnish *Kalevala*. But above all these achievements towered his impressively rich personality, his originality, and his intellectual independence from all fashionable currents of thought and art styles. Perhaps this "bullheadedness" was responsible for his works being underestimated before the

Revolution of 1917, and for his migration from Communist Russia to Latvia where he died in the 1920's.

Our long and lively conversation was concluded by his promise to arrange with Mr. Tscherniaeff for my free admission to the school and by his invitation to me to visit the Jakovs and to attend the monthly literary *soirées* in their apartment. This first visit was the beginning of a long and close friendship that lasted up to the deaths of the Jakovs in the 1920's. They helped me in many ways during my first year in St. Petersburg. They also introduced me to several philosophical, literary, and artistic circles. Later on Jakov and I together made several anthropological and economic field-studies of the Komi people. Among other things, it was at one of the Jakovs' *soirées* that I met my wife, then a young and beautiful student at the Bestudjeff Women's University in St. Petersburg.

Happy and encouraged, I walked seven miles back to the room of Pavel and there, bidding the company goodbye, I moved that evening to my pupils' apartment. Since all my belongings were contained in my small bundle, moving was easy: I simply walked to my new residence, carrying my bundle with me. The Latin saying, *omnia mea mecum porto*, which I learned later on, accurately describes this easy form of "residential mobility," as the sociologists call it. I felt fortunate indeed. In two days I had succeeded in procuring a place to live, daily sustenance, and admission to the night school to continue my education. In those days, in her inscrutable way, Dame Fortune seemed to be smiling at me.

Night School Years

I was fortunate also in the family of my pupils. It was a modest, reasonably traditional but very decent family. Despite a difference in our political ideologies, our relationship rapidly grew friendly and remained good during the year I stayed with them. Perhaps by affluent American standards, my breakfast consisting of a glass of tea and a roll and my dinner of soup, cereal or meat, and tea would appear somewhat meager, and my corner in the room of the pupils somewhat crowded, but for me, with my economic background, all this was quite acceptable and comfortable. Satisfactory also was the twelve-mile-long walk to and from the night school which I attended six times a week. The walk was good exercise for a young man and—what was more important—in these evening and midnight walks I learned a great deal about the shady side of big-city night life.

Soon, through Jakov's recommendations, I obtained additional tutorial work and with it an additional income of a few rubles for my simple needs. I felt quite content with these perhaps somewhat Spartan conditions. Having settled these small matters, I earnestly devoted myself to the task of my mental, moral, and cultural development. With this objective in mind, I worked hard over my courses at night school, read and thought a great deal outside of it, participated in various discussions, and absorbed as much culture as I could in the metropolis.

Three semesters of attendance at night school helped me greatly in this task. Most of the teachers there were college professors, and their lecture courses were not much different from the college courses for freshmen and sophomores. Attendance at courses and lessons was optional. Tests and examinations were few but quite rigorous and searching. This system of instruction, similar to that of the Russian universities before the Revolution, was free from the drudgery of high school instruction as well as from the boredom of obligatory attendance and other largely fruitless "compulsory requirements" still prevalent in American colleges and universities. I liked this free system and profited by it to the best of my capacity.

The students of the school were composed of a heterogeneous group of predominantly young men and women from different walks of life. Side by side with the dull mediocre students, there happened to be a small group of bright ones. Subsequently some of these distinguished themselves in science, the humanities, and politics. Community of interest in these fields, including the common anti-Czarist political position, established my friendship with some of these bright students. Together we discussed various problems, participated in "subversive" activities and now and then had convivial gatherings over a bottle of beer or a glass of vodka. These friendships endured for many years until some of us either were killed or scattered over the planet by World War I and the Communist Revolution of 1917.

The closest of these friends was Kondratieff. As I mentioned before, we were together in the Teachers' Seminary. Several months after my discharge from it, Kondratieff was also expelled for his revolutionary activities. Informed of my attendance at the night school, he moved to St. Petersburg and enrolled in that school in the spring semester of 1908. In the fall semester of that year, we rented a room (together with a Komi student of the school, Kusbodjeff), and Kondratieff and I continued to be roommates during several years of our university studentship. Eventually he became a distinguished professor of economics and a high official in the department of agriculture in the Kerensky and the Communist governments. Under the Soviet regime he was led several times from his high office to prison and from prison back to the office. We met for the last time at the University of Minnesota in 1927 during his scientific tour of the main universities of the United States. At that time he stayed with us as our guest for some ten days. During these days we pleasantly reminisced about our past experiences and exchanged views on basic problems of common interest, particularly about Russia and the Communist revolution. This visit happened to be our last. A few years later Kondratieff was accused by Stalin of instigating and carrying out anti-Communist agricultural policies. He was included among the anti-Stalin faction of the Communist and anti-Communist leaders and purged with them after the famous mock-trial of 1931-32. He was banished to Turkestan or Siberia and there perished under circumstances unknown to me and his other friends. Once more I have to say *Requiem eternam* to my dearest friend and a wonderful man.

My mental and cultural development was advanced not only by school but also by my avid absorption of the great cultural values accumulated in St. Petersburg. During these years I was like a sponge thirstily drinking in as much as I could of the immortal achievements of human genius in science and technology, philosophy and the fine arts, ethics and law, politics and economics. Any great city has, along with an accumulation of hollow and poisonous pseudo-values, a gigantic treasury of universal, eternal, and immortal values stored in its schools and laboratories, cathedrals and libraries, in its museums and art galleries, in its theaters and symphony halls, in its great buildings and historical monuments. In this sense any great city is an immense school for man's ennoblement or degradation, for the development or stultification of his creative potentialities. Unfortunately, many urbanites, especially in this age of commercialized and vulgarized pseudo-culture, do not select what they absorb from the rich culture of the great cities. In such an age huge masses and a crowd of "sophisticated barbarians" take in from this culture—mainly through the press, radio, television, advertising, and other means of communication—empty trivia, glittering nothings, poisonous toys, and short-lived "successes." As a result they largely remain "the groomed manikins of civilization" hardly superior to uncivilized savages in their intelligence, moral conduct, and creativity.

Whether because of my previous experience with hard realities that did not allow dilly-dallying with trivia or because of my revolutionary frame of mind—whatever the reason—seductive false values did not attract me at that time, nor have they hypnotized me up to the present moment. Their rapid change from one fashionable form of vacuum to another never fascinated me. Even now if a book or record or play is sold in millions of copies, this is sufficient reason for me not to bother myself with that kind of mental or cultural "chewing gum." There are few exceptions to the rule but, as I have shown in my *Social and Cultural Dynamics* (Vol. IV, Chap. V) the exceptions do not invalidate the rule: the overwhelming majority of short-lived "hits," "successes" and "best-sellers" represent merely vulgarized intellectual fare, and nothing more.

Instead of cluttering my mind with such pap I gorged upon the immortal masterpieces of literature, music, painting, sculpture, architecture, religion and philosophy, science and technology, social and humanistic disciplines. This sort of general education I pursued by voraciously reading classic works and, so far as my time and meager resources allowed, by visiting museums, attending plays and symphony concerts, and participating in various literary, artistic, philosophical, and political groups and societies. Through the Jakovs and other professors I soon became acquainted with several Russian leaders in these cultural fields. I also established personal relationships with some of the leaders of the Social-Revolutionary, the Social-Democratic, and the Constitutional-Democratic parties, and resumed cultural and educational activities among the workers of Putilovsky and other factories. In a truly democratic regime these activities would merely be regarded as regular work in the field of adult education and popularization of positivistic, progressive, and socialistic views; under the decaying Czarist regime they could not help being viewed by the agencies of that government as "subversive" and "revolutionary." However, until 1911 no arrest or imprisonment was imposed upon me for this kind of "subversiveness." Along with this absorption of new knowledge and values I also strove to integrate my ideas into a consistent, unified *Weltanschauung*. There are persons who seem to feel no urgent need to organize the heterogeneous contents of their minds into a consistent system. Their mentality reminds one of a dump where diverse and contradictory bits of knowledge, philosophies, and ideologies, various odds and ends of imcompatible values and aspirations peacefully squat side by side. In their own way such scatterbrained individuals, with their unintegrated or splintered personalities, often appear to be content and run their life-course without crises and tragedies.

In contrast to this type there are individuals with a strong "strain toward consistency" of their ideas, values, and aspirations. This type of person cannot help trying to unify them into a more or less consistent whole. I seem to belong to this "integrated" type. After the crumbling of my early view of life in the Teachers' Seminary, I felt somewhat confused and discontented and spontaneously began to grope for a new philosophy to restore the unity and integrity of my "self." My increased knowledge of the natural sciences, a better acquaintance with positivistic philosophy and revolutionary-socialistic doctrines, gave me the first directions for building the new *Weltanschauung*. Considerable progress in this tasks was made during my study in night school. But even then the new system of ideas, values, and aspirations was only half-built. Its construction had to be continued in my years of study at the Psycho-Neurological Institute and the University of St. Petersburg.

* * *

All in all, these two years of study in the metropolis were productive for my mental, moral, and cultural development. At the end of that time I began to feel that I was essentially prepared for the examination of maturity, sufficiently oriented in the main fields of culture, and to a notable degree advanced in integration of my basic ideas, values, and aspirations. This intellectual development was paralleled by emotional and volitional maturation. I was satisfied with the results, and being still young and in good health, I felt contented and hopeful.

In this frame of mind, in February, 1909, I decided to go to Veliki Ustyug to prepare for the final examination which I intended to take there in May of the same year. I moved to Ustyug because there I could devote all my time to this task and could live with my Uncle Mikhail and Aunt Anna more cheaply than I could in St. Petersburg. I went to Ustyug and stayed there for several months before and after the examination. In May, 1909, I passed the examination with the mark of "5" (excellent) in all its subjects. The diploma opened the door to my university education, which until then had been completely closed. It entitled me to enroll in any Russian university I chose. There still remained one hindrance, namely, the procurement of "the certificate of loyalty" (*svidetelstvo o blagonadejnosti*) from the Czarist government. However, this requirement did not worry me much: I was sure that despite my officially ascertained "subversiveness" and "political disloyalty" to the Czarist regime, somehow or other I would obtain this certificate from the officials of the disintegrating political regime. Eventually, indeed, I obtained it from the governor of St. Petersburg.

The months spent in Ustyug prior to and especially following the examination were fruitful and enjoyable. My uncle and aunt were simple but very good persons. They earned their living by baking and selling bread and cookies in their booth in the city market place. Their earnings were limited but sufficient for their modest needs. Both of them were traditionally religious, honest, and kind in the best sense of these terms. Their small house on "Red Hill" in the outskirts of Ustyug had a beautiful view over the city and lower valley of the countryside. The house was unpretentious but fairly comfortable inside. A small flower and vegetable garden in the backyard increased its attractiveness. The atmosphere of kindness, peace, and harmony in the mutual relationship of my relatives somehow permeated the whole atmosphere of the house.

During the same months I established close friendships with many young students and elder citizens of Ustyug. Some of the students, Peter Zepaloff, Vassiliy Bogatyreff, and a few others, became my lifelong friends until some of them perished in, or were scattered by, the Communist Revolution. After this first long stay in Ustyug, I visited it several times in later years. Like Rymia, it became one of the focal points for my recreational, educational, and revolutionary activities. Eventually it turned out to be the city in which I was imprisoned and condemned to death by the Communist rulers.

This last event, however, still lay in the laps of the gods during my first stay in Ustyug. After the examination I was elated with the open road to university education, and, bubbling with energy and hopes, I lived an enjoyable life of conviviality with my Ustyug companions and in warmest friendship with my uncle and aunt. Dame Fortune was still smiling at me. In September, 1909, I left Ustyug for St. Petersburg.

CHAPTER FIVE

Undergraduate University Years

The Psycho-Neurological Institute

Back in St. Petersburg, after some hesitation, I decided to enroll not at the University of St. Petersburg but at the newly opened Psycho-Neurological Institute. Its program appeared to me less rigid that that of the University, although its faculty was as distinguished. Among other things, the Institute offered courses in sociology given by two international leaders in this field, M. M. Kovalevsky and E. de Roberty, while the University did not offer any instruction in this discipline. At that time, of all the scientific fields, chemistry and sociology interested me most. Despite the very different character of these disciplines I hesitated for a considerable time as to which of these sciences to choose as my major. Finally I decided the matter in favor of sociology. The student body of the Institute, unlike that of the University for the most part impressed me as being more alive, revolutionary, and, like myself, recruited from the lower, peasant-labor classes. These and similar reasons determined my choice. So in the fall of 1909 I became a student at the Institute.

In contrast to American universities and colleges, the Russian universities and institutions of higher learning in those days did not require undergraduate attendance at lectures, seminars, or quizzes. This matter was left to their free choice. Likewise, with a few exceptions, in the psycho-social sciences and humanities there were practically no quizzes during the whole semester or even the academic year. Instead, there was one very thorough examination at the end of a semester or the academic year. Usually May and part of June were the months especially allotted for examination of students in all the subjects they had taken during the year. Students who failed were automatically dropped from the universities. The higher institutions were not interested in how students acquired the knowledge necessary for passing the stiff examinations at the end of the year or semester, nor did they assume that this knowledge could be acquired only through regular attendance of lectures and classes and through frequent quizzes. Quite reasonably, the institutions believed that there was not one but several different ways for different students to obtain the required knowledge and to meet the other demands of the school. The universities also assumed, quite justifiably, that spontaneous enthusiasm for learning supplemented by one rigorous examination at the end of a semester or academic year, were more efficient stimuli for acquiring knowledge and for testing it than too many superficial quizzes with their accompanying strain and rush which tend to interrupt systematic study and to impose an unnecessary burden upon both professors and students. This system was more free, fruitful, and creative than our prevalent system of obligatory attendance of lectures and frequent superficial tests. In my opinion our system is especially detrimental to capable undergraduates and graduate students.

I myself went beyond even this free system of the Russian universities. After enrolling at the Psycho-Neurological Institute I decided to attend only those courses in which: *a*) the professor offered something original, *b*) this original theory or knowledge was important and significant, and *c*) his theory was unpublished. Following this rule, I attended only half a course in the Institute, and throughout four years of undergraduate study at the University of St. Petersburg, I also attended only half a course. All other courses I studied, with a much greater economy of time and effort, from the books of the eminent professors or from the dependable texts recommended by mediocre professors. The advantages of my system of study were and are fairly obvious. In their books the distinguished scholars formulated their theories more precisely than in their lectures; I could study their writings more carefully, if necessary rereading unclear or difficult passages, a thing I could not do when listening to an incessantly unfolding lecture; then while reading the books I could make very comprehensive notes and summaries which would have been impossible in the process of listening to the lecture. Furthermore, my study schedule could be flexible, while the dates and duration of lectures were fixed, and often quite inconveniently for my time schedule and circumstances. Finally, to attend lectures I had to spend at least two hours walking to the buildings where they were given and then back to my "residence." For all these reasons, following my self-imposed rule, I mastered all my courses in a much shorter time and with greater economy of effort than through regular attendance of lectures and recitations. For instance, the famous course of Professor Petrajitzki, General Theory of Law and Morality, given three times a week throughout the academic year, I learned well in two weeks by a careful study of his substantial volume, *Introduction into General Theory of Law and Morality*, and two volumes of his *General Theory of Law and Morality*. With a similar economy of time and effort I mastered other courses at the Institute and at the University. On the basis of my experience I strongly recommend this method of study to all capable university and college students; it is more efficacious, economical, and productive than the wasteful system of obligatory attendance of all the lectures of the courses taken: most lectures and courses hardly offer anything new and original that cannot be found in a good relevant text.

One important shortcoming of my system of study was a lack of personal interaction with the professors. I easily remedied it by active participation in seminars and by direct consultation with the eminent professors. Like most real scholars they eagerly welcomed participation of capable students in their seminars and personal discussion of the students' scientific problems. It was precisely through my study of books, my work in the seminars, and personal discussions with professors E. de Roberty, M. M. Kovalevsky, and V. M.

Bekhtereff at the Institute and with Leon Petrajitzky, M. I. Rostovtzeff, Ivan P. Pavlov, N. Rosin, and other professors at the University of St. Petersburg, that I acquired the reputation of an outstanding student and promising young scholar, was elected chairman of their seminars, was invited to publish some of my papers in scientific journals; and even during my undergraduate years was given the position of assistant in some of their courses, or secretary and research assistant to M. M. Kovalevsky; and finally, in the first year of my graduate work, was appointed a lecturer in sociology at the Psycho-Neurological and Lesgaft institutes.

Besides these advantages my "short-cut" system of study left more time for me to earn my living and greater freedom for my extracurricular scientific, cultural, and political activities.

After enrollment in the Institute, I still had to earn my living, which I did by tutoring and writing occasionally for a few periodicals. The income I earned was very modest but it somehow kept body and soul together. With N. D. Kondratieff and his younger brother, I rented a room in an old apartment house. Three other rooms were rented by three other male students, by two girl students from the Women's College (*Bestujevskiye Kursy*), and by a lady-member of the chorus of the People's Opera Company (*Narodny Dom*). The rent amounted to only a few rubles per month for each of us. Our typical diet was tea and a roll, now and then supplemented by a piece of sausage or cheese. Food did not cost more than 10 to 12 rubles a month. All in all, a monthly income of some 25 to 30 rubles ($12.50 to $15.00) was sufficient to meet our basic needs. To be sure, this standard of living was not affluent, but it kept us going and, among other things, prevented us from becoming fat and soft. Of course, Kondratieff and I could have earned more but we preferred to spend most of our time and energy in enjoyable, creative activities rather than wasting our life in the more gainful but boring occupational pursuits we considered sterile for our mental, moral, and cultural development. The sound attitudes of "first things first" and "the means should never replace the end-value" resulted for us in their usual by-products: progressive improvement of our income and material conditions during the subsequent years of our university life. The next year both of us were granted fairly good university scholarships, then teaching and research assistantships, then lectureships, with their increasingly ample remunerations. The modest standard of living in this first year in no way prevented us from feeling young, bubbling with vitality, and enjoying life in its creative richness.

We lived an intense intellectual life through our concentrated study of the problems and sciences we were interested in, through hearty discussions with our professors, fellow students, and friends, and through the writing and publication of our first scholarly papers. We satisfied our moral demands by trying not to have too many vices and by not pretending to have too many virtues. Our political duties we discharged in the form of "subversive" educational activity among the workers of factories, fellow students, and other groups. This sort of work, for which nobody paid us a single kopeck and which involved the risk of being arrested, imprisoned, and penalized by the Czarist government, we considered as the important moral and political duty of every "critically thinking and morally responsible person," to use the popular expression of P. Lavrov, one of the leading ideologists of the Social-Revolutionary Party. Besides reading masterpieces of literature, we met our esthetic needs by occasionally attending symphonic concerts, operas, and literary recitations; by visiting museums, exhibitions, and galleries; by taking part in students' literary and musical "matinées and soirèes"; by participating in various associations of poets, literati, musicians, painters, and actors; by singing and reciting our own poems or short stories at the convivial gatherings of friends, around some "eats" and "drinks"; and, finally, by flirting with charming girl students.

Despite our modest material conditions, we lived a meaningful, vigorous, and felicitous life of creative efforts and hopeful expectations. To be sure, side by side with its joys and achievements, our life had its sorrows and disappointments, but these only enhanced its depth and plenitude.

Among the leading students of the Institute with whom I became friendly there were several who a few years later distinguished themselves either as notable literary critics, as did V. Polonsky and V. Spiridonov, or as prominent Communist writers and leaders such as Koltzoff, Smilga, Eliava, or as capable psychologists and psychiatrists, like G. Zilboorg (whom we then called the "director of corps de ballet" because of his engrossment in the organization of various dancing parties of girl students), and several others.

During the same year, I established particularly good relations with the founder of the Institute, the internationally known psychologist and psychiatrist V. Bekhterev, and with the international leaders in sociology, philosophy, anthropology, and economic history M. M. Kovalevsky and E. de Roberty, not to mention several other professors. These friendly relationships grew stronger during subsequent years and led to close scientific cooperation between these distinguished scholars and myself—a cooperation which continued up to their deaths.

In spite of the fruitfulness of my studies at the Institute, at the end of my first year there I decided to leave it and to enroll in the University of St. Petersburg. The principal reason for this change was my deep reluctance to be drafted into the armed forces of the Czarist regime. The students of all Russian state universities were exempt from such a draft, while students of the newly established private institutions of higher learning, like the Psycho-Neurological Institute, did not have this privilege—especially the "subversive" students. If I remained in the Institute I would assuredly be drafted the next year. Regarding compulsory military draft as the worst form of coercive servitude imposed upon a free person by the Czarist regime, and military service as training in the art of mass-murder, I neither had any desire to be drafted nor regarded a positive response to the draft as a moral duty. In this attitude I was strongly supported by my friends and professors.

They unanimously advised me to avoid the draft by enrolling in the University. Following my own conviction and the advice of my teachers and friends, in the late spring of 1910 I enrolled in the University. To my surprise, the University soon informed me that on the basis of excellent records in my maturity examination and at the Institute, I was granted a scholarship that paid not only the tuition fee, but a part of my living expenses. Dame Fortune continued to smile.

Lighthearted and encouraged, I went to Ustyug and Rymia for the summer vacation. There in the company of my relatives and friends I rested, helped Aunt Anyssia with her harvesting and haying, and started my field-research on the forms of marriage and the family of the Komi people. For this study I had to visit several villages where I had worked before with my father and brother. The familiar scenery of a still unspoiled nature, the warm company of my previous friends, the agricultural and scientific work—all these greatly refreshed my body and mind fatigued by tense city life. The summer was happy and fruitful indeed. At the end of August, I returned to St. Petersburg.

The University of St. Petersburg

Before the Revolution of 1917 there was neither a department of sociology nor any course given under that name at the University. Despite this official lack of recognition of the field, many basic sociological problems were substantially discussed in courses dealing with law, economics, the theory and philosophy of history, political science, criminology, ethnography, and others. Most of such courses were given in the faculty of law and economics (*Iuridichesky fakultet*), which determined my choice of this department for my concentration and specialization. Among its professors at that time, besides M. M. Kovalevsky, there were Leon Petrajitzky, possibly the greatest scholar of law and morality in the twentieth century; M. I. Tugan-Baranovsky, internationally known economist, particularly in the field of business cycles, problems of socialism, and theory of value; N. Rosin and A. Jijilenko, distinguished criminologists and penologists; and N. Pokrovsky and D. Grimm, eminent professors in the history and dogma of Roman Law. Under the friendly guidance of these scholars, particularly of Leon Petrajitzky and M. Kovalevsky in the department of law and economics, of E. de Roberty in the Institute, and of M. I. Rostovtzeff and N. O. Lossky in the departments of classics and philosophy, I did most of my studies in the University. I was fortunate in having such a splendid galaxy of great scholars as teachers, and, later on, as friends. Being truly eminent professors, they did not require blind acceptance of their theories, as mediocre scholars often do. On the contrary, my *maitres* rather encouraged a reasonably critical attitude toward their viewpoints and heartily welcomed manifestations of creative originality on the part of their students.

My high estimation of the scientific contributions of my teachers, my criticism of the weaknesses of their theories, and some constructive ideas I happened to express in their seminars and in personal discussion seem to have favorably impressed my *maitres*. This impression was reinforced by several anthropological, sociological, juridical, and philosophical studies which I published in respective scientific journals during my undergraduate years, and by the publication of my first substantial volume, *Crime and Punishment, Service and Reward* in my junior year (1913). As a result of their unduly high appreciation of my scholastic achievements, in my sophomore and junior years M. M. Kovalevsky offered me a position as his private secretary and research assistant, de Roberty the position of assistant in his courses and of co-editor of the series "*New Ideas in Sociology*," while Petrajitzky and Bekhterev invited me to be co-editor of *New Ideas in Science of Law* and of *Journal of Psychology and Criminal Anthropology*.*

* In the American Sociological Forum, Vol. I, *Pitirim A. Sorokin in Review*, Duke University Press, 1963, edited by Professor Philip Allen and devoted to analysis, evaluation, and criticism of my sociological, psychological, philosophical, esthetic, juristic, and ethical theories by distinguished American, European, and Asiatic scholars, there is

Generally, the years of my undergraduate study at the University were years of intense and profitable scientific study and development. During this period I acquired a substantial knowledge of philosophy, psychology, ethics, history, and the natural sciences, not to mention sociology and law. In these last two fields I mastered all the important theories of law, Russian and European; history of Roman, Western, and Russian law, the dogmas of the constitutional, civil, and criminal law, by a careful study of the codes of law and of the most important Russian and Western works in these fields. Still more importantly I studied most of the classical works in sociology, philosophy of history, and related disciplines, including the recent Western works in these fields, such as those of Durkheim, Tarde, Simmel, Max Weber, Pareto, and Westermarck, to mention but a few.

Along with the enrichment of my knowledge in these disciplines I continued the work of integrating this knowledge into a unified, more or less consistent system or *Weltanschauung*. Philosophically the emerging system was a variety of empirical neopositivism or critical realism based upon logical and empirical scientific methods. Sociologically it represented a sort of synthesis of Comteian-Spencerian sociology of evolution-progress corrected and supplemented by the theories of N. Mikhailovsky, P. Lavrov, E. de Roberty, L. Petrajitzky, M. Kovalevsky, M. Rostovtzeff, P. Kropotkin, among the Russian social thinkers, and by the theories of G. Tarde, E. Durkheim, G. Simmel, M. Weber, R. Stammler, K. Marx, V. Pareto and other western social scientists. Politically, it was a form of socialistic ideology, founded upon the ethics of solidarity, mutual aid, and freedom. All in all, it was an optimistic *Weltanschauung* fairly similar to the prevalent "world-view" of a majority of the Russian and Western thinkers of the pre-

given a fairly complete chronological bibliography of my scientific publications, including most important papers published during my undergraduate years. A similar bibliography is given in the E. Tiryakian volume; *Sociological Theory. Essays in Honor of Pitirim A. Sorokin,* The Free Press of Glencoe, 1963.

catastrophic decade of the twentieth century. I did not foresee then that this "scientific, positivistic, and progressively optimistic" *Weltanschauung* soon would be found wanting by the crucial test of historical events and would engender the second crisis in my world-outlook and its second basic revision similar to the first crisis and reintegration. This second crisis was hidden in the darkness of the future. In these undergraduate years I was satisfied with this *Weltanschauung* of "a young calf looking through pink glasses at the rosy world," as I used to call it in my later years.

To finish this dry chronicle of my undergraduate academic activities I can briefly mention that in 1914 I graduated with the first-class diploma from the University of St. Petersburg. At graduation the University offered me the position of a "person left at the University for preparation for professorship." I gladly accepted the offer because it fully satisfied my own choice of professorial and academic activities as the main vocation of my life. A fairly good stipend, granted for at least four years of preparation for the magister degree and privat-docentship, was quite sufficient to cover my living expenses and allowed me to give all my time to my scientific work. Since sociology was still absent from the list of disciplines approved by the University, I had to choose one of the fields taught there. After some hesitation, I chose criminal law and penology as my major and constitutional law as my minor fields. This choice determined the disciplines to which I gave most of my time during the next two years of my graduate study. My concentrated study of these disciplines in no way interrupted my labors in sociology. During the next two years of my preparation for teaching I devoted as much time to sociology as to my official field of specialization. All in all I was fairly well satisfied by the results of my undergraduate study; it earned me not only the University diploma and the privilege of being "left at the University for preparation for professorship" but also a reputation of a capable young scholar expected to grow into an outstanding scholar and creative thinker in the years to come.

Politics

The preceding account of my undergraduate academic activities must not convey the false impression that my life, as well as that of many other students, was confined within the quiet and narrow limits of academic learning. Social and political conditions in Russia during the years 1910-14 did not permit such confinement. Though the Revolution of 1905-6 was over, its consequences were still operative and continued their double work of undermining the remnants of the Czarist regime and of preparing, planning, and beginning to build the new regime to come. The whole cultural, social, and political life of the country was in a state of intense inner excitement which manifested itself in the emergence and blossoming of new currents in the arts; in intense pulsation of philosophical, humanistic, and social thought; and in a proliferation of diverse political discussions and movements, both legal and illegal. Being a kind of interloper interested in many cultural fields, I naturally followed these currents and movements as a member of various groups and associations, as a listener to, and participant in, many private and public discussions. These activities brought me into contact with a number of leading poets, writers, musicians, artists, philosophers, columnists, and other cultural celebrities.

Still more active was my participation in the political life of the country. Through Kovalevsky, who was an influential member of the State Council (which corresponded somewhat to the Senate of the United States) and a leader of a liberal party, and through Petrajitzky, who was one of the leaders of the Constitutional-Democratic Party, I met many influential officials and statesmen, members of the *Duma* (Russian House of Representatives), and other leaders of conservative and progressive political parties. Kovalevsky, Petrajitzky, de Roberty, and other professors knew of my affiliation with the Social-Revolutionary Party and of my past and present "subversive" activities; however, this knowledge in no way spoiled our good relations. If anything they rather approved of my political views as being quite natural for a young man of my background. Kovalevsky often half-humorously introduced me to political leaders as "a young Jean Jacques Rousseau," while Petrajitzky, de Roberty, and others commented favorably on the broad and idealistic-realistic character of my political ideology which was free from a narrow fanaticism and intolerance.

Still closer grew my relationships with the ideological and political leaders and members of the Social-Revolutionary and other Socialist parties. My "subversive" lectures, political discussions, and social work among factory workers, students, and various groups of intelligentsia; political articles I began to publish in both highbrow and popular periodicals congenial to the Social-Revolutionary ideology; my work of organizing the Social-Revolutionary "cells" and "groups"—these and similar activities soon earned me the reputation of a notable ideologist and young leader of the Social-Revolutionary current of thought.

These activities naturally developed my contact and cooperation with the leaders of the party in the Duma (Kerensky and others) and in other national institutions, with editors of journals congenial to the party, like *Russkoyie Bogatstvo* and *Zavety,* and with the weekly and daily periodicals (legal and illegal)—not to mention my cooperation with a multitude of ordinary members and fellow travelers of the party.

These political activities, plus participation in the same seminars and scientific work in the University, were responsible for the establishment of friendly relations and cooperation with the leaders and members of the Social-Democratic (Bolshevik and Menshevik), the People's Socialist, and other radical parties. At that time all these parties did their anti-Czarist revolutionary work together, as one revolutionary front fighting the common enemy. This did not preclude many a heated discussion of basic theoretical differences between the Social-Revolutionary and the Social-Democratic ideologies. But these discussions, with the exception of a few public disputes, we had mainly in our rooms in the most informal and friendly atmosphere of convivial gatherings around food and drink. Despite their casual character, in these informal discussions we probed deeper, learned more, and sharpened our pro and con arguments more fruitfully than in many a public dispute between various leaders, or in lecture courses. It was through participation in these seminars of Petrajitzky, Kovalevsky, and Tugan-Baranovsky, through shared revolutionary work, and eventually through many heated, informal discussions that a mutual friendship developed between myself and several Social-Democratic students, such as Piatakov, Karakhan, and others, who later became Communist leaders and members of the first Communist Council of the People's Kommissars headed by Lenin. (Karakhan was the Secretary of Foreign Affairs, Piatakov, Secretary of Industry and Commerce, and so on).

We could not then foresee that a few years later we would be fighting on opposite sides of the civil war, and little did I suspect that these friendships and my "subversive" work among the factory-workers would one day save me from being shot by a Communist firing squad.

That episode often reminded me of the wisdom of the biblical saying about bread cast upon the waters. One seldom knows all the consequences of one's actions; but all in all good actions seem to bring good consequences while evil actions tend to react upon the doer with disastrous results. Perhaps some law of the preservation of energy of human actions—somewhat similar to the physical laws of preservation of energy and matter—is operative also in the human world; possibly none of our actions vanish completely and all our activities continue to function in the form of their short- and long-term consequences.

New Arrests

My political activities increasingly attracted the attention not only of various anti-Czarist groups but also of the Czarist police and secret agencies. Their "watch and ward" over my political conduct soon brought me trouble. Already during my freshman year at the University the police had invaded a purely convivial gathering of my friends in my room, had searched, arrested, and conveyed the whole party to the nearest police station. Being in high spirits (partly because of vodka and beer we had consumed) and having no respect for the agents of the crumbling order, we decisively refused to be interrogated. Instead we showered the police with invectives and started singing and dancing so noisily that in a short time the police chief yelled at us: "Get out of this station, get out of this place!" which we obligingly did, our songs reverberating through the streets.

This kind of treatment of political offenders by police agents is hardly possible in strong and sound political regimes, but it frequently occurs in crumbling regimes that have outlived their usefulness. Their obsolescent values cease to inspire its agents with self-confidence, self-respect, and deep conviction in the righteousness of their official duties and bureaucratic orders. Disintegration of the dying political order usually demoralizes that order's agents. Confronted with the enthusiastic proselytes of new, ascending values, they become hesitant, confused, and frequently fail to execute their official functions. I have already noted above this kind of failure on the part of Kineshma prison guards, and I observed it many times during my encounters with Czarist agents. Similar demoralization has taken place in practically all "decaying regimes" on the eve of their reformist or revolutionary liquidation, beginning with the oldest recorded revolution in Ancient Egypt (*ca.* 3000-2500 B.C.) and ending with the recent revolutions against or reconstructions of the defective governments in Cuba, South Korea, South Vietnam, Japan, and in some Latin-American countries. As in Russia, the anti-government movements in these countries have been spearheaded by student demonstrations and clashes with the police forces of the decaying regimes; and, as in Russia, these police forces often failed to oppose vigorously student demonstrations and anti-government activities. The episode of the arrest and release of our party is therefore rather typical of dying political regimes and their police forces.

During these years similar arrests and releases of myself and other revolutionary students occurred so frequently that we used to regard them as a mere routine nuisance and took them in our stride without particular anxiety.

Besides these nuisances, occasionally much longer imprisonments, banishments, and other punitive measures were inflicted on some of the young and old revolutionaries. An imminent threat of this sort of punishment arose for me in my freshman year at the university. The threat originated in connection with the nation-wide student demonstrations against the Czarist government occasioned by the death of Leo Tolstoi on November 20, 1910. In the highly charged political atmosphere of Russia, Tolstoi's departure from his family and estate before his death, and then his death itself, served as an igniting spark for an explosion of serious anti-Czarist disorders among the students and the faculties of universities and higher institutions of learning. These "disorders" continued for a few weeks and interrupted the academic life of many such institutions. The Czarist government attempted to suppress the disorders by the harsh measures of mass arrest, imprisonment, and banishment, especially of the leaders of these "subversive" movements. Being one of these leaders, I naturally expected attempts to arrest and imprison me if I were to let myself be caught. Having no desire to be jailed again, I took the necessary measures to elude this danger by spending the night in the rooms of friends and by visiting my room only for a few moments and only when the agreed signals indicated that it was neither being watched by police nor were they there to trap me.

In January, 1911, gendarmes ("'archangels'") indeed came to arrest me. Not finding me at home, they carefully searched the room and, discovering no incriminating evidence (which I had removed), they left it to arrest other "subversive" leaders. Promptly informed about their visit, I redoubled, with the help of friends, my precautionary measures. For a week or so I successfully eluded "the archangels" and the "pharaohs," who intensified their hunt and increasingly interfered with my active participation in the "disorders."

I do not know whether I would finally have been arrested had I remained in St. Petersburg, but an unforeseen event saved me from this unwelcome lot. One of my friends, an engineer, became gravely ill in his advanced state of tuberculosis. Among other medical measures, doctors prescribed a trip to the Italian Riviera, accompanied by a nurse or friend to help him during the trip. Looking for such a companion, the engineer and friends conceived the idea of suggesting me for this role. My sick friend told me that my company would be more enjoyable to him than that of someone unknown and that I could save myself from pending arrest and help him at the same time. At first I objected to the plan on the ground of my incompetence in nursing. Friends, doctors, and the engineer himself countered my objection by assurances that, supplied with the necessary medicines and with instructions concerning their use, the diet, and other conditions, I would be able to serve the sick friend as well as any nurse-companion. Once I had accepted the offer, my friends proceeded to obtain a false passport, a uniform of a student-officer of the Military Medical Academy (*Voienno-Medizinskaia Akademia*), and all the other certificates and paraphernalia necessary for a successful impersonation. They even drilled me in how to salute and handle a sword and in other manners and sayings expected of a student of the Academy. The plan went through without a hitch. No suspicions were aroused throughout the whole trip, including the perfunctory questioning and checking of our luggage and passports at the boundaries of Russia, Switzerland, Austria, and Italy. After a few days travel in a comfortable compartment of the International Sleeping Cars (*wagon-lit*) we safely arrived at San Remo. There my friend entered the sanatorium prescribed by his doctors while I stayed in one of the local hotels for two weeks or so.

In this unforeseen way I had my first visit to Western Europe and my first impression of the "highly civilized" (as I thought then) countries. All in all these impressions were favorable. Farms, countryside, and cities seemed quite attractive to me, prosperous and well ordered as they were; the standard of living was much higher and the people more dignified, free, and satisfied than their counterparts in Russia. The sunny Riviera, the Mediterranean, the mountains, the resort cities—all appeared beautiful and delightful. The Russians and foreigners whom I met in the hotel were kind and helpful in many ways, particularly in taking me sight-seeing in Nice and Monte-Carlo where, following their suggestion, I even gambled at the Casino for a few minutes and won a few hundred francs. After two weeks of enjoyable vacation I said goodbye to my sick friend and started back to Russia. I stopped overnight in Vienna and, among other things, bought there the recently published *G. Simmel's Soziologie*. I reached St. Petersburg safely and resumed my normal way of living.

The climax of student "disorders" was about over. With their decline the police search for subversives and revolutionaries had also abated. Academic life resumed its normal course with the exception of a few stubborn students who remained faithful to their previous pledge of not resuming their academic functions or taking their examinations until the required minimum of academic freedom was secured for the universities and higher institutions. I was among these stubborn subversives. I continued my studies, and at the end of the academic year was well prepared for the examination, but as a sign of my protest against the Czarist regime and its suppression of academic freedom I did not take the examination at the end of the year. This stubbornness cost me my university scholarship for the next year: regardless of their personal wishes the university authorities had to deprive me of the scholarship for flunking the examinations. I took this penalty in stride as a small price for keeping my pledge and self-respect. Eventually the scholarship was renewed for my junior and senior years.

My last imprisonment by the Czarist regime took place in 1913, the tercentenary year of the Romanov dynasty in Russia. At the suggestion of my party I agreed to write a critical pamphlet about the crimes, misdeeds, and misrule of this dynasty of Russia. Unfortunately one of the members of the party cognizant of this plan happened to be an *agent-provocateur* of the Czarist *Okhranka* secret service. (At that time the Social-Revolutionary and the Social-Democratic parties were successfully penetrated by the agents of the Okhranka. Some of these spies even succeeded in becoming top leaders of these parties, like Aseff in the Social-Revolutionary Party and Chernomasoff, an intimate friend of Lenin and the editor-in-chief of Lenin's *Pravda,* in the Social-Democratic Party.) This *agent-provocateur* promptly informed the Okhranka about the projected pamphlet and its author. Returning to my room on a late evening in March, 1913, I found "the "archangels" of the Okhranka there waiting for me. They promptly arrested and took me to the modern reformatory (*"Predvarilka"*) with which I was acquainted from having visited some professors, students, and revolutionaries prevoiusly incarcerated there. (Arrests and short-term imprisonment of scholars and students were fairly frequent during these years.) They put me in a clean and fairly comfortable cell, so far as prison cells are "comfortable." After their routine interrogations, I settled down to live and work there as well as I could. From a fairly good library of the reformatory I took out several books, among these Mark Twain's *Life on the Mississippi* which I had not read before. I thoroughly enjoyed this book by my favorite American writer. It did not occur to me then that sometime in the future I would be living on the banks of this river (in Minneapolis) and would see it from its beginning in Itasca Park, Minnesota, to its end in Louisiana. However, we rarely foresee many important consequences of our actions and many events destined to happen in our life. The Czarist authorities held me in the reformatory for about three weeks. Having no proof that I had written the pamphlet and being hard pressed by M. Kovalevsky and other influential statesmen, such as the members of the Duma and the State Council (*Gosudartvennuy Soviet*), they were obliged to set me free.

This was my last imprisonment by the Czarist regime. In

all these imprisonments I was treated quite decently and humanely—something I cannot say for the Communist penological methods that I experienced a few years later. These methods were indeed cruel, inhuman, and deadly not only for the prisoner but also for his relatives, friends, and the groups to which he belonged. The Czarist prisons could be called a purgatory in comparison with the inferno of Communist prisons and camps.

Fortunately, in 1913 the hell of Communist imprisonments was hidden in the darkness of the future. When I stepped out of the gates of the reformatory, I felt intoxicated with the joy of regained freedom. Happy and energetic, I resumed my normal activities the very next day.

All in all my life (and the lives of my friends) during these years was eventful, exciting, and meaningful. No boredom, no feeling of emptiness, no sense of aimless drifting, and no fear of adverse winds seriously marred it. It was a rich life of *per aspera ad astra*.

CHAPTER SIX

Preparation for Professorship: 1914-16

Requirements for the Master's (Magister) Degree*

The "preparation for professorship" in Russian universities remotely corresponded to graduate and postgraduate study in our American universities. However, the similarities between these two types of advanced training were hardly greater than their dissimilarities. Young scholars "left for preparation for professorship" were not required to take courses, attend lectures or seminars, undergo any examination, or submit any term papers until they actually presented themselves at the oral examination for master's (magister) degree. At least 99 per cent of the candidates for professorship had first to pass oral examinations for this degree, and second to submit and successfully defend their master's dissertations after they had been "accepted for defense" by a special committee of eminent specialist-professors of several universities. Only in the exceedingly rare cases of already eminent scholars applying for a master's degree were they granted a doctor's degree instead, on the grounds of their significant achievements and the outstanding importance of their dissertations. Such was the case with the great Russian philosopher Vladimir Solovoyev, with an eminent statistician and scientific methodologist, A. A. Tschuprov, and with the outstanding economic historian, Peter B. Struve. With these extremely rare exceptions, all candidates for professorship had to meet successfully the outlined requirements for master's degree.

* The requirements for the master's (magister) degree in the Russian universities were notably higher than for the Ph.D. degree in American or German universities.

Once he had taken this degree, any magister could attach himself as a privat-docent (lecturer) to any university he chose and could hold any lecture-course or seminar in his field, not excluding those parallel to and competing with the same kind of course offered by "ordinary" (full) professors. The salary of lecturers was much lower than that of full professors. But if a privat-docent was an outstanding scholar and a popular lecturer, he often had a much larger body of students registered in his course and consequently a larger income from the student fees than a less eminent full professor. Such precisely was the case with privat-docent M. Tugan-Baranovsky and Professor Georgievsky at the University of St. Petersburg. Both of them offered parallel courses in political economy, but the number of students registered in Tugan-Baranovsky's course was many times larger than that in the course of Georgievsky, and their respective incomes from the course varied accordingly. Eventually a talented privat-docent was promoted to the position of an "extraordinary" or "ordinary" professor. Generally, fair competition in scientific creativity played a more important role in Russian universities than it does in our American higher institutions.

Because of the much more stringent requirements for the master's degree in Russian universities than for the Ph.D. degree in our universities, most Russian professors held only a master's degree. The doctor's degree was granted only to outstanding professors whose dissertations were of far greater scientific importance than the rank-and-file of master's theses. The dissertations for the master's and doctor's degrees were invariably submitted in the form of a substantial printed volume or volumes. No oral examination was required for the doctor's degree.

After my appointment for "preparation for professorship," professor of criminal law N. Rosin gave me a list of some five hundred titles of Russian and foreign volumes in the field of criminal law, Professor A. Jijilenko handed me a list of some 250 titles in the field of criminal procedure, and Professor N. Lazarevsky added a list of some 150 titles in constitutional law.

Some of these titles, such as the German *Vergleichende Darstellung* of criminal law and procedure (prepared by eminent German professors for the new project of German criminal code), consisted of almost one hundred substantial volumes. As they gave me these lists the professors told me: "You must show a good knowledge of these works to pass your oral examination for master's degree successfully. We are not interested in how you master them. But master them you must. If from time to time you would like to have conferences with us or with other professors, we will be glad to be of service to you." These lists and the very brief instructions accompanying them constituted all the requirements for the master's oral examinations.

Before World War I preparation for these oral examinations ordinarily took some four or more years. During this period the candidates used to go abroad for one or more years to work with eminent foreign scholars in their fields. But my "preparation" occurred in the years of World War I, a period during which trips abroad and work with foreign scholars became impossible. For this reason I had to pursue my preparatory studies in Russia, without the benefit of the personal consultations and guidance of foreign scholars. Some of their wartime works, however, continued somehow to reach the university libraries. For instance, as early as December, 1916, I managed to find there Pareto's *Trattato di sociologia generale,* just published in Italy.

Other candidates for the master's degree were in a similar situation during the years of the war. Despite this isolation from Western scholarship and science during the years of World War I, and the still greater isolation during the first period of the Communist revolution, several internationally known scholars emerged from our group of candidates. Among them were Dr. George Gurvitch, now a successor to Durkheim's chair in the Sorbonne; N. S. Timasheff, a distinguished sociologist of Harvard and Fordham universities; and Max Laserson, professor of constitutional law at the universities of Riga (Latvia) and Tel-Aviv, and researcher for the Carnegie

Foundation of Peace, like the abovementioned professors N. Kondratieff, T. Rainov, and several others. Also from our group came several political leaders: Dr. Piip, first prime minister of Latvia, the first high officials of Estonia, and the Communist leaders Piatakov, Karakhan, and others.

Despite enormous obstacles, many of the candidates of our group (which hardly exceeded some twenty or so members) succeeded in overcoming the difficulties inherent in these times to become internationally known scholars or political leaders. This seems to indicate that the selection of the candidates for future professorship or leadership by the University was quite careful and valid. It may also possibly mean that the complete freedom given to the candidates in their preparation for the advanced degree was probably a much better method than our "compulsory" system of graduate training with its numerous course requirements to be fulfilled and the hosts of other requirements of an essentially undergraduate nature. If the fruitfulness of this "regimental system" of education is doubtful even for undergraduate students, for graduate students it appears to me quite poisonous to the development of potential creativity and originality. The sooner the American universities discard this "undergraduate" system of graduate training, the better for the talented students, the universities, and the nation at large.

Freed from financial worry by a decent fellowship granted to me with my appointment, during the years 1914-16 I was able to give all my time to preparation for master's examinations as well as to my sociological research. With youthful vigor I earnestly devoted myself to these tasks, and in a record period of two years, instead of the usual four or more years, I succeeded in passing my master's oral examinations in October-November, 1916. Perhaps it should be stressed again that these examinations were much more rigorous than the American oral examinations for the Ph.D. degree. First, the examination took four days, one for criminal law, one for criminal procedure, one for constitutional law, and finally, one for writing a substantial extemporaneous essay on a topic assigned by the examining body. Each of these examinations lasted from three to five hours. Second the examining body consisted not only of the members of the special committee appointed for this purpose but of most of the professors of the entire Juridical Faculty (roughly corresponding to our Law School plus the departments of economic and political science). The range of the questions posed by this comparatively large body of professors was much wider and the character of their questions from related fields was often more surprising and therefore more difficult to answer than the questions of some three or four members of the examining committee for the Ph.D. degree in our universities.

Passing these examinations conferred upon me the degree of "magistrant of criminal law," and entitled me to become a privat-docent of the University of St. Petersburg. To receive the degree of "magister of criminal law" I had to submit a magister's dissertation, have it approved by the committee of the University and then to defend it successfully in an exceedingly rigorous dispute with all the official opponents appointed by the University, unofficial faculty opponents, and public challengers. The day of the defense of a master's or doctor's dissertation was "the red-letter day" in university life, much more important than "home-coming day" or the day of the big football game in the life of our universities. The date of the dispute was advertised in advance in the university publications and in all the important newspapers. One of the biggest auditoriums of the university was especially reserved for the dispute. With the rector or pro-rector of the university presiding, the defense was carried on in the presence of all the professors of the Juridical Faculty (or another big division of the University), other professors who wished to attend, many specialists outside of the university, a multitude of students, and a large body of the interested public.

In the presence of this large audience the dispute was opened by reading the *curriculum vitae* and a list of the main publications and achievements of the defender of the dissertation. Then each of the official opponents presented his criticism, emphasizing all the weak and doubtful points of the thesis. Each of the criticisms was answered point by point by the defending scholar. The attacks of the official opponents were followed by the criticisms of the unofficial opponents—members of the faculty who wanted to take part in the dispute, then by the critical remarks of the outside experts and, finally, those of any member of the public and the student body. Each of these criticisms was again immediately answered by the dissertators. The whole dispute ordinarily lasted from five to seven hours.

At its termination all the members of the faculty present at the dispute cast secret ballots for or against granting the student the degree of magister or doctor. The majority of votes decided the matter.

The interchange of these criticisms and repartee was one of the most exciting and inspiring spectacles I have ever witnessed. In this scientific debate, the disputing parties impressively displayed their deepest knowledge, their brilliant logic, their humor, wit, and sparkling originality. It was indeed a magnificent battle of mature and competent minds clashing in their common search for truth and verifiable knowledge. It was a most enlightening exhibition of intellectual fireworks and a real educational feast for the participants as well as for the public at large. No wonder, therefore, that each of these disputes was comprehensively reported by the press and served as a topic for vital discussion in the university as well as in the intellectual circles of the whole nation for many days and weeks. I can but deeply regret that our universities and colleges do not have this kind of dispute as their "red-letter" days, instead of the big "football-baseball-screwball" days devoid of any mental stimulation, inspiration, or intellectual activity. On this point, as well as in the policy of granting advanced scientific degrees mainly to influential financiers and politicians innocent of any contribution to science, philosophy, or the fine arts, our universities and colleges have gravely deviated from their real task and have inadvertently degraded the value of scientific degrees as well as of the scientific prestige of the universities and learning in general.

Having received the degree of "a magistrant of criminal law," I planned to submit my substantial volume: *Crime and Punishment, Service and Reward,* published in 1913, as my dissertation for the degree of magister of criminal law. The preliminary reactions of the professors of criminal law of the University of St. Petersburg, as well as of some other universities, were for the most part favorable for acceptance of the volume as my magister dissertation. As a matter of fact the committee of these professors tentatively designated some day in March, 1917, for the public defense of this thesis. The plan, however, was cancelled by the violent disorders occurring in January and February of 1917 and then by the eruption of the Russian Revolution in March of 1917. The preliminary disorders and eventual explosion of the Revolution completely disrupted university life, including all procedures for granting advanced scientific degrees. The Communist Revolution in October, 1917, and the ensuing civil war prolonged the cessation of practically all functions of the University for 1917 and 1918. In 1918 the Communist government decreed complete abolition of scientific degrees in all institutions of higher learning. These revolutionary circumstances explain why the plan for my magisterial dispute fell through and why I had to wait until April 22, 1922, to defend two volumes of my *System of Sociology* (published in 1920) which I submitted as a dissertation for the degree of doctor of sociology.

Public Defense of My Dissertation

In a highly subdued and abnormal form, the universities gradually began to revive in the years of 1919-21. With the resumption of their functions, the old members of the faculties—that is, the pre-revolutionary scholars and scientists, in contrast to "the red, Communist professors" appointed by the Communist government—slowly succeeded, if not legally then at least practically, in re-establishing the advanced scientific degrees with their requirements and procedures similar to those of the pre-revolutionary period. The new requirements, however, were somewhat less rigorous than the old ones; the faculties of the universities knew well through their own experience the near physical and mental impossibility of carrying on serious scientific work under conditions of acute starvation, lack of the basic necessities, amidst endless waves of various epidemics and the "abomination of desolation" of the civil war, in an atmosphere of continuing persecution of the non-Communist scholars, and in the climate of fierce governmental terror and complete insecurity of scholars and scientists themselves. During these years only a small fraction of the non-Communist scientists and scholars were able to do any significant work. Most of them busied themselves mainly with routine teaching activities. Under these circumstances the relaxation of requirements for the advanced scientific degrees was quite comprehensible and certainly excusable. Another element of the new requirements was that, in view of the governmental abolition of scientific degrees, at the end of the public defence of a dissertation the faculty could not vote for or against granting the appropriate degree to the dissertator, but rather voted for a "successful" or "unsuccessful" defense of his dissertation. This verdict did not formally violate the governmental abolition of the degree but in fact did signify a verdict of granting or not granting the scientific degree to the dissertator.

Despite the very adverse conditions of my personal life in the years of 1918-20 (described in subsequent chapters), somehow I succeeded in writing, besides two elementary texts *General Theory of Law* and the *Popular Text of Sociology,* (*Uchebnik Obschei Teorii Prava* and *Obschedostupnuy Uchebnik Soziologii,* Jaroslavl, 1920), two substantial volumes of my *System of Sociology* (*Sistema Soziologii,* 2 vols., Isdateltvo Kolos, Petragrad, 1920). I succeeded not only in writing but, what was much more difficult, in publishing the "subversive" volumes illegally. The extraordinary feat of illegal publication, especially of the *System of Sociology* in times when even a mere visiting card or "exit" sign could not be printed without the approval of the Communist censors, was accomplished through the heroic efforts of my friends—F. I. Sedenko-Vitiazeff, publisher of the Kolos firm, and the workers and printers of two nationalized printing establishments in St. Petersburg ("the Second and the Tenth State Printing Houses").

In sympathy with my political and social views and bound by the ties of personal friendship, they secretly printed the books (360 pages in Vol. I and 460 pages in Vol. II), forged the Communist censorship permission, stamped the necessary letters "R.V.C." ("Permitted by the Communist censorship") on the title pages of the volumes, then published ten thousand copies of each volume and sold and distributed the entire edition within a short period of two or three weeks. When the Communist government learned of the publication it ordered all printed copies to be confiscated. Its agents, however, scarcely found a copy to seize and destroy. Of course the Communist police tried to arrest me and Sedenko, but, expecting the arrest, we "ducked underground" and remained there until we could safely re-emerge. (During these years the Communist agents had to arrest so many people that they could not afford to spend too much time and energy searching for a single individual. If they could not find him in a few days, they soon had to abandon their search in favor of some of their many other victims.)

With the restoration of the advanced scientific degrees and their requirements at the end of 1921, the deans and faculty members of the University of St. Petersburg urged me to submit two volumes of my *System of Sociology* as a dissertation for the doctor's degree in sociology. (Sociology had been introduced into the university curriculum under Kerensky's regime in 1917, and in the years of 1919-22 was expanded into a separate department with myself as its elected chairman.) After some hesitation I followed this suggestion and submitted my volumes to the Juridical Faculty. The special committee of the University approved the work and fixed April 22, 1922, as the day for its public defense.

By a lucky chance I saved the editorial "The Dispute of Professor P. A. Sorokin," published in the *Ekonomist,* Nos. 4-5, 1922. The article gives a detailed account of the public defense of my dissertation. It says that the dispute was presided over by the chairman of the faculty, a distinguished professor of medieval history, I. M. Grevs, and that it took place in the large physics auditorium filled to capacity with members of the faculty, students, outside scholars, journalists, and interested public. According to the editorial, at the beginning of the memorable session the secretary of the faculty read Sorokin's *curriculum vitae* and a list of his publications. This was followed by the introductory address of the dissertator in which he summed up the basic principles, uniformities, methods, and purposes of his volumes. These preliminaries over, the dispute opened with a general evaluation of Sorokin's work and was followed by detailed criticisms of its weak and ambiguous points delivered by "the official opponents" of the University, namely by a notable professor of sociology, K. M. Takhtareff; a distinguished professor of history and sociology, N. Kareeff; and an eminent professor of philosophy, I. I. Lapshin. The official opponents unanimously hailed the *System of Sociology* as an outstanding contribution to the field and then presented their point-by-point criticisms of its shortcomings. Each of their criticisms was vigorously answered by the dissertator. Following the long debate with the official opponents, several other scholars took part in the dispute: former vice-president of the first Duma, Professor N. Gredeskul, Professor of Economics S. I. Tkhorjevsky, and others.

The whole debate lasted about six hours and was terminated by the secret vote of the faculty. The article of the *Ekonomist* ends with the statement: "In view of the abolition of the advanced scientific degrees at the present time, the dispute was closed by the official announcement by presiding professor Grevs that the faculty vote unanimously approved the *System of Sociology* as fully meeting the requirements for which it was submitted, and that Professor Sorokin's defense of his dissertation was unanimously voted quite satisfactory. A big audience rewarded the verdict and the dissertator with a long and thunderous ovation."

That evening I was tired but happy that the felicitous ordeal was over. Subsequent events revealed that the date for my public dispute was happily chosen; if it had been postponed for a few months the dispute could never have taken place because soon the Communist government renewed its attempts to arrest me, and in September, 1922, I was banished from Russia, which I have not visited up to this time.

Some forty-four years have now elapsed since the publication of my *System of Sociology*. Unless there is an urgent need for it, I rarely reread my books after they are published. During these forty-four years, while writing my volumes: *Social and Cultural Dynamics* (1937-41); *Social Mobility* (1927); *Contemporary Sociological Theories* (1928); and *Society, Culture and Personality* (1947), I had to reread various parts of these volumes. As a result of these rereadings I find that, despite several defects, the volumes gave what appears to me the first logically systematic and empirically detailed theory of social structures: "The Structure of the Elementary Social Systems," developed in Volume I, and "The Structure of the Complex (Multibonded) Social Systems," expounded in Volume II.

If in these later works I virtually reiterated in concise form the theory developed in my *Sistema Soziologii*, the reason for such repetition was that I found my early theory more logically consistent, more empirically valid, and more scientifically adequate than any other theory of the social structure in the world literature of sociology and social sciences. In addition to the theory of the social structures, the *Sistema Soziologii* contained the skeleton of a theory of social mobility later developed in my pioneering monograph on *Social Mobility*.

Considering the fact that these later volumes have been translated into many languages, have served as advanced texts in the universities of many Western and Eastern countries, have opened new fields of social research, and have produced a large literature dealing with my theories, these "social facts" testify favorably to, and confirm the verdict of the faculty vote of the University of St. Petersburg that *Sistema Soziologii* fully met the requirements for which it was submitted and was well defended by the dissertator from the criticisms of its "official" and unofficial opponents at the dispute, as well as of various opponents who have attacked it during the forty-four-year period since its publication.

With this remark I conclude the account of my public defense of the *Sistema Soziologii*. This story tells of an event that happened in 1922, not in the period 1914-16 with which the chapter deals; but I inserted the story here in order to complete the narrative of my labors for the advanced scientific degree in Russia. Now that this matter is disposed of, I can return to a brief account of other aspects of my life during the years of 1914-16.

Life Amidst the Fury of War and the Rumblings of Revolution

The preceding story of my academic life in 1914-16 should not give a false impression that my activities, as well as those of other Russian scholars, were confined to our scientific pursuits. Such complete dedication to science or the arts was impossible amidst the conflagration of the World War and first thunderings of the approaching Revolution. In Czarist Russia university professors and students were free from compulsory draft into the armed forces (a very wise rule for the welfare of any nation). Despite this freedom, they willingly took an active part in defending the fatherland from the invading enemy—each scholar or student working in the field in which his special training was most useful. Like many other social scientists I worked on many committees to organize and mobilize the economic resources of the nation, supplies for the armed forces, recreational and educational arrangements for invalids and veterans and active units of the army and navy.

Besides participation in various committees I lectured extensively in the line of duty to various military groups and civic audiences.

Side by side with these patriotic activities many of us carried on the no less urgent work of charting the plans, ways and means of what we ourselves and the nation at large should do in the case of the imminent downfall of the Czarist regime and the defeat of Russia by the German forces. If at the beginning of the war the Czarist government was supported by the nation, the government's unpreparedness and growing incapacity to cope successfully with the defense of the country rapidly undermined the patriotic support, the trust, and the very prestige of the Czarist regime. Already in 1915 many of us were quite certain that the days of this regime were numbered and that some plans for a basic reconstruction of the nation should be made as well as decisions of what to do about the increasingly devastating war and the further invasion of the country by the enemy.

At the end of 1916 and in January, 1917, the over-all situation of the nation became quite critical. A few lines from my *Leaves from a Russian Diary* vividly describe it.

"It is clear that we are now entering the storm of the Revolution. The authority of the Czar, the Czarina, and all the Government has terribly broken down. Defeat of Russian arms, poverty, and wide discontent of the people inevitably call forth a new revolutionary clamor. The speeches of Shulgin, Milyukov, and Kerensky in the Duma, and especially Milyukov's denunciation of the "stupidity and treason of the Government," have awakened a dangerous echo throughout the country. . . . University life tends to become more and more disorderly. On the walls of the lavatories one reads such sentences as: 'Down with the Czar!' 'Death to the Czarina of Rasputin!' . . . The newspapers have become audacious in attacking the Government. Prices are rising frightfully. Bread lines before the shops are longer and longer. Bitter complaints from poor people waiting for hours in these lines become more and more rebellious. . . . The soldiers returning from the front speak of the Government with hatred and extreme indignation. . . . Street demonstrations by poor women and children demanding "bread and herrings" became larger and noisier. . . . The rioters today stopped tram cars, turning over some of them, plundering a good many shops, and even attacking policemen. Many workmen have joined the women; strikes and disorders begin to proliferate. . . . The Russian Revolution was begun by hungry women and children demanding bread and herrings. They started by wrecking street cars and looting a few small shops. Only later did they, together with workmen and politicians, become ambitious to wreck that mighty edifice—the Russian autocracy. The orderly routine of life is broken. Shops and offices are closed. Political meetings are held in the University instead of lectures. Revolution has set one foot over the threshold of my country. . . . The police are idle and irresolute. Even the Cossacks have refused to disperse the crowds. This means that the Government is helpless and their machine broken. Rioters have begun to kill policemen. . . . The end is very near . . . or is it only the beginning?

"Politicians of all parties, intellectuals of all currents of thought, and the mentally and morally bankrupt nobility busy themselves with endless political discussions and plans.

"At a meeting yesterday of deputies, politicians, scholars, and writers at the house of Shubin-Posdeeff, even the most conservative men talked about the coming Revolution as a certainty. Counts and barons, landlords and businessmen all applauded scathing criticisms of the Government and acclaimed the approaching Revolution. To see these men—weary, effeminate, accustomed to lives of comfort—calling for revolution was a curious spectacle. I had a vision of the French ruling classes on the eve of the great French Revolution. Like these Russians, so their emasculated aristocracy greeted the storm with laughter, not reflecting that it might rob them of their property and even of their lives." (*Leaves from a Russian Diary,* Chap. 1.)

With my revolutionary background as an ideologist of the Social-Revolutionary Party, I actively participated in these discussions and plans for the new democratic constitution of Russia, the basic social reforms to be carried on after the fall of the regime, and the most advisable steps to be taken in regard to the World War. This last point sharply divided all the Socialist parties into the "Social Patriots" and the "Internationalists." Both factions wanted to end the war as soon as possible, but the Social Patriots were against a separate peace with the German forces and for continuation of the war until the Western allies of Russia were ready to declare the general peace with the enemy. Opposed to this standpoint, the Internationalists were in favor of a separate peace with Germany regardless of the policies of our allies: if they were also willing to end the war—well and good; if they were not ready to do so, then the Internationalists wished to arrange without delay an armistice and separate peace with the German-led coalition. The greater part of the Social-Revolutionary, the Social-Democratic (Menshevik) and of other Socialist parties supported the position of the Social Patriots. An overwhelming majority of the Bolsheviks and of the "Left Social-Revolutionaries" took the position of the Internationalists. Led eventually by Lenin, they wanted to replace international war by global "class war." "Peace to huts and war to palaces!" was their motto (*Mir khijinam i voina dwortzam*!).

Rightly or wrongly, I adopted the position of the Social Patriots. At that time I still held a highly idealistic opinion of the Western allied governments. I still believed in the non-Machiavellian, honest, democratic, and moral nature of their policies, in their keeping their pledges and treaties unbroken, and in their readiness to help Russia in the hour of her sickness as she had helped—and saved—them in the hour of their mortal danger. I must remind the Western reader that in the first as in the second World War Russia alone fought a much greater proportion of the enemy armed forces than all the Allies together, that she took upon herself the main blows of the war, paid for this a terrific price in terms of human lives, devastated cities and villages, destroyed economic and natural resources—a price many times higher than that paid by all the

Allies together. By this sacrifice Russia undoubtedly saved the Allies from probable defeat and ruin, not to mention the saving of millions of lives of Western allies who might have had to fight the German coalition by themselves, had Russia not borne the main burden of the fighting.

Later on I was disillusioned in my idealistic conception of the Western governments. Instead of helping Russia in the hour of her need they tried to weaken her, to incite her to civil war, to dismember her by seizing any part of Russia they could cut out for themselves. They broke their pledges and obligations, and, after the second World War started all sorts of cold and hot wars against her; and even at the moment of this writing, they, in cooperation with the former enemy, are still trying to destroy, not only the Russian Empire and the Soviet government but the backbone of the Russian nation itself. Even in my personal fight with the Communist government I almost perished through the duplicity of the leaders of the Allies' expeditionary force in Arkhangelsk: by breaking their solemnly given promises to our group that engineered the overthrow of the Communist government in Arkhangelsk, they greatly contributed to my imprisonment and condemnation to death by the Communist agents in Veliki Ustyug.

If in 1915-17 I had held my present opinion of the Western governments as mainly a power machine just as cynical, Machiavellian, rapacious, shortsighted, and selfishly tribal as the power machine of other governments—including the Soviet —I would probably have joined the Internationalists. As the matter stood then, my idealization of the Western regimes and democracies placed me among the Social Patriots. Along with the Kerensky government and with most of the members and leaders of all the Socialist and liberal parties—including the "grandmother" and "grandfather" of the Russian Revolution, E. Breshkovskaia and N. Tchaikovsky; the most eminent leader of the Social-Democratic party, G. Plekhanov; and even one of the greatest leaders of anarchism, P. Kropotkin—I defended this position as a member of Kerensky's government, the Council of the Russian Republic, the Constituent Assembly, the Russian

Peasant Soviet, and as one of the main editors of the Social-Revolutionary newspapers *Delo Naroda* and *Volia Naroda*, as a scholar, popular orator, and as a lecturer before and during the Revolution until I was banished from Russia.

These lines may give an idea of the many non-academic activities I was engaged in during the war and on the eve of the Revolution. During the years of 1914-16 life was uncomfortable but truly exciting. In the rapidly unfolding events there was no possibility of confining one's activities to purely scientific or any other specific pursuits. With the explosion of the Revolution such confinement became still more impossible.

Of other personal events of these years I must mention the death of my teacher friends M. Kovalevsky and E. de Roberty. Their passing explains why neither of them participated in my master's examinations and dispute. My third great teacher, Professor L. Petrajitzky, stayed in Russia until September, 1917. Since university life was completely shattered, and the Communist ascendance to power imminent, I helped arrange his transportation to Warsaw (as secretary to Prime Minister Kerensky I still could help in these matters); he safely left Russia for Poland. As an eminent Polish-Russian scholar he was offered a professorship at Warsaw University; but for various reasons he did not feel as happy there nor was he as highly appreciated by the extremely "nationalistic" circles of newly born Poland, as he had been in Russia. Depressed by the destructive trends of increasing wars and revolutions and by the unleashing in man of "the worst of the beasts" he finally committed suicide by opening his veins. The deaths of these great men were a great personal loss to me as well as to all mankind. Their deaths were the precursors of many other deaths of a legion of creative spirits to be devoured by the gigantic wars and revolutions of this bloodiest and most inhuman twentieth century.

PART THREE

CHAPTER SEVEN

Holocaust: The 1917 Revolution

In the full development of their life-cycle all *great* revolutions seem to pass through three typical phases. The first phase is usually of short duration. It is marked by the joys of liberation from the tyranny of the old regime and by great expectations of the reforms promised by all revolutions. This initial stage is radiant, its government humanitarian and benign, its policies mild, vacillating, and fairly impotent. "The worst of the beasts" in man begins to awaken. This short overture is ordinarily succeeded by the second, destructive phase. The great revolution now turns into a furious tornado indiscriminately destroying everything in its path. It pitilessly uproots not only the obsolescent institutions but also the vigorous ones which it destroys along with the dead or moribund values; it murders not only the uncreative power elite of the old regime but also a multitude of creative persons and groups. The revolutionary government at this stage is ruthless, tyrannical, and bloodthirsty. Its policies are mainly destructive, coercive, and terroristic. If the tornado phase does not utterly ruin the nation, its revolution eventually enters the third, constructive phase. With the destruction of all counter-revolutionary forces, it now begins to build a new social, cultural, and personal order. This order is constructed not only of new, revolutionary ideals but includes the restoration of the more vital of the pre-revolutionary institutions, values, and ways of life which had been temporarily destroyed by the second phase of revolution and which revive and reassert themselves regardless of the wishes of the revolutionary government. The post-revolutionary order, therefore, usually represents a blending of the new patterns and way of life with old but vital and creative patterns of pre-revolutionary times. Roughly after the end of the 1920's, the Russian Revolution began to pass into this constructive phase and is at the present time in full development of this phase. Its internal and international policies are now more constructive and creative than those of many Western and Eastern countries. It is highly regrettable that this momentous change is still ignored by the politicians and the "power-elites" of these countries. (See the detailed analysis of the destructive and constructive phases of great revolutions in my *Sociology of Revolution; Social and Cultural Dynamics*, Vol. III; and *Society, Culture and Personality*, Chaps. 31-33).

As a participant I observed the sequence of all three phases in the revolution of 1905-8. In 1917 I experienced directly only the first and the second stages of the life-cycle of that epochal revolution. The subsequent passages taken from my *Leaves from a Russian Diary* give not only concrete examples of the early destructive phases of a great revolution but vividly depict what happened to me and to my compatriots during the most destructive phase of the Russian Revolution in the years 1917-22.

The First Day: February 27, 1917

It has come at last. At two o'clock in the morning, just now returned from the Duma, I hasten to set down the stirring events of this day. Because I did not feel too well and since lectures at the University had virtually ceased, I decided to stay at home and read the new work of Vilfredo Pareto, *Trattato di Sociologia Generale*. From time to time I was interrupted by friends phoning me for news and in turn giving theirs to me.

"The crowds on the Nevsky are bigger than ever today."

"The workmen of the Putylovsky factory have gone out into the streets."

At noon telephone service was discontinued; about three o'clock one of my students rushed in with the news that two regiments, armed and carrying red flags, had left their barracks and were marching on the Duma.

Hastily leaving the house, we hurried to the Troizky Bridge. Here we found a large but orderly crowd listening to the firing and greedily drinking in every bit of news. Nobody knew anything definite.

Not without difficulty did we cross the river and reach the Economic Committee of the Union of Cities and Zemstvos (County Councils). It occurred to me that if the regiments did reach the Duma they would probably have to be fed. So I said to my friends, the members of the Committee: "You try to get some food together, and at a message from me send it to the Duma." An old acquaintance, Mr. Kuzmin, joined us at this moment and we set off. Nevsky Prospekt near the Ekaterina Canal was still quiet, but as we turned into the Liteiny the crowd grew larger and the shooting became louder. The frantic efforts of the police to disperse the crowds were utterly without effect.

"Ah-h! Pharaohs! Your end is coming!" howled the mob.

Advancing cautiously along the Liteiny, we came upon fresh bloodstains and saw two dead bodies on the pavement. Skilfully maneuvering, we finally reached the Tauride Palace to find it surrounded by crowds of peasants, soldiers, and workmen. No attempt had yet been made to enter the Russian Parliament, but cannon and machine guns were everywhere in evidence.

The hall of the Duma presented a striking contrast to the tumult without. Here was comfort, dignity, order. Only here and there in corners could be seen small groups of deputies discussing the situation. The Duma had actually been dissolved, but an executive committee had been appointed as a temporary government.

Confusion and uncertainty were evident in the utterances of the deputies. The captains who were steering the Ship of State into the teeth of the hurricane were not yet sure of their own course. I went back to the court of the Duma and explained to a group of soldiers that I was trying to have provisions brought for them. They found an automobile with a red flag flying from it, and we drove off through the crowd.

"This is enough to hang us all if the Revolution is put down," I said jestingly to my guards.

"Don't worry. All will be right," they answered.

Near the Duma lived the lawyer Grusenberg. His telephone was working and I got in touch with friends who promised that food for the troops would soon be forthcoming. Returning to the Duma I found the crowds massed closer than ever. In the courtyard and in all adjacent streets excited groups surrounded orators—members of the Duma, soldiers, and workmen—all holding forth on the significance of the day's events, hailing the Revolution and the fall of Czarist despotism. Everyone exalted the rising power of the people and called on all citizens to support the Revolution.

The hall and corridors of the Duma were packed with people, soldiers stood behind rifles and machine guns. But order still prevailed; the street had not yet broken in.

"Ah, comrade Sorokin, at last, Revolution! At last the day of glory has arrived!" cried one of my worker-students as he joyfully approached me with others in whose faces shone the light of hope and exaltation.

Entering a committee room I found several Social Democratic deputies and about twelve workmen, the nucleus of the future Soviet. From them I received an urgent invitation to become a member, but I felt no call just then to join a soviet, so I left them for a meeting of writers who were organizing an official press committee of the Revolution.

"Who elected these men as representatives of the press?" I asked myself. Here they were, self-appointed censors, assuming power to suppress whatever, in their judgment, seemed to be undesirable newspapers, preparing to stifle liberty of speech and the press. Suddenly the words of Flaubert came to my mind: "In every revolutionist is hidden a gendarme."

"What's the latest?" I asked of a deputy shouldering his way through the crowd.

"Rodzianko is trying to make contact with the Czar by telegraph. The Executive Committee is discussing the organization of a new Ministry responsible jointly to the Czar and to the Duma."

"Is anybody in charge of this Revolution?"

"Nobody. It's developing spontaneously."

Food was being brought in, a buffet was set up, and girl students began to feed the soldiers. This produced a sudden lull. But outside, I learned, things were going badly. Fires continued to break out. The people were growing hysterical with excitement and, as for the police, they had retreated. It was midnight before I could tear myself away from the place.

As no trams or cabs were to be had, I walked to the Petrogradskaia, a long distance from the Duma. I could still hear incessant shooting but it was very dark and no street lamps were burning. Then, on the Liteiny, I saw a burst of flame. The magnificent building of the Okroujny Soud (the High Court) was blazing fiercely.

"Who started that fire?" someone exclaimed. "Is it not necessary to have a court building for New Russia?" The question went unanswered. We could see that other government buildings were also burning, among them police stations, and that no efforts were being made to extinguish the fires. In the red blaze the faces of many spectators looked demonic as they shouted, laughed, and danced. Here and there were heaped wooden carvings of the Russian double eagle, and these emblems of Empire, torn from government buildings, were being thrown on the fires as the crowds cheered. The old regime was disappearing in ashes and no one regretted it. No one cared even when the fire spread to private houses. "Let them go," one man said defiantly. "When wood is chopped chips fly."

Twice I came on groups of soldiers and street loafers looting wine-shops with no one attempting to stop them.

At two o'clock I reached home and sat down to write these hurried notes. Am I glad or am I sorry? I can hardly tell, but certainly there are persistent apprehensions in my mind.

I looked at my books and manuscripts. I suppose they will

have to be put aside for a time, I reflected. This is no time for study. Action is the thing.

Shooting has started again.

Following Day

Next morning, with two friends, I started on foot for the Duma. The streets were full of excited people. All shops were closed, all business suspended. The sound of shooting came from several directions. Motor cars full of soldiers and young men with rifles and machine guns zoomed up and down. They were searching for police and counter-revolutionaries.

Today the Hall of the Duma presented quite a different picture from yesterday. Soldiers, workmen, students, citizens —young and old—crowded the place. Order, cleanliness, and restraint were conspicuous by their absence. His Majesty the People was master of the scene. In every room and corner were extemporaneous meetings and much loud oratory. "Down with the Czar!" "Death to all enemies of the people!" "Long life to Revolution and the democratic Republic!" One grew tired of their endless repetition. Today the existence of two centers of power was apparent. One center was the Executive Committee of the Duma with Rodzianko as its leader, the other was the Soviet of Workmen and Soldiers, sitting at the opposite end of the Russian Parliament. With a group of my workmen students I entered the Soviet room. Instead of the original twelve there were now three or four hundred men present. It seems that anyone who desires can become a member of this body—a very informal "election" indeed. In the overcrowded room full of tobacco smoke, wild harangues were being delivered, more than one at a time. The dominant question being discussed as we came in was whether or not Rodzianko, president of the Duma, should be arrested as a counter-revolutionary.

I was astounded. Had these people lost their minds overnight? I asked for a chance to speak and was recognized by the chairman.

"You foolish men," I addressed them. "The Revolution is only beginning, and if it is to succeed we must have complete union and accord of all anti-Czarist forces. There must be no anarchy. In this hour of peril you, a small group of men, debating such a question as the arrest of Rodzianko, are simply wasting time."

Maxim Gorky followed me, speaking in the same strain, and for the moment the question of Rodzianko's arrest was put aside. However, it was only too plain that mob mentality was beginning to assert itself and that not only the beast but the fool in man was striving to gain the upper hand.

On the way to the room where the Executive Committee of the Duma was sitting I met one of its members, Mr. Efremoff, and learned from him that the struggle between the Committee and the Soviet had begun in earnest, and that a dual power was now contending for control of the Revolution. "But what can we do?" he asked despairingly.

"Who is acting in the name of the Soviet?"

"Sukhanoff, Nakhamkes, Chkeidze, and a few others," he answered.

"Is it not possible to order soldiers to arrest these men and to disperse the Soviet?" I asked.

"Such aggression and conflict cannot take place in the first days of the Revolution," was the reply.

"Then get ready for your own dismissal very soon," I warned him. "Were I a member of your Committee I would act immediately. The Duma is still the highest authority in Russia."

At this moment Professor Gronsky joined us. "Can you write the proclamation of the future Government?" he asked me.

"Why should I do it? Nabokoff is a specialist in such matters. Go to him." In the midst of our conversation an officer burst into the room demanding to be conducted to the Committee of the Duma. "What has happened?" we asked.

"All the officers of the Baltic Fleet are being murdered by soldiers and sailors," he cried. "The Committee must interfere."

My heart turned to ice. But it would be madness to expect a revolution without some bloodshed. I reached home very late at night. No joy was in my soul, yet I bade myself hope. Tomorrow things might be better.

"Tomorrow"

Tomorrow things were not better. The streets were teeming with the same unruly crowds, the same motor cars full of men firing wildly, the same manhunt for policemen and counter-revolutionaries. In the Duma we received definite news that the Czar was to abdicate in favor of the Czarevitch Alexis.

Today the first copy of a newspaper, *Isvestia,* was issued.

The Soviet has grown to four or five hundred members. The Committees of the Duma and the Soviet are organizing the Provisional Government, Kerensky acting as mediator and liaison between the two bodies. He is vice-president of the Soviet and Minister of Justice. I met him. He was exhausted.

"Please send a telegram to the wardens of prisons throughout Russia to liberate all political prisoners," he said.

When I had written the telegram, he signed it, "Minister of Justice, Citizen Kerensky." This "citizen" is new, a little theatrical, but perhaps appropriate. I am not sure how strong Kerensky's mediating powers will prove, and I fear that this dual rule by the Provisional (or Visionary) Government and by the extremists of the Soviet cannot last long. One will certainly swallow the other. Which? Certainly the Soviet. Monarchy has fallen. The mind of the people has become solidly republican. Even a simple bourgeois republic is not radical enough for many. I fear these extremists. I fear the mob mentality.

Frightful news! The massacre of officers increases. In Kronstadt, Admiral Wiren and many officers of the fleet have been killed. They say that officers are being murdered according to lists prepared by the Germans.

I have just read "Order No. 1," issued by the Soviet and in

essence authorizing disobedience of soldiers to the orders of their officers. What madman wrote and published this thing?

In the library of the Duma I met, among others, Mr. Nabokoff who showed me his draft of the Proclamation of the Provisional Government. All liberties, all guarantees are promised not only to citizens but to soldiers. Russia is to be one of the most democratic countries and the freest in all the world.

"What do you think of it?" he asked proudly.

"It's an admirable document, but—"

"But what?"

"I fear it is a little too inclusive in time of Revolution, in the midst of a world war," I was forced to admit.

"I have some apprehensions too," he said, "but I hope it will be all right."

"I can only echo your hope."

"Now I am about to write a declaration of the abolition of capital punishment," said Nabokoff.

"What! Even in the army, in wartime?"

"Yes."

"But this is madness!" cried one man present. "Only lunatics would think of such a thing in this hour, when officers are butchered like sheep. I hate Czarism as much as any man, but I am sorry that at this precise time it had to fall. In its way it knew how to govern better than all these visionary fools."

In spite of myself I felt he was right.

The old regime has undoubtedly perished. In both Petrograd and Moscow the populace is as joyful as at Easter. Everyone acclaims the new regime and the Republic. "Liberty! Holy Liberty!" is everywhere shouted and sung. "Wonderful Revolution! Revolution without blood, pure as the robes of sinless angels!" I have heard this last from crowds of students parading the streets.

It is true, of course. Bloodshed has not been very terrible. If there are no further victims of the fanatics, our revolution may yet go down in history as the Bloodless Revolution.

"Since Freedom, Everything is Permitted"

The old regime has fallen throughout Russia and very few regret it. The whole country rejoices. The Czar has abdicated for himself and for his son. Grand Duke Michael has refused the throne. A Provisional Government has been elected, and its manifesto is one of the most liberal and democratic documents which has ever been issued. All Czarist officers, from ministers to policemen, have been dismissed and replaced by men devoted to the Republic—for no one doubts that we shall have a republic. The majority of people are hopeful and expect the war to be carried on more successfully. Soldiers, statesmen, students, citizens, and peasants—all display immense activity. Peasants are bringing corn to the towns and to the army, sometimes free of charge. Military regiments and workmen groups display standards: "Long Life to the Revolution!" "The Peasants to the Plow, the Workers to the Looms and Presses, the Soldiers to the Trenches!" "We, the Free People of Russia, Will Defend the Country and the Revolution!"

"See how splendid the people are!" exulted a friend of mine, pointing to one of these demonstrations.

"It certainly seems to be all right," I answered.

But while trying to convince myself that it is all right, I cannot shut my eyes to certain realities. The workers bear aloft such signs as "The Workers to the Looms and Presses"; yet they have ceased to work and they spend almost all their time at political meetings. They have begun to demand an eight-hour, and even a six-hour working day. The soldiers are apparently ready to fight, but yesterday when one of the regiments was ordered to the front the men refused to go, under the pretext that they were needed in Petrograd to defend the Revolution. In these days we have also received information that peasants are seizing private estates, sacking and burning them. In the streets I have seen many intoxicated men, bawling obscenities and crying: "Long Life to Freedom! Since we have freedom, everything is permitted."

Passing a house near the Bestuzhevsky Women's University,

I saw a crowd of men laughing and gesticulating wildly. In the shadow of the gate, in plain sight, were a man and a woman behaving in the most indecent manner. "Ha, ha!" laughed the crowd, "since freedom, everything is permitted!"

Last night we held the first meeting of old members of the Social Revolutionary Party, twenty or thirty tried and trusted leaders. I challenged the proposals of the extremists and finally forced through a resolution to support the Government. This resolution was accepted by the majority, with a characteristic reservation, "Provided the Government adheres to its program." This meeting showed me that the equilibrium of mind in the members of old and reliable men of the Party had begun to waver. If it is so even with these men, what will happen in the mob? Truly we have entered a critical period, more critical than I had feared.

Today there was another meeting of Social Revolutionary leaders to found a newspaper and to appoint its editors. The discussion was heated and disclosed clearly the existence within the party of two different elements, Social Patriots and Internationalists. After a long and tedious debate, the five editors of the newspaper, to be called the *Delo Naroda* (the *Affair of the People*), were elected. They are Russanoff, Ivanoff-Razumnik, Mstislavsky, Gukovsky, and myself. I can't quite see how we are to agree on the policies of the paper, Gukovsky and I being very moderate Social Patriots, the others Internationalists.

Alas! at the very first meeting of the editors to arrange for the paper's initial appearance, five hours were wasted in vain dispute. Articles submitted by the Internationalists were rejected by us, and all our articles were denounced by them. Three times we started to leave the room, but each time we returned. At last we all began to reread the leading editorials, pitilessly blue-penciling the most telling passages of each. As a result both moderate and radical articles were shorn of value without losing any of their contradictions. An auspicious beginning! *Delo Naroda,* as issued, has proved to be a newspaper in which one article appears denouncing another on the same page. This sort of thing cannot go on, and we all admit it. All monarchist newspapers have been suppressed and their printing establishments confiscated. The Socialists agree that this is perfectly proper, but how does this square with the liberty of the press once so ardently advocated by them? As soon as "ambition's debt is paid" it seems that radicals become even more despotic than the reactionaries. Power incites tyranny.

At meetings of workmen I hear more and more demands to end the war. The ideas that the Government must be purely socialistic and that a general massacre of all "exploiters" must take place are rapidly spreading among the people. Every attempt of engineers and managers to maintain discipline in works and factories, to keep up the scale of production, or to discharge slackers is considered counter-revolutionary. Among the soldiers the situation is no better. Obedience and discipline have almost disappeared.

As for the *muzhiks* (the peasants), even they begin to grow restless and may soon join the Soviets. My God! These adventurers, self-elected deputies of soldiers and workmen, these destitute intellectuals, play-acting the drama of revolution, assuming the characters of French revolutionaries. Talking, talking, talking endlessly, all their energies devoted to the destruction of the provisional Government and to preparations for the "dictatorship of the proletariat." The Soviet interferes in everything. Its acts lead only to disorganization in government and the unleashing of wild instincts in the mob.

The Government? It may be better to say nothing about these men. Highminded and idealistic, they do not know the *ABC's* of the science of government. They do not appear to know what they themselves want done, and even if they did know, they could accomplish nothing.

Today the funeral was held for the victims who died for the Revolution. What a moving spectacle! Hundreds of thousands of people moved behind thousands of red and black banners emblazoned with the words: "Glory to Those Who Perished for Liberty." Marvelous music—voices and bands—joined in the funeral hymn. There was perfect order and discipline as, for hours, the endless procession wound through the streets. The faces of the marchers were solemn and uplifted. Such a crowd thrills me; it is so human.

Tonight it was my turn to act as editor-in-chief of *Delo Naroda*. The paper went to press at about three o'clock in the morning and, as usual, I went home on foot. The streets are not so crowded at night and it is easier to observe the changes which have taken place in Petrograd during this month of Revolution. The picture is not very pleasant. The streets are littered with papers, dust, dung, and sunflower seeds (the Russian equivalent of peanut shells). The bullet-shattered windows of many houses are stuffed with paper. In every side street soldiers and prostitutes behave with revolting indecency.

"Comrade! Let the proletarians of all countries unite. Come home with me," a painted creature accosted me. A most original application of the revolutionary slogan!

All political prisoners have been released and are flocking home from Siberia and from abroad. They are met triumphantly by government committees, soldiers, workmen, and the general public. Bands, flags, and speeches greet each new group of arrivals. The return exiles bear themselves like conquering heroes who deserve to be worshipped by the people as liberators and benefactors. There is an amusing aspect to the case, for a large number of these people were never political offenders, but common convicts, thieves, murderers, and ordinary swindlers. All, however, are treated alike, as victims of Czarism. It appears that among other forms of vanity there is a revolutionary vanity which claims everything for itself.

Many of these returned "politicals" show evidence of disturbed minds and unbalanced emotions. Having spent years in prison and exile, at hard and degrading labor, they inevitably begin to introduce into society the methods and cruelties they themselves have suffered. They perpetuate hatred, cruelty, and contempt for human life and suffering.

The Soviet, packed with these "heroes," increasingly loses its sense of reality. It directs its energy toward obstructing the Government, preaching Socialism, and doing nothing at all toward the re-education and reorganization of Russian society. Its proclamations are addressed "To All, All, All" or "To the Whole World." The speeches and demeanor of the leaders are absurdly pompous. They seem to possess no sense of humor, and are unable to see how comic is their pose.

As for the Government, it is equally chaotic and impotent. Division of authority is now complete, and the Government loses ground every day.

Light and Shadow

Today, April 22, 1917, a conference was held by the Social Revolutionary Party of Petrograd. The frame of mind of the new "March" Socialist Revolutionaries is radical in the extreme. New "revolutionists" today are treating the older leaders as their servants. The new ones had a majority in the conference and passed a resolution that the war be brought to an immediate end, and that a Socialist government be established. I declared that I could not accept their program, walked out of the conference, and resigned my position as editor of *Delo Naroda*. Many old members followed me, most of the right wing abandoning the conference. Sooner or later this had to happen, so it was better to let it happen now.

Gukovsky and I are organizing a right-wing Socialist-Revolutionary newspaper, *The Will of the People* (*Volia Naroda*). "Grandmother" Breshkovskaia, Mirolyuboff, Stalinsky, and Argunoff will be our co-editors. To hope for success at this time is impossible; still, we have to do what we think is right.

The political immigrants continue to return. Of our party leaders these have appeared: Chernoff, Avksentieff, Bunakoff, Stalinsky, Argunoff, Lebedeff, and others. In a few days the Bolshevist leaders, Lenin, Trotsky, Zinoviev, and others are expected to return. They are coming through Germany with the assistance of the German government, which has loaned them a special "plombiert" wagon. Some of our people are indignant that the Provisional Government has permitted these persons to return. The rumor is spreading that Lenin and his companions (about forty men) were hired by the German staff to incite civil war in Russia and to demoralize the Russian Army still more. I am convinced of the necessity of summoning an All-Russian Peasants' Soviet to counterbalance the Soviet of idle workers and soldiers of the town.

Night. . . . Wearied by speeches, meetings, and a hundred depressing incidents, I have returned home feeling like a man who tries to stop with his bare hands a great movement of ice from the mountains. A hopeless task.

With my friends we began the organization of the All-Russian Peasants' Conference.

I started yesterday from Petrograd to Veliki Ustyug, summoned there by the peasants and other inhabitants of the district. What a relief to leave the capital with its constantly moving crowds, its disorder, dirt, and hysteria, and to be again in the tranquil places I love! The steamer is gliding swiftly along the Sukhona. Above me is the blue sky, under and around me the gleaming river and the beautiful scenery. How perfect is the calm of it all! How pure and still the air, as if no revolution exists! Only the constant chatter of the passengers recalls its presence.

At my beloved Veliki Ustyug a group of friends met me. From the steamer I was driven to the market place where thousands of people were assembled. My speech evoked great patriotic enthusiasm. Hundreds pressed forward to subscribe to the State Loan of Freedom issued by the Government for the economic improvement of the State. Many peasants who had come to town to sell their grain gave it to the army without charge. I had a similar triumph at a meeting of teachers and among the simple people of three neighboring villages.

To return to the unhealthy atmosphere, I found the disorder and unrestraint of the capital to be frightful.

Lenin and his companions have arrived. Their first speeches

at the Bolshevist Conference embarrassed even members of the extreme left. Lenin and his group are now very rich men, and as a consequence the number of Bolshevist newspapers, pamphlets, proclamations, etc., have greatly increased. Trotsky has taken a very expensive apartment. Where did all this money come from?—that is the question.

"Socialization" has begun. The Bolsheviki have forcibly taken possession of the dancer Kshessinsky's villa, the anarchists have seized the villa of Durnovo and other houses, the proprietors being summarily evicted. Although the owners have appealed to the courts and to the Government, nothing has been done to restore their property.

April 21, 1917. Today we have had a real taste of mob revolt. The Foreign Office note to the Allies, stating that the Provisional Government would be faithful to all treaties and obligations undertaken by Russia, was furiously attacked by the Soviets and by the Bolsheviki. About noon today two regiments, fully armed, had left their barracks to support the rioters. Firing began. Sacking of shops by criminals became general. The situation resembled the first days of anti-Czarist revolt, but in those days citizens were able to control the masses. The Government has announced that Milyukoff is to be dismissed.

This means that the Government has fallen, for this first concession to the mob and to the Bolsheviki is the beginning of the end of the Provisional Government. We are all living on the edge of a volcano, and at any moment an eruption may burst forth. Not a pleasant situation, but step by step we manage to adapt ourselves to it. At any rate it is all interesting enough.

Today we published the first copy of *The Will of the People*. The organization of the All-Russian Peasants' Conference is proceeding successfully and is approaching achievement.

Vandervelde and De Brouker, leaders of the Belgian Socialists, paid a visit to our office today. "You are the first Russian Socialists not to denounce our patriotism and our 'bourgeois' opinions," said Vandervelde while shaking hands with me.

This evening we gave a dinner for Albert Thomas. He, like Vandervelde, regards the situation rather pessimistically, but he treated the rudeness of the Soviet with good humor. "They are like irresponsible children," he said.

My manner of living has become regular in its irregularity. I have no definite time for dinner, for sleeping, rising, or working. Day after day I tire myself out in agitation, excitement, and in carrying on a great deal of business. I sometimes feel like a homeless dog.

Agony

May–June, 1917. The Peasants' Conference has opened with about one thousand representatives of real peasants and loyal soldiers from the front. The peasants' frame of mind is incomparably more sound and balanced that that of the workmen or of the soldiery. Patriotism, a real desire to suppress disorders, and even a willingness to abstain from seizing the land until a definite settlement of this question has been reached, a perfect readiness to support the Government and to oppose the Bolsheviki—all these sentiments were heartily expressed by the Conference.

An interesting episode was the appearance of Lenin at the Conference. Mounting the platform, he dramatically threw off his overcoat and began to speak. This man's face has something in it which recalls religious fanatics of the Starover (old Orthodox Church). He is a dull speaker and his efforts to arouse enthusiasm for Bolshevism fell absolutely flat. His speech was received coldly, his personality excited animosity, and in the end he retired in evident embarrassment. The Bolshevist *Pravda* and other Internationalist newspapers renewed their attack on the Peasants' Conference, calling it a "citadel of the social patriots and the little bourgeois." Well, let them attack it.

The Peasants' Conference adjourned after voting to organize a special Peasants' Soviet, electing deputies, an executive committee, and representatives of its organization in different institutions. I was elected a member of the executive committee and a delegate to the "Commission for Elaboration of the Law for Election of Members of the Constitutional Assembly."

On my way downtown I passed the Villa Kshessinsky which has been seized by the Bolsheviki and is being used by them as a headquarters. Day after day they deliver orations to crowds of workmen and soldiers, from the balcony of the palace. All efforts of the Government to expel the intruders from this place have failed. The Durnovo Palace, taken by the Anarchists, as well as other villas illegally held by criminals calling themselves anarchists or communists, are still in their possession. In vain the courts have ordered the intruders to vacate, and equally in vain the Minister of Justice has issued his orders. No results. I stopped before the Kshessinsky Palace to listen to Lenin. Although a poor speaker, it seems to me that this man may go far. Why? Because he is prepared and determined to encourage all the violence, criminality, and obscenity which the mob, under these demoralized conditions, is straining to let loose.

"Comrade workers," thus went Lenin's speech, "take the factories from your exploiters! Comrade peasants, take the lands from your enemies, the landlords! Comrade soldiers, stop the war, go home. Make peace with the Germans and declare war on the rich! Poor wretches, you are starving while all around are plutocrats and bankers. Why do you not seize all this wealth? Steal what has been stolen! Pitilessly destroy this whole capitalistic society! Down with it! Down with the Government! Down with all war! Long life to the Social Revolution! Long life to class war! Long life to the dictatorship of the proletariat!"

Such a speech always calls forth a lively response. Zinoviev followed Lenin. What a disgusting creature this Zinoviev! In his high womanish voice, his face, his fat figure, there is something hideous and obscene; he is an extraordinary moral and mental degenerate. Lenin has found a perfect pupil in this man.

After listening for about an hour, I crossed the Troitzky Bridge to my office. The day was beautiful. The sun shone brilliantly, and the Neva reflected a cloudless sky. But my soul was full of dark foreboding. These men, I knew, presaged terrible things. If I were the Government I would arrest them without hesitation. Poor Kerensky does his best. He delivers one eloquent speech after another, but wild beasts cannot be controlled by speeches, however eloquent. In the towns starvation threatens, for work has practically ceased. I must say that as a propagandist newspaper their *Pravda* is very ably edited. Especially brilliant are the sarcastic articles of Trotsky in which he lashes and jeers at his opponents, myself among them. Excellent satire.

The Peasants' Soviet is still a bulwark. Most of the *muzhiks,* representatives of the peasant majority, have retained their mental balance.

May 26, 1917 was my marriage day. It was a real revolutionary wedding. After the ceremony in the church, to which I came straight from an important meeting, my wife and our friends took only half an hour for luncheon; then I had to hurry off to another cursed conference. Only during war or revolution could such a thing have happened. In the evening I consigned revolution to the devil and returned home to my beloved. The tornado approaches, but in spite of everything I bless this day.

Today Professor Masaryk of Prague visited me in my office. It was a great pleasure to talk with this rational, intelligent, serious, and broad-minded man. We discussed the Czech problem, about which I had written. Surely with such leaders as Masaryk, Czechoslovakia will regain its independence. In the *Will of the People* we support this cause.

Work in the Peasants' Soviet goes on satisfactorily. The principal problems of future Russia—agrarian reform, the constitution, organization of government, defense of the country, and so on—are already tentatively arranged. Meetings of the Soviets—the Workmen's and Soldiers' and the Peasants'—are conducted separately. The old Soviet at first tried to dominate, but now it has been obliged to recognize the equal status of the peasants' organization. In the Hall of the Duma the members of our Peasants' Soviet occupy the right side, while on the extreme left are seated the small group of Bolsheviki, the Internationalists, and the leftist Social Revolutionaries. As our men enter, these Red greet us with derisive cries: "Here come the little bourgeosie!" And we retaliate: "There are the traitors!"

A very grave crisis has arisen. While the Executive Committee of the Peasants' Soviet was in session, we were suddenly informed by telephone that the Bolsheviki had organized for the next morning an armed demonstration of soldiers and workmen with the demand: "Down with the Capitalistic Government!" There was no doubt that such a demonstration would mean the fall of the Government and the final breakdown of the offensive. It would mean civil war, bloodshed, death. As a counter to their action we voted to take part in an unarmed demonstration planned for the following week. We have thwarted the attempted armed demonstration. Next morning *Pravda* announced that the Bolsheviki would join in our peaceful march. This time we won, but I fear that the next victory will be theirs.

In the evening, riots and several street murders took place. The bloodless skirts of the Revolution became more and more blood stained. Starvation is increasing.

Our offensive on the front began brilliantly, and at once the spirit of the people was immensely uplifted. Patriotic demonstrations filled all the streets, and Kerensky's popularity was widely acclaimed. The Bolsheviki, for the moment, suffered complete eclipse.

Yes, the catastrophe has come. Our revolutionary army is defeated. In mad panic it has broken, fled, and in its flight it is destroying everything in its path; murders, violations, looting, devastated fields, and destroyed villages mark its way. No discipline, no authority, no mercy for innocent women or civilians. General Kornilov and B. Savinkov demand the reinstatement of capital punishment for deserters. In vain! The impotent Government and the Soviets, even in this emergency, have no will to act. Again Bolsheviki and anarchy prevail.

A significant thing has happened. At a meeting today, addressed by "Grandmother" Breshkovskaia, Savinkov, Plekhanov, Tschaikovsky, and myself, the audience of soldiers and workers suddenly broke out in hisses and denunciation of these leaders of the Revolution. Against such martyrs as Breshkovskaia and Tschaikovsky were hurled such epithets as "Traitors!" "Counter-Revolutionaries!" Springing to his feet Savinkov shouted: "Who are you to treat us in this way? What have you slackers ever done for the Revolution? Nothing at all. What have you ever risked? Nothing. But these men and women here" (pointing to us) "have lain in prison, starved and frozen in Siberia, risked their lives over and over again. It was I and not any of you who threw a bomb at the tyrant Czarist Minister. It was I and not you who for that deed heard the death penalty pronounced against me by the Czarist Government. How dare you accuse me of being a counter-revolutionary? What are you anyhow but a mob of fools and loafers who are plotting the ruin of Russia, the destruction of the Revolution and of yourselves?"

This outburst somewhat awed and impressed the mob. But it is plain that all the great revolutionaries are facing tragedy. The work and sacrifices of their lives are forgotten. In comparison with the "March Revolutionaries" they are now considered reactionary and out of date.

"Have you ever thought of yourself as a reactionary counter-revolutionist?" I asked G. Plekhanov.

"If these maniacs are revolutionists, then I am proud to be called a reactionary," replied the founder of the Social Democratic Party.

"Have a care, Mr. Plekhanov," I said, "lest you be arrested as soon as these people, your own pupils, become dictators."

"Since these people have become even greater reactionaries than the Czarist Government itself what have I to expect but arrest?" he asked bitterly.

I like Plekhanov. It seems to me that he grasps the truth of conditions better than do his pupils in the Soviet who will not even admit him as a member. All the old revolutionaries and the founders of Russian Socialism count themselves as moderates, or, in the patter of the Bolsheviki, "counter-revolutionists." I see that my "conservation" is identical with what in all revolutions and social upheavals comes to be called by the mob "counter-revolution." All of us are beginning to see that revolution and radicalism in practice are quite different from the same ideas in theory.

The disintegration of Russia is beginning in earnest. Finland, the Ukraine, and the Caucasus have declared their independence. Kronstadt, Schlisselburg, and many districts in various parts of Russia have voted their own independence.

Yesterday I published an article on the impending catastrophe, which I called "The Damnation of the Russian Nation." Today all the other newspapers commented on it, the Bolshevist sheets uttering threats against me. Many citizens, however, called to thank me for the article. Their sympathy cannot save the situation, which is now quite hopeless. As for me, I have no personal fears.

Life in Petrograd becomes more and more difficult. Riots, murders, starvation, and death are everyday commonplaces. We await the next eruption, knowing that it will surely come. Yesterday I disputed at a public meeting with Trotsky and Madame Kollontay. As for this woman, it is plain that her revolutionary enthusiasm is nothing but an indirect gratification of her nymphomania.

Trotsky, granted favorable conditions, will certainly rise to the top. This theatrical brigand is a true adventurer. His comrades in the Social Democratic Party (*Menshevik*) used to say of him: "Trotsky brings his own chair to every meeting. Today he sits with this party, tomorrow he sits with another." For the moment he places his chair in the Communist Party. The Bolsheviki will probably give him all he longs for.

Tragedy

July 3–5, 1917. The eruption has come. On the afternoon of the third, when the Peasants' Soviet was in the midst of an afternoon session, we were summoned by telephone to the Tavrichesky Palace for a joint session with the Workmen's Soviet. "Come as soon as possible," we were urged, "a new Bolshevist riot has broken out." We left immediately. The streets surrounding the Palace and its large courtyard were full of soldiers and sailors, and standing up in an automobile was Trotsky, haranguing the men from Krondstadt:

"You, comrade sailors, are the pride and glory of the Russian Revolution. You are its best promoters and defenders. By your deeds, by your devotion to communism, by your ruthless hatred and massacres of all exploiters and enemies of the proletariat, you have written deathless pages in the history of the Revolution. Now there is before you a new task—to push revolution to its ultimate limits, to create the kingdom of communism, the dictatorship of the proletariat, and to start a world revolution. The great drama has begun. Victory and everlasting glory call us. Let our enemies tremble. No pity, no mercy for them. Summon all your hatred. Destroy them once and forever!"

A wild animal roar was the answer to this speech.

With extreme difficulty we forced our way into the Palace where in the Hall of the Duma we found many representatives of the Workmen's Soviet and of the Social Democratic Party. The atmosphere was tense with excitement. "This is terrible!" "This is a crime against the Revolution!" cried these leaders of the left.

To the explosion of gunfire and demoniac shrieks from without, the joint meeting of the Soviets—the Soldiers' the Workmen's and the Peasants'—was called to order by Chkeidze.

"In the name of the board of the Soviets," said Dan, "I offer the following motion: that all members of the Soviet here present must swear to do everything—even to die, if necessary—in order to suppress this criminal revolt against the Soviet and the Revolution. Those who are unwilling to take this oath shall immediately withdraw."

Deep silence for a moment, and then deafening applause. Around me I saw the pale faces of the deputies. I heard fervent murmurs: "Yes, we are ready to die." Something tragic and heroic took possession of us all. Surrounded by the unbridled mob, amid roars of cannon and rattle of machine guns, defended only by two soldiers guarding the door of the Hall, the members of the Soviet for the first time rose to that height of grandeur and nobility when man is indeed ready to vanquish or die.

The next moment groups of Bolsheviki, Internationalists, and leftist Social Revolutionaries, led by Trotsky, Lunacharsky, Gimmer, and Kamkoff, pressed forward. "We protest this motion," they shouted in unison. "Look at the sea of workers and soldiers surrounding this building. In their names we demand that the Soviet declare the Provisional Government dismissed. We demand that the war be ended at once. We demand a dictatorship of the proletariat, and that a communistic state be established. If you don't accept this willingly, we will force it down your throats. The time of hesitation is past. What the revolutionary proletariat commands, you must obey."

Such was the essence of their speeches. The Bolsheviki, feeling themselves victorious, no longer appealed to the Soviet; they issued orders. Trying to control their indignation and anger, the Soviet listened calmly.

"What is it that you demand?" asked the chairman. "The dictatorship of the Soviet or your own dictatorship of the Soviet? If the former, then stop threatening, sit down, wait for the decision of the Soviet, and obey it. If, on the contrary, you are seeking to dictate to the Soviet, why are you here? Nobody in this hall has any doubts as to what you mean. Not 'All power to the Soviets,' but all power to yourselves is your object. For this you have inflamed the ignorant and misguided masses. For this you have incited civil war. Very well, we accept your challenge. Go out and do your worst."

Such was our reply to the Bolsheviki. After a few minutes of hesitation they blustered out, and Dan's resolution was unanimously adopted.

One fiery speech succeeded another. My head bursting with excitement in the close atmosphere of the room, I went out into the yard of the Duma. In the grey twilight of the July night I saw a stormy sea of soldiers, workmen, sailors. . . . Here and there cannon and machine guns pointed at the Palace, and everywhere red banners floated and there was the sound of incessant firing. It was like a madhouse. Here was the mob demanding "All power to the Soviets" while at the same time they trained cannon on the Soviets, threatening them with death and extinction.

As soon as I was recognized a crowd surrounded me and hot questions and fierce threats were hurled at my head. I tried to tell the crowd that the Soviets could not wield all the power because the Bolshevist demands were impossible. I tried to tell them what calamities might result from their excesses. But I spoke not to a crowd but to a monster. Deaf to all reason, crazed with hate and insensate fury, the monster simply howled aloud the idiotic slogans of the Bolsheviki. Never shall I forget the faces of this maddened crowd. They had lost all human traits and had become purely bestial. The crowd yelled and shrieked and furiously shook their fists.

"The Soviet members have sold out to the capitalists!"

"Traitor—Judas!"

"Enemy of the people!"

"Death to him!"

I shouted over this din of voices: "Will my death bring you land or fill your empty stomachs?"

Strangely enough this caused a number of the animals to burst into roars of laughter. So easily is the mob swayed one way or another!

In the Hall of the Duma speeches, speeches, speeches, were still going on. . . . By dawn some of the members lay sleeping the sleep of exhaustion. Others staggered up and down, still talking. The mob was still outside, reinforced now by several more regiments. One strategic position after another was occupied by mutinous soldiers. The firing sounded more heavily than during the night, and very frequently bullets struck the walls of the building. Exhausted after a sleepless night, I went out again into the garden of the Duma. Here I saw three armored cars. For or against us? Against, of course. Soldiers and sailors with rifles were crowding the garden. Suddenly there came a loud explosion, and all these valiant warriors threw themselves in panic to the ground. The panic had been caused by the Bolsheviki themselves. One of their soldiers had dropped a hand grenade, killing several people. Thinking their forces attacked by the Government, the Bolshevik machine-gunners opened fire, killing more people. After this some of the rioters decided to go home.

At five P.M., the Soviet reconvened, the Bolshevist deputies and their followers being present. They knew that the moment had arrived when they must either conquer or be conquered, and in order to conquer they were resolved to apply the utmost force. But just as one of them was roaring out a speech full of bloody threats, the door was flung open and three officers, their uniforms white with dust and caked with mud, marched into the hall and advanced with rapid steps to Chkeidze's seat on the rostrum. Saluting him formally, they turned, and the ranking officer addressed the Bolshevik groups with these words:

"While the Russian Army has been gathering all its forces to defend the country from the enemy, you soldiers and sailors who have never faced war, you idlers and traitors who spend your time in vicious babblings, you adventurers and turncoats—what have you been doing here? Instead of fighting like men against an invading enemy you have been murdering peaceful citizens, organizing riots, encouraging the enemy, and meeting us, the soldiers of the great Russian Army, with machine guns and cannon. What infamy! But all your treachery is in vain. I, the commander of the regiment of bicyclists, inform you that my troops have entered Petrograd. Your rioters are dispersed. Your machine guns are in my hands. Your fighters, so brave in the face of unarmed citizens, when confronted with real soldiers have fled like the cowards they are. And I tell you that those who make the first attempt to continue or to repeat this uprising will be shot down like dogs."

Turning to the chairman and saluting once more, he added: "I have the honor to declare to the Soviet that we are at the disposal of the Government and the Soviet, and that we await their orders."

The explosion of a bomb could scarcely have produced such an effect. Wild, joyous applause on the one hand, shrieks, groans, maledictions on the other. As for Trotsky, Lunacharsky, Gimmer, Katz, and Zinoviev, as one of my colleagues expressed it, they "shriveled like the Devil before holy water!" One of them did make an effort to say something, but was instantly shouted down. "Out of here! Away!" shouted the Soviet, and with their partisans at their heels, they left.

Half an hour later military music filled the halls and corridors of the Palace. Two fully armed regiments of Petrograd had entered the Duma. The Bolsheviki had been definitely defeated and once more the forces of order had won. When the crowds had been quickly dispersed, the mutinous soldiers were disarmed and arrested. About two o'clock in the morning I reached home, fell on my bed, and was instantly asleep.

July 5–6, 1917. Today's newspapers published documents proving that before their return to Russia the Bolshevik leaders had received large sums of money from the German Military Staff. The news created universal indignation.

"Traitors! German spies! Murderers!"

"Death to them! Death to the Bolsheviki!"

Thus roared and howled the mob, which yesterday had been just as lustful for the blood of Bolshevik enemies. The public mind had veered so completely that now it was necessary to defend the Bolshevist leaders from violence. Some of them voluntarily sought arrest in order to save their lives. To prevent lynching of the Krondstadt sailors, Tschaikovsky and I were obliged to accompany them from Petropavlovskaia Fortress to their ships. Realizing the fate in store for them if they fell into the hands of the fickle mob, the "pride and glory of the

Revolution," as Trotsky had called them only a few days ago, now cringed like dogs under the hoots and curses of the street crowds.

"Are you alive? Is everything all right with you?" This was a telegram from my wife, who was in Samara. Of course I was all right.

Today Trotsky, Kollontay, and others were arrested. Lenin and Zinoviev escaped. Now the question is, what to do? We moderates are not bloodthirsty, yet in order to prevent repetition of these murderous uprisings we must exercise great firmness. The Soviet is inclined to leniency. I think leniency at this juncture is nothing but weakness.

Riot is put down but nothing is done to suppress the orators or to punish the riotors. And the arrested Communist leaders were soon released.

I have been offered three posts under the Provisional Government—that of Assistant Minister of the Interior, Director of the Russian Telegraphic Service, and Secretary to Prime Minister Kerensky. After due reflection I have decided to accept the secretaryship, although in present circumstances I doubt if I can be of great service to the country. However, as Kerensky's aide, I shall do my utmost.

The elaboration of the law regarding elections to the Constitutional Assembly is almost complete. It is most democratic, allowing for full proportional representation—only it seems to me that it is about as suitable for poor Russia as evening dress would be for a horse.

A few days before I assumed my responsibilities as secretary to Kerensky an event occurred which deeply impressed all sober-minded Russians, even those who had been committed to the Revolution for years. I refer to the exile of Czar Nicholas II and his family to Tobolsk in Siberia. This was done secretly, but several days before, my old friend and colloborator, Mr. Pankratoff, called on me at the office of *The Will of the People* and told me that he had been appointed as chief of the Emperor's guard to escort the Czar into exile. Pankratoff was an old revolutionist who had spent twenty years of his life in close confinement in the Fortress of Schlisselburg. Notwithstanding this, he was a thoroughly humane man, having not the slightest animosity toward the Czar or toward the old regime. Therefore I was glad that he had been chosen and I felt sure that he would do all in his power to make the Imperial Family as comfortable as they could be under confinement. The motivation for this banishment was not in any way malicious. On the contrary, I know that it was Kerensky's desire that the family be sent to England. His plan failed simply because the Soviet would not consent to it. It was the extremists who were guilty of the worst features of the Czar's imprisonment in the Palace at Czarskoe Selo. His position there finally became entirely unsafe, and had the July riots lasted even a few days longer I am positive that he would have been murdered by the Bolsheviki. It was really necessary to send the family someplace where their lives would be safe, and where at the same time there would be no quarrel with the extremists concerning the safety of the Revolution. At Tobolsk there was little revolutionary sentiment, and no fanaticism at all, and under the guard commanded by Pankratoff there was no danger of attempts at assassination. Yet, if the Bolsheviki ever gained an upper hand, said Pankratoff, God alone knew what might befall.

New Crisis

Mingled with the telegrams expressing devotion to the Government from cities, Zemstvo, peasants, and workers, there are disturbing telegraphic reports of strikes among workmen, riots of soldiers, and anarchistic conditions among the peasants. I read all these and refer all important communications to Kerensky. To little purpose, however, as Kerensky does almost no constructive work, busying himself instead with the framing of resolutions which get the business of government nowhere. The wheels of the State are moving in a vacuum.

It has arrived at last, the catastrophe, the titanic cataclysm. On August 26, General Kornilov began it by marching an army on Petrograd with the intention of overthrowing the Soviet and the Government, and making himself dictator. This, at least, was Kerensky's version of the events; but to me Kornilov appeared less culpable.

I knew that relations between Kerensky and Kornilov had long since reached the breaking point and that Kornilov's group of non-Socialists were absolutely opposed to Kerensky's government, which they charged with the responsibility for Russia's rapidly approaching disintegration. Kerensky, for his part, characterized Kornilov and his following as traitors against the State. New forces had been organizing for defense against the Bolsheviki, but instead of uniting against the common foe, here was an army of patriots divided into three separate camps. The Bolsheviki, of course, were beside themselves with joy. What better fortune could they have asked for? In the Soviets there was feverish activity. A High Committee of twenty-two members "For the Struggle with Counter-Revolution" was elected, I being included in its membership. Characteristically, the Soviets elected a few Bolshevist members, and we found ourselves in the anomalous position of working with Reds for the suppression of patriots. The first thing these committee members demanded was the release from prison of their Bolshevist associates, Trotsky, Kollontay, and others; and against my energetic protests this was granted.

The Bolshevist Ryazanoff was one of the busiest members of the High Committee, writing proclamations and issuing bulletins. One of the members observed: "Who would ever believe that Ryazanoff and Sorokin would ever be seen working together? Myself, I find this encouraging."

But I do not feel particularly encouraged. My only thought was that revolution, like politics, sometimes makes strange bedfellows.

The High Committee had received information that our propaganda had been so successful that Kornilov's troops were already wavering and showing reluctance to continue the march to Petrograd. Two or three hours later came definite assurance that the Kornilov army was on the point of mutiny.

Next morning General Krymoff, commander of the "counter-revolutionary" troops, came to see Kerensky, and after a short conversation with him went straight out and shot himself. To me, the whole Kornilov affair was a tragedy. His motives and those of Krymoff, his chief aide, were absolutely pure and patriotic. They were in no sense "counter-revolutionaries."

Now the triumph of Bolshevism was merely a matter of time. The Government, having lost the confidence of all non-Socialist groups, now hung by a hair, and its downfall was imminent.

* * *

I have to endure the sight of my wife and all our friends suffering from slow starvation. No one complains, but by gay conversation we try to forget the lack of food in our stomachs. Well, it is discipline of a sort.

In all regiments the Bolsheviki have organized "Military Committees of the Revolution." This means new uprisings. I have bought a revolver, but would I shoot anybody? Hardly.

People are fleeing from Petrograd by the thousands, and indeed why should they remain? They face starvation, if not massacre by the Bolshevik mob.

"I advise you go too," said a friend to whom I bade farewell at the railway station. "Get away as soon as you can, for soon you won't be able to leave."

But leave Petrograd now? I must not and cannot.

The Abyss

October–December, 1917. The abyss has opened at last. Bolshevism has conquered. It was all very simple. The Provisional Government and the first all-Russian Soviet were overthrown as easily as had been the Czarist regime. Through their Military Committees of Revolution the Bolsheviki gained control of the regiments. Through the Petrograd Workers' Soviet they became masters of the working classes. These soldiers and

Petrograd workmen commandeered all automobiles in the street, occupied the Winter Palace, Petropavlovskaia Fortress, the railway stations, the telephones, and the post offices. To destroy the old Government and to establish the new had taken a mere twenty-four hours.

On October 25, in spite of illness, I set out for the Winter Palace to get news. As I approached I found it surrounded by Bolshevist troops. It would have been sheer folly to walk into their arms, so I turned around and sought, in Mariinsky Palace, the Council of the Republic. There I learned that while Kerensky had fled to the front to seek military assistance, Konovaloff and other ministers, with the Governor of Petrograd, Palchinsky, were barricaded in the Winter Palace defended only by a regiment of women soldiers and three hundred military cadets.

"This is outrageous!" stormed a Social Democrat deputy. "We shall certainly protest against such violence."

"What! Are we going to pass another resolution?" I asked.

"In the name of the Soviet, the Council of the Republic, and the Government we shall appeal to the country and to world democracy," he replied, offended at my levity.

"And what is that but another resolution?" I asked banteringly.

"We shall appeal to the military forces."

"What military forces?"

"Officers and Cossacks are still faithful."

"The same men whom the revolutionary democracy treated as counter-revolutionaries and reactionaries," I persisted. "Have you forgotten how you insulted them, especially after Kornilov's failure? After that do you imagine that they will be willing to defend us? I think, on the contrary, that they will be rather delighted at what has happened."

The besieged Ministers had not been murdered but had been whisked off to Petropavlovskaia Fortress to join the Ministers of the Czar. But the fate of the women was even worse than our imaginations had been able to picture. Many had been killed, and those who had escaped merciful death were savagely raped by the Bolsheviki. Some of these women soldiers were so vilely abused that they died in frightful agony. Some of the officials of the Provisional Government were also murdered with sadistic cruelty.

In my newspaper office I wrote my first article on the conquerors, branding them murderers, rapists, brigands, and robbers. I signed this article with my full name despite the protests of my colleagues and even of the compositor. "Let it stand," I said. "We all face death anyhow." As a matter of fact my article had such success that we had to print three times the usual number of papers. My friends begged me not to spend the night at home, and I decided to follow their advice. I also consented to change my appearance by ceasing to shave. Many were doing the same, clean-shaven men appearing with beards, bearded men clean-shaven.

Kerensky is defeated. The Bolsheviki have taken over the banks, state and private, and my former friend Pyatakoff has been made Commissar of Finance. From the front come new tales of horror. Generalissimo Dukhonin has been murdered along with hundreds of other officers. Our army is now a wild flying mob which destroys everything that stands in its path. German invasion is inevitable.

Today my colleague Argunoff, one of the founders of the Social Revolutionary Party, fell into the claws of the cat. Management and publication of newspapers will now be carried on under great difficulties. Invasion of editorial offices and printing plants has become an everyday routine. Bolshevik soldiers destroy copy and even presses. As a matter of form, we obey orders to cease our publications, but they reappear immediately under slightly altered names. *The Will of the People*, suppressed yesterday, appears today as *The Will*, and later on as *The People, The Wish of the People,* and so on. The newspaper *The Day* appears as *Morning, Midday, Afternoon, Evening, Night, Black Midnight, One O'Clock, Two O'Clock*. What is important is that our newspapers are eventually published. The readers who fail to get one in the morning read one at night.

Again today I narrowly escaped arrest.

Our daily menu at home has become exotic to say the least. There is no bread, but yesterday at a small shop we found a few tins of preserved peaches. For bread we prepare "cake" from potato skins, and find it not too awful to swallow. Long life to the Revolution, which stimulates invention and makes the people more modest in their appetites and desires!

Elections to the Constitutional Assembly are being held all over Russia. These elections are the country's challenge to the Bolshevist Revolution. If the Bolsheviki are right, they will receive a majority of votes. Very soon we shall know Russia's verdict. Of course, the Bolsheviki are doing everything in their power to block the elections, and all the "hunted mice" are doing their best to facilitate them. During the past week I have spoken at twelve meetings.

The first results of the elections have been published, and the Bolsheviki are beaten. They, together with the leftist Social Revolutionaries, are far behind the right wing of the party, and both are in a minority in the Constitutional Assembly. My name and those of other comrades in Vologda Province gained about ninety per cent of all votes. Last night we celebrated with a most extravagant banquet, each of us having a bit of bread, half a sausage, preserved peaches, and tea with sugar.

The Bolsheviki are decisively beaten. Yet we know they have no intention of accepting the verdict. As long as they had hopes of gaining a favorable vote they were willing for the Constitutional Assembly to meet. Now they will try to prevent its meeting.

Meanwhile I play the role of mouse against cat. Legally all deputies are immune from arrest; but the law is one thing, Bolshevist practice another. All roads now lead to prison. I am tired, exhausted, partly from work and excitement, partly from hunger.

November 27. The legal opening day of the Constitutional Assembly dawned beautifully clear, blue sky, white snow, an auspicious background for the huge placards displayed everywhere: "Long Life to the Constitutional Assembly, the Master of Russia." Crowds of people, bearing these standards, welcomed the highest authority of the country, the real voice of the Russian people. As the deputies approached Tavrichesky Palace, thousands of people hailed them with deafening cheers. But when the deputies reached the gates they found them closed and guarded by Bolshevist Lettish soldiers, armed to the teeth.

Something had to be done, and at once. Climbing the iron fence of the Palace, I addressed the people while other deputies climbed and scrambled after me. They managed to unlock the gates and the crowds rushed in, filling the courtyard. Staggered by the audacity of this move, the Lettish soldiers hesitated, and as a result the doors were opened and we walked in, many citizens following. In the Hall of the Palace we held our meeting and called upon the Russian nation to defend its Constitutional Assembly. A resolution was passed that in spite of every obstacle the Assembly would open on January 5.

To ensure its success, we hold daily meetings in the factories and among soldiers. At the same time the leaders continue their work of preparing fundamental laws and decrees, methods of procedure, etc. These conferences are usually held in my apartment.

The hand of the destroyer lies heavily on Petrograd. All commercial life has long since ground to a halt. Night and day we hear the noise of guns. The devastating madness and plundering has spread to the towns and even the country. The army no longer exists, and the Germans can walk in whenever they choose.

This is the last day of 1917. I look back on the year with feelings of bitterness and disillusionment.

At New Year's we meet together, the Social Revolutionary leaders and deputies. Dull sorrow mingled with the grim resolution to die fighting for liberty mark all our speeches. This morbid enthusiasm reached its climax after the speech of my friend K—, while we listened to the words of the famous aria from Moussorgsky's opera, "Khovanshchina" ("The Streltsy Sleep").

"My poor Russia sleeps; she is surrounded by enemies! Aliens are robbing her. Long years ago she lay under the yoke of the Tartars, groaned under the yoke of the aristocrats. My poor Russia! Who now will save you from your foes? Who will save you from your misfortune? O loved and unhappy Russia!"

The words moved us profoundly.

"We do not know who will save Russia. But whatever sorrows lie before you now, dear country, you shall not perish. From these ashes you will rise, a great country and a great nation, a power among the powers of the earth. If for this it is necessary for us to lay down our lives, we are ready."

Such were the words of the eloquent K— which closed our New Year's celebration.

The prospects for 1918 are very dark, but come what may I believe in my country and its historical mission.

CHAPTER EIGHT

De Profundis: 1918

In the Fortress of Peter and Paul

Trapped! At last the Bolshevist cat has caught his mouse, and now I shall have plenty of time for repose. I was arrested on January 2, 1918. After a meeting of the Committee of the Constitutional Assembly, Argunoff and I went to the offices of *The Will of the People*. When we arrived at our office on the third floor of the building we found everything apparently normal. But when we opened the door we were confronted by five or six men with leveled revolvers.

"Hands up!" they cried.

"What's the matter?"

"You are all under arrest."

"Members of the Constitutional Assembly are immune from arrest," I said, knowing full well the futility of my words.

"Never mind. We are ordered to arrest you. That is all."

An hour later, driven by car, we found ourselves inside the walls of Petropavlovskaia Fortress, the Bastille of Petrograd.

In the Commandant's office we found six or seven Bolshevist soldiers idly chatting. For some time they paid no attention to us, but one, toying with his revolver, pointed it once or twice in our direction. Finally we broke the silence.

"Are prisoners allowed to see their relatives and receive food, blankets, books, and linen from them?"

"Generally, yes. But in your case, no."

"Why?"

"Because you deserve not only imprisonment but immediate execution."

"For what offense?"

"Attempt on Lenin's life."

This was interesting news indeed. While we were digesting it, Commandant Pavlov, a man noted for his abnormal cruelties, entered the room and, after an icy glance at us, ordered the soldiers to lead us to Number 63. A few minutes later the door of a cell in the Trubetskoy Bastion clanged shut behind us. We were prisoners of Peter and Paul.*

Number 63 of this celebrated bastion of the fortress was a small cell with one heavily barred window. It was cold and dirty, with streaks of half-frozen water on the walls. There were no chairs or bed. Instead there was simply a ragged straw mat on the floor. When our eyes grew used to the half-light, we discovered the silhouettes of two men drawn in pencil on the wall, and underneath them a scrawled legend: "In this cell were imprisoned the Rumanian Ambassador and the Attaché of the Rumanian Embassy." They had been arrested some days before, and now we were in the cell where they had first been confined. "Some consolation, at least, to find ourselves in such aristocratic quarters," said Argunoff.

"Well," said I, "I have been a prisoner of the Czar and now I am a prisoner of the Communists. From this varied experience I should emerge a practical as well as a theoretical criminologist."

"I should call you a recidivist criminal," suggested Argunoff jocosely.

"If so, I am in good company," I retorted.

Thus we jested, and when Argunoff mentioned hunger I reminded him that since the Communists were the most advanced people in the world, they must know what was good for us. After an hour of this banter we "went to bed" by huddling together on the damp and ragged straw mat. In silence and darkness our souls wrestled with secret apprehensions. I thought of my wife waiting at home for me in vain, of her anguish when she would learn the cause of my absence; the difficulties of the Assembly; the fate of our newspaper. These troubled thoughts, combined with cold, dampness, and hunger,

* The name of the Petragrad Bastille was the Fortress of Peter and Paul.

murdered sleep. Suddenly my companion, also sleepless, began to laugh.

"Did any of us who prepared and welcomed the Revolution ever expect to be arrested by a Revolutionary government?"

We both laughed, and then I asked Argunoff: "How does this cell compare with your Czarist prison?"

"Just about as a country inn compares with a first-class hotel," he answered truthfully.

"Ah, that proves you are a counter-revolutionary."

Silence again, broken by the dripping of water from the walls and by the periodic staccato of machine-gun fire and the melodic chimes of the fortress, ringing every hour. "How Glorious is our God!" What hundreds of revolutionists of the past have listened to those chimes! What tragedies have been enacted beneath them! In the course of two centuries these dumb walls have witnessed despair, fever, death, and execution. Within these fortress walls lie the bones of many revolutionists. Here in the church of the fortress lie the mortal remains of the Romanoffs, beginning with Peter the Great and ending with Alexander III. Rebels and autocrats alike, their shades watch this hurricane of revolution which furiously rages above the ashes. The Revolution will pass, its actors disappear, but the shades will remain while new tragedies and comedies enact themselves upon the earth.

At seven the next morning the cell door opened and the warden appeared bringing hot water, a small quantity of sugar, and a quarter pound of bread for each one of us. "You will soon be moved to a more comfortable cell," he said encouragingly. "At least, I shall try." And sure enough, in about an hour he returned with the cheerful summons, "Come along."

The new cell was indeed much better—warmer and drier, with two beds and a sort of table attached to the wall.

"How do you do?" A voice greeted us through a small hole in the door. "Could we ever have imagined meeting here?"

Looking up, I beheld Professor Kokoshkin and Dr. Shingareff, former ministers in the Kerensky Government.

"Representatives of the sovereign people, welcome to this shrine of liberty," said Mr. Avksentieff, former Minister of the Interior. Others soon came to our door to congratulate us: Ministers Tereschenko, Kishkin, Bernatsky; Prince Dolgorouky, leader of the Constitutional Democratic Party; Palchinsky, recent Military Governor of Petrograd; and Ruthenberg, now one of the principal organizers of the Jewish State in Palestine. They brought us bread, tea, sugar, some books, and also news of the prison. Arrested immediately after the Bolshevist Revolution, these men had been in the fortress for two months and were old residents, privileged characters, so to speak. With them, in the most friendly spirit, mingled representatives of the old regime: Purishkevitch, leader of the Monarchists in the Duma; Shcheglovitoff, former Minister of Justice; and Sukhomlinoff, Minister of War in the Czar's government. They all met us and, I imagine, obtained some pleasure from seeing members of the new government in the same predicament as themselves.

At four o'clock we were taken out for exercise in the yard of the prison and had the good fortune to meet our friends. Their appearances had altered sadly, Kokoshkin and Shingareff looking really ill. Tereschenko, a man very *comme il faut,* always clean-shaven and exquisitely dressed, was transformed into a bearded man in shabby trousers and a sweater. Purishkevitch looked like the janitor whose work he actually performed in prison. Kokoshkin and Shingareff proved to be in an acute stage of tuberculosis and were soon to be removed to the Mariynskaia Hospital. Walking up and down the yard, our comrades warned us that our position in the fortress was extremely perilous. The wardens of the bastion, Social-Democrat Internationalists, were decent men, but the garrison itself was governed by Bolsheviki. In connection with the alleged attempt on the life of Lenin, they had issued a proclamation threatening a St. Bartholomew's Night and a September Massacre of all prisoners in the fortress. "The sooner all these counter-revolutionaries are killed the better," concluded this proclamation.

Later, we all learned the truth about this attempted assassination of Lenin. A tire of his motor car had blown out and Lenin, terrified, had taken this for the report of a pistol. That was all there was to it.

Little by little we adapted ourselves to the routine of the prison. At seven o'clock we got up and received hot water, a little sugar, and a quarter pound of bread for the day. At noon we had our dinner, consisting of hot water with some cabbage and a bit of meat. At four o'clock there was afternoon tea—hot water; and at seven, supper—more hot water.

Our diet consisted of too much water and too little anything else, but as we received a little extra food from friends, we did not want. The gloom of the prison was hard to bear. In our cell, with its one high window looking out on the fortress wall, it was difficult to read or to write even at noon. In the morning and afternoon the place was quite dark. Sometimes the electric light was turned on between six and ten o'clock, sometimes for not more than an hour during the whole day. Much of our time had to be spent in dreary idleness. The hardships of life under the Revolution, however, had developed in us all a keener sense of humor which enabled us to meet all our new trials with a certain philosophical detachment.

Talking with our friends during the half hour of exercise every day, exchanging news, cleaning the snow and ice from the yard and gazing at the blue sky, we kept ourselves in fair health and spirits.

The dark hours of the late afternoon and of the night were very irksome; we spent them lying down or pacing the cell and thinking endlessly of family, friends, and our unhappy country. It was a week after our arrest before we had news of our wives. Mrs. Argunoff had been arrested with us, and I feared that my wife also might have been taken. Where? If free, how did she fare? Life in Petrograd was so full of danger that it is no wonder my mind was distraught.

With great anxiety we looked forward to January 5, the opening day of the Constitutional Assembly. Intense firing around noon of that day disquieted us, but we tried to believe that it was only the everyday music of the Revolution. At eight o'clock word came, partly through the warden, partly through the evening newspapers he brought us. The Constitutional Assembly had opened. The opening ceremony, election of the president, first speeches, turbulent behavior of the crowds in the galleries, and the calm behavior of the deputies under terrible conditions—these we had expected. In the same newspaper I was astonished to read the speech I had planned to deliver at this first sitting. It was so fully reported that only those who knew I was in the fortress were aware that it had not been given at all. While this paper was being printed, the real condition of the Assembly was extremely critical. That morning thousands of people had gone out to welcome it, but Bolshevist machine guns met them and killed and wounded many. The streets, we afterwards learned, were strewn with bullet-ridden bodies. Such was the reception the Bolsheviki gave to the Russian Constitutional Assembly and to the unarmed citizenry who went out to see the realization of their cherished dreams. "The dispersal of the Assembly and arrest of the deputies is only a question of hours," we agreed after reading and hearing this terrible news.

Next morning being the feast of Epiphany, we were allowed to attend services in the Cathedral of Sts. Peter and Paul in the fortress. We listened as we stood among the tombs of the Russian emperors lying peacefully in their eternal sleep.

"The Constitutional Assembly is dispersed," we read that day in the newspaper. Utterly depressed in spirits, we met that afternoon in the prison yard to say good-bye to Kokoshkin and Shingareff, who were to go to the hospital that evening.

The next day one of the wardens, bringing our dinner, said: "Have you heard about your friends?"

"No. Has anything happened?"

"They were killed last night by Communists who broke into the hospital."

In utter horror we listened to the story. The plan to murder Kokoshkin and Shingareff had been made while they were still in the fortress, and through the connivance of Commandant Pavlov. "I must tell you," added the warden, "that attempts may be made to kill you also. We shall try to prevent them, and the only thing for us to do in case the men come in great numbers, is to open the doors of your cells and of this passage to the yard. Only there is no way out of the yard."

"At least do that," we begged. "It would be better to die in the open than inside like rats in a trap."

Thoughts of Kokoshkin and Shingareff returned to torment us. Anything more wantonly cruel than this murder was difficult to imagine. Both men had devoted their lives to social and patriotic service, and now, sick to death, they had been butchered in their sleep as "enemies of the people." Night came but we could not sleep.

About eleven o'clock we heard voices, the sound of opening and closing doors, the rattling of keys. "Don't be alarmed," said a warden at the door. "It is only new prisoners who have just been brought in."

The Devil's Pepper Pot (*Tchortova Pereshnitja*), an anti-Bolshevist magazine published the following "social notes" at this time: "The winter season in the health resort of Petropavlovskaia Fortress has opened brilliantly. Prominent ministers statesmen, politicians, representatives of the people, writers, and other distinguished gentlemen of the Czarist and Provisional governments, members of the Soviets and of the Assembly, leaders of the Monarchist, Constitutional Democratic, Social Democratic, and Social Revolutionary parties are taking vacations in this celebrated resort with its well-known methods of medical treatment by cold, hunger, and compulsory rest, interrupted at times by surgical operations, butcheries, and other excitements. There is reason to believe that in the near future this exclusive circle will become even larger and more brilliant."

In some ways our conditions grew a little better. We received letters and twice a week were permitted visits from close relatives. The weekly meetings with my wife and with one dear friend were the happiest moments of my prison life. Once I was deeply touched by a visit from a peasant from Vologda Province.

"Devils! What are they doing to you?" he cried furiously.

"Be careful, my friend," I warned. "They may arrest you."

"Let them arrest me. I am sixty-seven years old. What can these scoundrels do to me? Nothing."

My wife and our friends tried their best to effect our release. Up to this time their efforts had failed, but they were not altogether hopeless.

It was encouraging to hear as we did at this time, that the murder of Kokoshkin and Shingareff had aroused such a storm of indignation in Petrograd that even Lenin realized he had gone too far and that repetition of such atrocities was temporarily impossible.

Nothing endures forever in this world, and our imprisonment in Petropavlovskaia came to an end. One evening a warden came to my cell with the abrupt announcement, "Your wife and a friend are in the office with an order for your release. Take your things and come along." The friend turned out to be a man quite unknown to me personally. He was an old revolutionist named Kramaroff. Now he was an Internationalist and was cooperating with the Bolsheviki. Nevertheless, he bravely opposed the methods of the Chekha, and when he heard of my arrest, he went vigorously to work to secure my release. Now, having been at last successful, he came in person to the fortress to see that I left the prison without violence from the guards. Leaving the fortress, we stopped at the office of the Commandant to have my order of release signed, and Kramaroff, addressing the brutal Pavlov, said contemptuously, "Well rogue, when do you expect to be hanged?" These insulting words, far from offending the Commandant, seemed to please him. "Who the devil can hang me?" he asked laughing. Kramaroff replied that he knew plenty of men who would enjoy doing so, whereupon Pavlov said complacently, "I know, but most of them are here now, in my hotel."

Ten minutes later, after fifty-seven days and nights of imprisonment, I drove out of the fortress.

The Cat and the Mice

After about a week in Petrograd, my wife and I went to Moscow. The city of Peter the Great was dying, and with it was passing an era of Russian history, the period which during two centuries had transformed Moscovia into the Russian Empire and had witnessed great achievements in art, literature, and science. Now it was all passing. Even the Bolshevist Government was moving to Moscow.

In Moscow the activity of all the anti-Bolshevist groups continued. "The League for the Regeneration of Russia," the "League for the Fatherland and the Revolution," the Social Revolutionary, Social Democratic, and Constitutional Democratic parties all worked zealously together. Plans for a general uprising against the Bolsheviki and the Germans were being matured. Friction was appearing and leftist Social Revolutionaries resented the abject surrender of the Bolshevist leaders to the Germans. Conflict between the Bolsheviki and the Czecho-Slovak legionaries had also arisen. In a word, the Bolshevik leaders found themselves so discredited that they turned for support to their military forces—the Lettish troops, troops made up of German and Austrian war prisoners, Chinese, and all kinds of adventurers and criminals. The real Bolshevist Reign of Terror began at this time and under this tremendous pressure of adverse public opinion.

We began publication of our newspaper, *Regeneration,* and no sooner had the first copy appeared than Bolshevist agents raided the office, seeking to arrest the editors. They destroyed all copy, broke up forms and matrices, and smashed the presses. Nevertheless we went on writing, and for a month we issued regular editions. The cat-and-mouse game began all over again, this time more ferociously.

In Moscow at this time I met Kerensky, whom I had not seen since the Bolshevist Revolution. Entering his apartment, I was met by a long-haired, bearded man wearing thick blue spectacles; his general make-up recalled the intellectual of the 1860-70 period. No stranger would have believed that this was the man who, a few months earlier, had been virtually the ruler of Russia.

By the end of May a great many members of the Constitutional Assembly and the League for the Regeneration of Russia began to leave Moscow to carry on their special missions as worked out by the new plan of liberation of Russia from the Communist government and the Germans. I was sent to Veliki Ustyug, Vologda, and Arkhangelsk [Archangel].

In Arkhangelsk the most horrible purge was going on. The Bolshevist Commissar Kedroff was executing people by the hundreds and thousands. Victims were being shot, drowned, or murdered with unnameable mutilations. Feeling the ground under their feet insecure, the Bolsheviki tried to strengthen their position by unrestrained terror.

In Vologda Province the situation was somewhat better, although presage of the Red terror was there too. I had therefore to move cautiously and to conceal the real character of my mission, which was to organize Ustyug and Kotlas in connection with the planned overthrow of the Bolsheviki in Arkhangelsk. The district Ustyug-Kotlas was important to the plan. Located between Vologda and Arkhangelsk at the mouth of three rivers—Vychegda, Sukhona, and Dvina—it was the center of concentration for enormous quantities of military supplies. Being a connecting link with anti-Bolshevist Siberia, this district had to play a very serious part in the re-establishment of the eastern front against the Germans, in the overthrow of the Bolsheviki, and in the re-establishment of the Constitutional Assembly. To liberate the north of Russia—Arkhangelsk, Ustyug, Vologda, and Yaroslavl on the one hand, and the Volga district and central Russia on the other—it was planned to form a union with Siberia, and in this way to surround the capitals occupied by Bolshevist forces. The fact that Ustyug-Kotlas was my native region where I usually spent my summers helped me greatly in carrying out my mission.

At the end of June, Nicholas Tschaikovsky left Vologda on a steamer. I altered my appearance and joined him at Ustyug. Our journey to Arkhangelsk was a dangerous undertaking. If the Communists discovered who we were, our fate would be fatal indeed. During our three-day trip on the steamer we had several narrow escapes from our real identities nearly being discovered by the Communists. Our difficulties were greatly increased by the delayed arrival of a British expeditionary force and by the resulting postponement of the overthrow of the Communist government in Arkhangelsk. Finally we decided that Tschaikovsky would continue his trip to Arkhangelsk while I would return to Ustyug to finish preparations for the liquidation of the Communist local government in the Ustyug-Kotlas region. A few days later the Arkhangelsk government was overthrown and Tschaikovsky became the head of the new Democratic government there. In Ustyug everything was ready for the overthow of the local Communist regime there. But the breach of promises on the part of the chiefs of the English expeditionary force radically changed the situation. After the overthrow of the Communist regime in Arkhangelsk, the Communists began a panicked retreat by steamer toward Kotlas-Ustyug and by train toward Vologda. The English and our forces did not meet any resistance from the fleeing enemy. Having pursued the Communists some two hundred fifty miles along the Dvina River and for a considerable distance along the railway from Arkhangelsk to Vologda, the chiefs of the English expeditionary force suddenly ordered a halt to the pursuit, although the Communists were still fleeing in panic and were offering no resistance at all.

When the Communists saw that they were no longer being pursued, they halted their retreat and brought in large reinforcements from other parts of Russia. We could easily have overthrown the Communists in Ustyug, but our local forces alone were not enough to cope with newly arrived large Communist forces led by great Communist military leaders. Instead of joining the Arkhangelsk Democratic government, as was planned, I and other anti-Communist fighters in the

Ustyug-Kotlas region found ourselves in the perilous situation of being hunted by the Communists with a price on our heads for delivery dead or alive.

Wandering

Further resistance on our part had become impossible, so we went into hiding in the woods near Ustyug. The only possible way for us to reach Arkhangelsk now was by forced marches. While preparing to go to Arkhangelsk, we decided to stay for some time near Ustyug; and so, dividing into several groups and having agreed on means of communication, we embraced each other and parted.

My first objective was a village where I spent two days with a peasant friend. I then continued on to another village, thus beginning a long series of wanderings around Ustyug. It was not easy to live secretly in a Russian village where every stranger excites curiosity. In the midst of civil war, when spies are everywhere, for a hundred friends who might be ready to give you shelter, you never know who is ready to betray you. In writing this history, I wish I could express my gratitude to those good and brave peasants who, at great risk to themselves, did shelter me and help me on from one place to another. If my head at this moment is on my shoulders, it is because of these faithful "Ivans" who warned me of every danger, gave me every comfort they could, arranged communications between me and my wife—in a word, tried in every way to help me.

With several narrow escapes from the Lettish Communist hunters, I wandered from village to village, from one hiding place to another, for about three weeks. (See the details in Chapter XI of my *Leaves from a Russian Diary*.)

Finally, when this sort of hiding became impossible, I decided to retreat with a fellow conspirator into the depths of the wild forest. From there, if the circumstances allowed, we hoped against hope to cross the distance of several hundred miles to Arkhangelsk. (Some fellow conspirators, including my brother Vassiliy, actually attempted to do this; so far as

I know, all of them were caught and shot by a Communist firing squad.)

About thirty miles from Ustyug I met my fellow fugitive, in fairly good spirits and quite prepared, as I was, for whatever might happen. With difficulty we bought flour, onions, and potatoes for four or five days, got an ax, rifle, and a few cartridges, a porridge pot, a teakettle, tobacco, needles and thread. These we put in bags with a change of linen, two or three books, and some canvas for sleeping bags. We spent the night in a hay-stack, and next morning we started to the forest, two peasants guiding us part of the way. In the afternoon of the same day a Red detachment galloped into the village to arrest me. But by that time we were far away.

Return to Nature

Forest! Endless forest! Thirty miles to the nearest village. After danger, a sensation of freedom. What happiness! Gaiety filled us and we began to sing and shout at the tops of our voices. We found a hut made by peasants who, in winter, came there to hunt squirrel, bear, and other game, and there we settled down. Above us was a roof, around us rough walls, and under us moss and dry grass and canvas. There was a good woodpile for fuel, a brook of good water. The air was healthful, and above there was no revolution, no "headhunters," no reminder of the cursed lunacy of communism. The incessant autumn rain spoiled our comfort a little but, after all, very little. Time flew by. Cutting more fuel, hunting, gathering berries and mushrooms, reading, writing, and conversation filled our time. Tired after a day of work, we slept all night like dead men. Five days passed thus, and then it was time to go to the villages for food and information.

My friend knew the country better than I and had more acquaintances, so it was decided that he would go first. We agreed that if he did not return by Sunday noon—this was Thursday—I would go to look for him. Sunday noon came and still my friend had not returned. I waited three hours and then, shouldering a few necessities, I set out. After walking five or six miles I saw a man on the path. But was it he? Yes, it was indeed, but what a figure! Clad in a shirt and nothing more!

"Where on earth did you leave your trousers and boots?"

"In the river," he answered cheerfully.

"Then let us be Communists and divide our clothes," I said, handing him my coat, boots, and trousers, and remaining in my undergarments. The man was fairly chattering with cold.

When we reached our hut he told me his adventures. In the first village he could get no food, so he crossed the river to another village where he had a peasant friend. There they gave him supper and a bed in the bath-house. But just as he was falling asleep he heard voices and saw men at his friend's door. He fled instantly to the woods, hoping that the men would leave and that he could get his bag of food, but in the morning he saw that three saddled horses remained at the door of the house. Stealing out of the woods, he ran along the banks of the Sukhona to the place where there was a boat, but when he looked back he saw the Reds riding after him. At once he shed his clothes and dove into the water. They shot at him, but he reached the opposite bank without mishap. He stayed half-naked in the woods until night and then started for our shelter. The exposure, excitement, and exhaustion had told on him terribly. I made a good fire to warm him and went out to seek some game, but was unsuccessful. Berries and mushrooms were all we had for supper, and berries and hot water was our breakfast. It was absolutely necessary to get food, so we started for the villages. In the darkness we cautiously approached the house of a relative of my companion, a peasant named Stepan. But, frightened to death of our sudden appearance, he whispered: "Go away, for God's sake. Red soldiers are in the village. Go away!"

He gave us some bread, a pair of bast shoes and trousers for my friend, who had walked barefoot the whole distance, and we went off with Stepan's promise that he would bring us provisions the next day. In the woods we ravenously devoured our bread and sat down to shiver under the shower until morning.

"It seems to me we take too many baths and too few meals," said my companion dolorously. But I reminded him that it was quite the other way around with less particular people.

Morning came, hour after hour passed, but no sign of Stepan. About noon we heard someone swearing at his horse, which was a conventional method of announcing the advent of provisions. Five or six pounds of flour and about a hundred pounds of potatoes, this was all that Stepan could bring us. Putting it in our bags, we tramped off toward our new objective, the basin of the Low Jerga. Avoiding villages, we walked for five hours through rain, carrying our burdens. It grew quite dark.

We spent five weeks moving from one place to another through this endless forest. When we came to a comparatively comfortable place, we built a rough shelter with hewn trees, moss, grass, and branches. Two tree trunks set closely together made us a fireplace. Our menu consisted of potatoes, flour-gruel, and what berries we could find. From time to time we shot a little game, but we were obliged to hoard our ammunition lest we should need it against two-legged beasts. We tried fishing, but it was an off season and we had no luck. By day we kept ourselves busy, but in the evening when darkness came on and we sat before the fire smoking our primitive cigarettes, we talked and thought and listened to the symphony of the forest. Composed of a thousand varying notes, this forest music was always fascinating to me.

Our nights were full of dreams. Almost all our waking hours we were hungry; our bodies, and most of all our feet in their bark shoes, were wet. We began to bloat and to feel very weak and tired. Sometimes our hunger and exhaustion, combined with our anxieties about those we loved at home, threw us into horrible despair. At other times we felt indifferent, almost happy.

One day we came to a huge swamp. For about five hours we walked through it in mud up to our knees. Our bark shoes fell to pieces, our feet were cut, our bodies ached, but still we came to no end of the cursed muck, no place where we could rest and eat. Everywhere we looked we saw a swelling, yellow-green surface with pools of open water, with small and half starved trees scattered here and there. Never shall I forget this damned swamp. The water was so cold that we lost all feeling in our feet. Often we collapsed and lay panting on beds of red berries. There were moments when we felt that we were perishing, that the last breath of life was leaving us, and that we would have to die in that red, endless expanse. Why not there? Yet by encouraging each other we managed to struggle on, and at last, O happiness, the red nightmare was over.

The next day we were rewarded by the discovery of a hunter's hut with a rude fireplace in it. Building a fire, we took off our rags, washed them in the river and, after hanging them up to dry, stretched ourselves out in our Turkish bath. As we lay there a wild duck flew by and lighted in the water just below us. My companion grabbed the rifle and fired. The duck was hit, but the stream began to carry it away. We ran and threw ourselves in the river after it. In this way we had a Turkish bath, a cool plunge, and a delicious duck dinner into the bargain. Afterwards we treated ourselves to a cup of hot tea, smoked dried-leaf cigarettes, and read Jack London's *Stories from Alaska.*

* * *

So we wandered over the bosom of Nature, occasionally wishing we might see a little civilization. In free moments we talked much about the Revolution, and doubts which had been born in my mind at the beginning of the upheaval grew to full size. During my meditation in the forest I lost many dazzling illusions, beautiful dreams in whose reality I had once believed. They vanished, I believe, forever. Healthy persons have no need for illusions.

"Lasciate Ogni Speranza Voi Ch'Entrate"

As winter approached, our situation grew much worse. Berries and mushrooms disappeared and the fetching of food from the villages involved the greatest difficulty. When snow began to fall the marks of our footsteps made it easier for the "headhunters" to trace us, and from merely hunting the country around settlements, they now extended their search far into the forests. Sometimes these hunters themselves were killed forty or fifty miles away from their detachments, but oftener they succeeded in killing their victims. All these things made it inevitable that we should leave our forest fastness and return to town. On the eve of our exodus we cautiously moved a little to the clearing. The next morning I embraced my friend, who was to start the following day, and set off. The distance to Ustyug was forty-seven miles, and I had to enter the town between six and seven in the evening. At six it was dark, and after seven I should have to produce a certificate.

Vigorously I set out, knowing that when one's life depends on his feet they usually hold out. Carefully avoiding all villages and hamlets, I made my way onward and at a quarter to seven I was safely in the appointed house. The first part of my revolutionary adventures was over. What was to come was mercifully hidden behind the veil of destiny.

In this place of refuge I lived an absolutely noiseless life, the existence of a fleshless phantom. Never to laugh, never to cough, never to approach a window, never to leave the house; to be ready at the slightest warning to fly to the lumber room, then remain motionless and still as long as a chance visitor remained; to listen night and day for dangerous sounds—this was the price of existence. I was like a hermit who has taken vows of perpetual solitude and silence. One day followed another, and the more I thought of it the more inevitable seemed the end of my safe confinement. I knew they were looking for me, knew that my presence in Ustyug was suspected. Sooner or later they would find me. Finally, I made a desperate resolve.

"My friends," I said that evening as we sat together, "I see no use in continuing this frightful existence. I know that I shall be arrested soon, and to stay here longer simply puts this whole household in jeopardy. It is not right for me to go on risking your lives and safety. So I am going to put an end to it all—my suffering and your danger."

"What are you going to do?" they asked.

"I am going to do what our northern hunters do as a last resort when they are fighting for life against a bear. They thrust one fist into the bear's mouth and with the other hand they try to stab him to death with their small knife. Something like this I intend to do. Tomorrow I am going to walk into the jaws of the Chekha."

"You are mad!" cried all my friends. But against their protests, I pointed out that my present situation was intolerable and that it did not even promise more than a few days' additional safety. I admitted that I had no more than one chance in a thousand, but that one chance I was determined to take.

I hope I shall never again in life have to go through such a scene of farewell as we endured the next evening. Good-bye, when it almost certainly means good-bye forever, is a terrible thing to say. A mother sending her son into battle knows something of what my wife and I, my brother Prokopiy and our faithful friends felt that night. Twice I said good-bye, and twice I turned back. Last good-byes, last kisses and embraces, last stifled sobs, last signs of the cross on my forehead, last looks—then they thrust into my ragged pockets a few cigarettes for comfort, and let me go. As I stumbled into the darkness the thought crossed my mind, "There is still time to return." But no, the die was cast. And on towards the dreaded Chekha I went.

Two Lettish soldiers in top boots met me in the anteroom. Pale faces with red lips and dull eyes that seemed to see and yet not see me, a thick odor of alcohol—this was my first impression of the Chekha.

"My name is Professor Pitirim Sorokin," I announced. "Please let them know that I have arrived."

In the dull eyes of the executioners something like astonishment glimmered. After a moment of silence one of them rang a bell. At once four armed men entered and stood staring at me. I lit a cigarette. After an interval one of the soldiers beckoned and I followed him into the office of the head of the Chekha. The house, and even the room, I knew very well. I had been there many times as a guest. But instead of a comfortable study with books and pictures, it was now a filthy den with ragged tapestries, broken furniture, and on the table a pile of dirty dishes and a litter of bottles. Pictures of Lenin, Trotsky, and Lunacharsky decorated the walls. At the table sat Sorvacheff, who was the temporary head of the Chekha. He was one of the local Communists, not a particularly bloodthirsty person, but weak before the higher authorities.

"Sit down," he invited, "and allow me to ask you some questions. Where did you come from?"

"From the forests."

"From which forests?"

"From the Dvina," said I, indicating a direction where I had not been.

"How long have you been in the forests?"

"About two months."

"With whom?"

"Alone."

"Where were you before?"

"In the villages."

"In which villages?"

"That does not matter."

"You must name them. I insist."

"You may insist as much as you like, I will not give any names."

"Well. Why did you go to the forests?"

"Because your agents paid too much attention to me. Besides, I like to be in 'the bosom of nature.'"

"Have you been in Arkhangelsk?"

"No."

"We have some evidence that you were."

"I say no. Let me see what sort of evidence you have."

"That does not concern you."

"Well?"

"Why did you come to us?"

"To know why I am persecuted and to learn what you are going to do with me."

"I think you well know why you are persecuted, and as to what we will do with you, I think you know that also. Personally, I would be ready to set you free. But your fate does not depend upon my desire. You will have to be shot immediately. But as you are too big a bird for us, and as your principal activity was carried on in Petrograd and Moscow, we must ask the Central Chekha what to do with you. You may be sure, however, that this only postpones your execution for a few days," he concluded.

"Thank you for your candor, at least," I said.

"Now I shall send you to the prison."

A few minutes later, accompanied by four armed men, in the darkness of night, I strode to prison. As I approached it, I looked in the direction where I had left my dearest people and sent them my last "good-bye."

Lasciate ogni speranza Voi ch'entrate—"Take leave of all your hopes, you who enter here," I remembered Dante's words above the gates of Hell as I entered the prison gates.

I was in the Kingdom of Death.

The Red Terror

In prison again! A little too much for one man in a year. Revolution takes no account of human sufferings.

* * *

In the cell of the prison at Veliki Ustyug, where I am confined, there are about thirty men. Some of them are known to me. There are three students who took my courses in the University of Petrograd, two teachers, two priests, two lawyers, four merchants. Most of the others are peasants and workers. The population of Russia outside of prisons is diminishing horribly, but inside the prison walls it is steadily increasing. Before the Revolution there were scarcely thirty prisoners in this prison; now there are more than three hundred. In addition, there are about two hundred in the cloister, which has been transformed into a prison. Is this not striking progress in the direction of freedom?

Some of the prisoners are lying on the floor in their rags. Some are sitting and hunting for insects. When I arrived, questions were hurled at me. What were the news and prospects for the future? In what way, why, and when was I arrested?

"In the usual way, for the usual crime," was my answer.

"But we don't know why we were arrested," some of them objected.

"You have been arrested in the name of the Revolution. You have been told that the Revolution is God and God cannot be questioned." I spoke in the humorous tone of a prospective gallows-bird.

Poor fellows! Especially the peasants and workers! The "bourgeois" students, lawyers, merchants, and priests know they are imprisoned as "hostages," but these laborers cannot understand why they were arrested by the "Government of the workers and peasants."

"What do you think they will do with us?" asked some of them.

"Probably you will be liberated very soon."

But I did not explain what I meant by this "liberation." If at the hour of their liberation, instead of the joyful faces of those they love they see the tragic face of Death, the final agony will be comparatively short. It takes an hour to go from here to the place of execution; another hour, perhaps, is consumed in awaiting one's turn to be shot. It is far better to suffer these two hours than to live many days and weeks as a man condemned to death.

I lighted a cigarette and offered the rest to my fellows,

leaving two for myself. I will keep two cigarettes for a special purpose—to smoke on the way to the execution. This seems a little strange, but human psychology generally is strange. Here in prison all is communal. Here exists a real communism, more effective than the communism introduced by force outside the prison. Food brought to this or that prisoner from outside is divided among all. Here complete equality is practiced. Death is the common fate of all of us. Our standards of life are the same.

However, in spite of communism and equality, all the prisoners are starving. Myself, as well. Many months of starvation have left me constantly hungry. But even this has its compensations. It again gives me the chance to continue my study of the psychology of starvation. I see that under any conditions it is possible to be an optimist. Everything depends upon the point of view.

"Dinner" is served. One-fourth of a pound of bread which bears slight resemblance to real bread, and some hot water with a few potatoes compose "dinner," "lunch," "breakfast" and "supper." Most of my comrades greedily eat their portions at once. Some try very hard to leave a little for the evening. But they cannot. Only four men in the cell are free from the sin of gluttony. They lie in a corner and pay no attention to the eating. Being in the delirium of typhus, they are unconscious of their environment.

Strange thing! My companions not only do not try to keep away from those poor creatures, but rather strive to be near them.

"My comrades, be careful and keep yourselves farther from the typhus," I warn them.

They smile. "It is not so bad to have typhus," says one. And they all agree. Very strange fellows indeed!

* * *

Night! About eight o'clock the people in the cell all "went to bed." That is, they stretched themselves out on the floor and became silent. I followed their example. In spite of my desire not to think of my position and of the future, my whole brain insists on thinking of these things. The nature of the inquiry in the Chekha today and the concluding remarks of the examiner do not leave any doubt as to my fate. I am to be shot.

I accepted the sentence quietly—if the term "quiet" is appropriate for such an occasion—but only my reason comprehended it, not my whole consciousness. Now, in the dark night, I realize all its dreadful significance.

After the prisoners had fallen asleep, the door of the cell suddenly opened and nine or ten Communists came in. The head of the executioners, a Lett named Petersen, gruffly commanded:

"Petroff, Diakonoff, Tachmeneff, Popoff, Sidoroff, Constantinoff, put on your overcoats and follow us."

"No, you don't need to take your things," he said to the peasants who, supposing that they were to be freed, wanted to take their "property" with them.

With pale faces, half-mad eyes, and quivering hands, the victims tried to put on their rags. All their movements were feverish. They move liked hypnotized somnambulists. Only two of them, the student Popoff and the peasant Petroff, kept to some extent their tranquility of mind. They shook our hands, and Petroff said: "Good-bye forever, my comrades. Don't bear me any ill will. If you come out alive, remember me to my family and give these things to my wife. Overcoat and boots are no longer necessary for me; to my children they may be useful." He crossed himself and genuflected "Good-bye forever!"

Popoff kissed the other students and me. "Long life to Russia and death to the Communist hangmen of the Russian people!" he exclaimed as he started out.

"Be silent, rascal!" roared Petersen, and struck the student's face with his revolver. A tiny stream of blood flowed down Popoff's cheek.

"Long life to Russia and away with Communist tortures!" shouted the student again.

"Then I will teach you, counter-revolutionary scoundrel!" said the executioner, pointing the revolver at Popoff.

"I am not afraid of your revolver. Fire!"

One, two, three shots thundered. The student fell. One life destroyed! Horrified silence suddenly fell upon us, but after a few moments it was broken by a wild and purely animal cry, a cry of terror and pain, a roar, a savage groan trailing off into murmurs of muted horror. Then Tachmeneff fell into a fit of hysterics and writhed with convulsions.

"Pick up this body and follow us!" ordered Petersen.

The executioners and their victims disappeared.

Deep silence filled the cell once more. How terrible this silence! And how terrible the pale faces of my comrades and their feverish looks! At last one of the lawyers spoke:

"All that must be, shall be," said he. "All that must not be, shall not be. Let us not dwell on this."

The prisoners began to talk in low tones. A priest was on his knees in a corner, continuing to pray. After some time we "went to bed" again, but nobody could sleep. Death was too near to every one of us.

* * *

"Today was their turn; tomorrow will probably be mine."

I have tried to visualize my own last moment. Do I fear it? I do not. It is not fear I feel, but a sense of outrage. I picture the way to the hill of execution. The place is well known to me. How many times have I stood on that lovely hill covered with beatiful pines. How often have I enjoyed the splendid view! How peaceful was this sight then, and how terrible is it now! Probably I will be led out with other victims, surrounded by twenty or thirty Communists. On the way I shall smoke my two cigarettes. I shall have to cross the street where my wife and brother are. Will they feel my last approach? Will their hearts tell them I am near? Perhaps! Perhaps they will come to the road and perhaps I will have the happiness of giving them one last look. Half an hour later we will arrive at the hill. Then we will be commanded to dig our own graves. I shall refuse to do it. If they want to bury me, let the Communists dig my grave. For my body I have no sentiment. It may lie in a grave or on top of the ground for all I care. After that they will order us to take off our overcoats and boots, which they will appropriate as "revolutionary perquisites." Finally they will make us all stand up. If the number of victims is large, some of us will be obliged to await our turns and to watch the others die. Then will come our turn. They will give the order to fire. I wonder if I shall hear the firing before I lose consciousness? There will be a sharp pain, but if they shoot straight all will be finished; if the shooting is bad, it will be necessary to suffer for some time. Do I fear this suffering? Not at all. Why, then, does all my organism, all my soul, all my "self" protest against this? Why do I feel so desperate? Why? Not because I fear but because I want to live!

In the cell is half-darkness. On the floor lie many bodies, the flesh of the Revolution. Silence. Only from time to time deep sighs and delirious exclamations from the men with typhus break the silence. Typhus! I begin to understand why my fellows do not fear typhus. Indeed it is not so bad to be in a delirium. All is relative in this world.

Seven men—young and healthy though emaciated—were brought in today. Their lives are over. If not tonight, then tomorrow they will be executed. They know it. Three of them are silent. They are kneeling in a corner, praying. This prayer is the last, deepest token of life and the highest and purest manifestation of Spirit. For whom, or to whose advantage is the destruction of these young men, these strong men, who have not yet lived half their lives? "Their death is necessary for the happiness of mankind and for the perfect well-being of future generations!" I wish I could see these happy generations who will build their happiness on the blood and sufferings of previous generations. I think that if they have even the most elementary morals they will not dare to be happy. Stop! I am beginning to philosophize. This is not quite proper now in this "Communistic Academy of Hell."

I have been moved from the common prison room to a lonely cell. It seems that my case is approaching its end. Here, alone, my thoughts are turning still more urgently to the question "To be or not to be." "My present reaction, from the behavioristic view," I say to myself, "is merely an expression of the instinct of self-preservation." For a moment my thoughts drift in the direction of scientific curiosity. I begin to analyze my situation, thus stimulating my reactions. I observe my own pacing to and fro, my restlessness, my general sensations. It would be interesting to investigate my physiological processes and to photograph my movements now. Probably they are a little unusual. Probably now I look quite unlike myself. I have not seen myself in a mirror for many weeks, but I can imagine how I must look in these rags—unshaven, bloated from starvation, pale and disheveled. Probably not very different from a real idiot.

Through the little hole in the door I hear a whisper.

"My friend, how are you?" I look out and see my friend Zepaloff. "My God!" I exclaim. "You, here too!"

"As you see."

"So your crossing the Red frontier was unsuccessful."

"I was caught."

"And now?"

"Now, in a few days I shall be dead."

A day or two later the warden told me that my friend had been shot.

One more valuable life gone. I wish I could see Smilga, Vetoshkin, and the other Bolshevist leaders whom he saved from arrest and to whom he gave such generous help. They "thanked" him then. Murderers!

Seven men from Vetluga died tonight. This voracious monster, the Revolution, cannot live without drinking human blood.

I am still alive. All my preparations are made. My last letters to my wife and friends are written. In this cell time passes very slowly. I sleep badly. Each morning I try to read and write, but with little success. I can concentrate on the pages for only a few minutes. From six o'clock in the evening until midnight I watch and listen feverishly to the sounds and the heavy steps in the prison. This is the time the Red "popes" of the Revolution come for the daily sacrifice to their God. For me, or not? When the steps are gone, I say to myself, "It is not yet my turn!"

* * *

Today the door of my cell suddenly opened and the Commissar of Justice came in. I had been told that he was a worker from Petrograd and a comparatively decent man. He carefully closed the door behind him, and in a low voice said to me: "Citizen Sorokin, you are our enemy now, but I remember your lectures for us in the workers' school in Petrograd, before the Revolution. Then you gave us a great deal and you really helped the workers."

"I fear that I taught you very badly if you, one of my students, are with the Communists."

"Let us not dispute vainly," he replied. "In spite of your present views, I think you may be useful to the country as a scientist. I will do my best to save you, though I have no real hope. Don't tell anybody about our meeting. Good-bye."

The door closed. An odd little "comrade" he is, this worker-commissar! At any rate, he is a brave man. If his friends in the Chekha should learn of his visit to me, he would soon be in my place.

* * *

Through the little window of my cell I can see part of a field beyond the wall of the prison. For many hours I have stood at this window, hoping I might see a friend or my wife, and today I was splendidly rewarded! Standing at the window I suddenly saw her. What happiness! I shouted and waved with my dirty towel to attract her attention, and I succeeded. My poor dear! For a few minutes we gazed at each other. That was all we could do, but what happiness! Thanks to Heaven!

The first anniversary of the Bolshevist Revolution—November 7—has arrived. Yesterday the Red priests offered their glutton god an extraordinary feast of human flesh. Twelve lives were sacrificed at once. Now we are told that for three days there will be no more executions. In the official newspaper this is announced as an "amnesty." Well, then, we all have three days to live while the Revolution is digesting its last heavy meal. After that, the god will probably be so hungry that it will demand extra rations.

I am back again in the common cell. Why? I do not know. I find many changes. Two have died of typhus; one man was liberated; about twenty-five others have been "liberated" on the hill of execution. In their place, new prisoners, principally peasants, have been brought in. This is the "sacred place of Revolution" and it must not be empty.

Three days of comparative quiet have passed. My apprehensions concerning the hunger of the Revolution were justified. Today at about ten o'clock the worshippers of the god of Revolution again came for food. But instead of three or five men—the average daily portion—they took sixteen at once. As usual the names of the victims were read aloud. All submissively began to put on their overcoats and to shake our hands. All but one. He did not move, but continued to lie on the floor. "I will not go," said he. "If you want me, you will have to carry me."

"Then, comrade, perhaps this will make you move," said the same Petersen, putting his revolver to the man's head.

"Fire! It is more convenient for me to die here than there!" stubbornly answered the prisoner.

"As you wish! Carry him out!" shouted the Communist.

Again the old terrible silence in the cell. Then—one, two, three, four shots in the prison yard!

"Great God, do not forget his soul in Thy blessed kingdom; give him peace and eternal life," prayed an old peasant kneeling and crossing himself. All the prisoners fell on their knees and began to cross themselves.

"We have no help, we have no hopes but You, O Mother of God," a priest began to sing. "Help us," joined in all the prisoners in full voice. "We have hope in You. We pray to You, we praise You! Don't leave us, poor creatures of the earth!"

This was real prayer. Never before have I heard such. In the voices echoed all man's love of life, all despair, all suffering, and all belief in the God of helpless human souls.

* * *

"Sorokin, put on your overcoat and follow us." This was the command today of four Communists who came into our cell. My turn had come at last. Well, I was ready. Only inside I felt as though something had suddenly snapped, and a cold shiver ran through my body. So, summoning all my courage and without haste, I shook hands with my fellows. "Good-bye, my friends . . . Good-bye."

"Come here." One of my escorts pointed to the door of the prison office. A man with a long nose invited me to sit down. I sat.

"Is this telegram known to you?" he stretched forth a bit of paper to me.

"On Thursday N. Tschaikovsky is starting from Vologda by the steamer *Uchreditel*," I read.

"No, I have never seen it."

"Nevertheless, it was addressed to you, was it not?"

"I might with equal justice claim that it was addressed to you."

"You may persist in denying what is obvious," said the inquisitor, "but it is all in vain. Your participation in the Arkhangelsk counter-revolution is known and your sentence has been passed."

"If that is final why trouble me further?"

"Take him back."

Congratulations met me in my cell, but they gave me no hope. Today's examination told me that my drama is approaching its end.

The days crawl like lice one over the other. Every night the same summoning of victims to the slaughter. Our suspense grows almost unbearable. It would be easier to walk out to meet death than to die thus slowly from day to day. It is difficult to keep one's outward calm for weeks on end. If one knew that in two days, or three or five—But weeks—weeks! It is very difficult even for the bravest. I try to catch a cold, to contract typhus—anything to hasten the end. All the others, I observe, do the same. There is actually competition among us to get near the typhus patients. Some of the men pick lice off the unconscious and dying and put them on their own skins.

Today seven victims.

Today three.

Today only one.

Today nine.

Death hovers over me but does not touch me yet. Today three more. My God! How long will this torture last? I remember descriptions of the French terror. This is quite like it. History repeats itself.

Sixty-seven new prisoners, among them five women and four children, have just come in. They are peasants who had the temerity to resist when the Communists came to "nationalize" all their grain, cattle, and other possessions. Artillery and machine guns were sent to the village to put down the revolt. Three villages were razed and burned, many peasants were killed, and more than a hundred arrested. The sixty-seven who have joined us here are in horrible condition—arms broken, flesh lacerated, bodies bruised. The bitter weeping of little children is heard now in our prison. I wonder how long they can live in this hell. If the fathers must suffer, why should these sinless little ones be punished? The prison is overcrowded now.

We are less crowded today. Most of the peasants have been executed. One of the children is left without father or mother.

Blessed be this day! For the first time I was permitted to go with some of the others to saw wood on the banks of the Sukhona. This great privilege was hitherto granted to all save myself and one or two other political prisoners. In a group of about sixty I went out, heavily guarded. From the streets the prisoners greedily picked up cigarette butts, cabbage leaves, and rotting potatoes. Some friends recognized me as I passed, and hurried to inform my wife and my brother. An hour later, at some distance, I saw them, those beings so dear to me. During two hours of hard labor I had the bliss of gazing at them. As we filed back to the prison we passed close to them. Tears streamed from their eyes. In my rags, unshaven, dirty, prison-pale, I must have been a sad sight for them to look upon. Yet I bless the day that gave me the unspeakable joy of seeing them once more.

Resurrection

Today, December 13, I am writing, not in prison but in the railway station of Luza. Yesterday at about three o'clock I was again ordered to go to the office. I entered the room. My wife! What does this mean?

"Please, Professor Sorokin, will you sit down?" This was my inquisitor, only today there was a note of servility in his voice.

"This article in *Pravda* may interest you." It was an article by Lenin about me. Its main theme was that men of my kind, representatives of the peasantry, in their origin and previous activities democratic, and only by unhappy chance enemies of the Communists, deserved special attention. The task of the Communists should be to convert them into allies. To have intellectuals and educated men in Communist Russia would be good for the country.

"We have received an order from Lenin himself," the Chekhist emphasized the last two words, "to send you to Moscow, where you will be at the disposal of the Central Chekha. Tomorrow morning you will leave. We will arrange whatever is necessary for you."

"May my wife go with me"?

"No, but she will have permission to join you within two or three days."

"May my wife bring me clean garments? These," I pointed to my filthy rags, "are a little soiled."

"Oh, certainly."

Next morning, followed by the Latvian head-executioner Petersen and a Russian Chekhist, I was driven to the Luza station. A clear winter sky was over my head, a clean, cold wind blew in my face. Life, wonderful life, summoned me again. I tried to imagine how the miracle had come about, but I gave it up.

When the train arrived at Luza we entered a car of "Special Designation," to quote the legend on its walls. This is a comfortable international wagon-lit appointed solely for agents of the government, while the people travel in, on top, on platforms, or above the wheels of trains. While the other travelers fast, the apostles of "equality" sit comfortably in their compartments eating caviar, meat, good bread, and drinking wine. Equality indeed!

For three days, closely guarded, I traveled with these Chekha officials. Quite casually they told me how they had hunted for me among the villagers, how many people they had killed, naming, among others, some of my friends.

On the morning of December 16, 1918, we reached the Central Chekha in Moscow. There I found, among other prisoners, Professor Kaminka, just down from Petrograd. Soon the rooms began to fill with "fresh fish," newly arrested girl and boy students, a priest, two literary men, workmen, profiteers, professional thieves, and two prostitutes. There being no chairs, we all sat on the floor. About seven in the evening the agent again entered the room and said to me, "You are free to go when you like."

Concealing my intense excitement, I followed him to the office, and while papers were being signed, I looked around at this center of the terrorist machine. There was a pretty woman in the room, exquisitely dressed and adorned with many jewels. Merrily chatting, she worked at a pile of papers. The others addressed her as "Comrade Peters," from which I inferred that she was either the wife or the sister of the great head terrorist

Peters. Apparently the Communists, if they could not bring about universal happiness, were looking after their own.

At last my papers were handed to me and, clasping them to my heart, I walked out into the streets of Moscow. The realization that I was saved, that I had actually risen from the dead, quite overwhelmed me. I wandered along for a time, unconscious of where I was going. Recovering myself with difficulty, I turned toward the house of an old friend. But in answer to my ring a stranger came to the door. He had no idea of what had become of my friend, so I went on to the apartment of another friend. Strangers were in his home also. The third visit brought to the door an intimate friend, Professor N. Kondratieff, who at first sight failed to recognize me. When I spoke my name he cried, "My God, but you have changed! You look twenty years older."

"It is the times that move so quickly," I laughed. "In a few months of this glorious era of progress one lives twenty years. Now please give me some clean undergarments. Mine are full of lice."

He gave me a room in which to bathe and change. The water was icy cold but I enjoyed the bath and, afterwards, the hot tea over which we discussed my adventures and those of our friends. Three days later I had the happiness of meeting my wife and the friend with whom I had wandered so long in the forest.

A few words about my unexpected reprieve. It was the work of my old student, the commissar who had visited me in prison. He had informed Piatakov and Karakhan—my previous friends, now members of the Lenin cabinet—about my death sentence, and they, old memories not quite obliterated, went to Lenin and demanded my liberation. Lenin, hoping to get credit for his magnanimity, wrote the *Pravda* article about me and ordered my release.

As I was not on parole of honor, I felt myself free to act as my conscience dictated. Therefore, if my activities since my resurrection have not entirely pleased the Bolsheviki, it is their affair, not mine.

Steps Toward the Communist Paradise

After a few days in Moscow I went to Petrograd. What I saw from the Nikolaevsky Station was the abomination of desolation. It was as though a devastating plague had swept the town.

Very hungry and sickened by such sights, I looked everywhere for a shop where I could buy a morsel of food. I found none. I went to my own apartment on Nadejdinskaia Street and found it occupied by a Jewish family.

Except for a few books and papers, all my property had disappeared. Some volumes lying close to the stove indicated the use to which others had been put.

"Please excuse us," said the woman. "We didn't know whether you would ever return. Besides, it was so cold and we had no fuel to burn."

Dressed in borrowed undergarments and in the torn boots and overcoat I had worn in the forest, I went to the home of old neighbors. As usual, I was greeted with, "How terribly you have changed!"

"Look at yourself," I retorted. "You have changed, too."

Mrs. Darmalatova laughed. "Oh, yes, my daughters and I wear our clothes several sizes smaller now." And when she had heard of my homeless plight she said, "Do take one or two rooms here. We are to have two or three Communists quartered on us, and it will be ever so agreeable to have you instead." Now it was only necessary to settle the problem of daily bread. With great difficulty I obtained the desired bread card, food card, tobacco card, fuel card, and clothes card. Professors, as a "semi-parasitic group," got second category cards, which entitled them to barely enough to keep alive.

After I had finished my card collecting, I visited the University and the Psycho-Neurological Institute to let my colleagues know that I was alive and to find out what had happened to my university position. My old professorship in the University and Institute was offered to me, and it was arranged that I should again begin my lectures and seminars after Christmas. I was also elected professor of sociology in the Agricultural Academy and the Institute of Public Economy, and I accepted both because it was necessary to have the extra allowances. At the same time two large cooperative organizations, not yet nationalized, asked me to write them textbooks in law and sociology.

Visiting the university dining room, I met another publisher, F. Sedenko, who asked me how much longer I was going to postpone writing my *System of Sociology*. I told him that all my material, gathered over a long period of years, had been lost. He urged that I should know from experience how foolish postponements in our circumstances were.

"Today one is alive, tomorrow dead. It is better to publish a needed book even if it has some defects," he said. "Begin your *System* at once, and I will publish it."

I knew he was right so I accepted his offer. Soon my wife arrived from Moscow and we settled down to live and work in the bosom of Communist culture.

On the night of December 31, 1918, we held a New Year's gathering with Mrs. Darmalatov's family and a few other intimate friends. Each of us had a piece of bread, some cakes made from potatoes, and a glass of tea with a morsel of sugar. It was so cold in the room that everyone sat in wraps and hats. Midnight struck, the hour for congratulations and speeches in other days. Now just one speech was made.

"The terrible year is over. Let us be thankful that it has gone. Let the memory of our dear friends who perished during its mournful months live forever. From the coming year we expect neither peace nor joy. If at its end, we, our relatives, and our friends are alive, we shall be happy. May we have courage to meet the coming trials."

We sat silent and melancholy. Each thought sadly of those who had died and prayed fervently for those who were still in the jaws of the Red monster.

CHAPTER NINE

Life in Death: 1919-22

In the Bosom of Communist Culture

"The Troglodytes," we called ourselves. Not that we lived in caves, but I am sure that the original cave-dwellers enjoyed more comforts than did ninety-five per cent of the population of Petrograd in 1919. Mrs. Darmalatov's apartment, for example, had eight large rooms, but in that bitter winter only two of them could be used. Mrs. Darmalatov and her two daughters lived in one, my wife and I in another. We always spoke of this as our "winter concentration." In Communist society everything had to be "natural," and we certainly had a natural temperature in our dwelling, which was heated principally from our lungs. We had fuel cards but no fuel. The water supply of Petrograd at this time was so full of typhus and other noxious germs that it was impossible to drink a drop without boiling it first. In 1919 the most valuable present one could give or receive was a piece of firewood.

As for sanitary conditions, they are simply not to be described in the language of decency. All water pipes cracked under the intense cold of unheated houses, and in the upper stories people could neither use toilets nor get water.

"This is communia," said a plumber, asked in to repair the disaster to our rooms. We experienced "communia" in many other areas. Broken window glass had to be repaired with rags. To wash or to take a bath was almost beyond anyone's power. The laundry, a bourgeois institution, disappeared. Soap was included in food cards, but it was never issued.

What was perhaps hardest to bear was the darkness. The electricity was turned on only for about two or three hours in the evening, and very often it was not turned on at all.

Our food cards gave us from one-eighth to one-half a pound of very bad bread daily, and sometimes we received even less. We used to go to "dinner" at the communistic dining room at the University, but even there we had only hot water with a few bits of cabbage in it. Professor Vvedensky, as a real scientist, accurately calculated that we wasted more strength in walking and waiting there than we received in vitamins and calories from the food. In time everyone grew thin. Many began to lose their memories, developed starvation psychoses and delirium, and died.

Each morning one of us began "breakfast" while another ran off to get a place in the bread line. These damned queues took two or three hours of our time each day, but gave us almost nothing in return. After breakfast we cleaned our room as well as we could, and then if there was no compulsory public work, no guard duty, no more queues, no sick or dead friends to attend to, I tried to write on my *System of Sociology* or to prepare my university lectures. I sat with all my wraps on, gloves on my hands, and my feet rolled up in rags. From time to time I got up and exercised to limber my half-frozen limbs. In the afternoon and evenings I went to my work, walking from one institution to another, from eight to ten miles a day. Exhausted from these exertions and from constant hunger, I went to bed early—unless it was my turn to stand guard all night. So we lived in the "Russian Surely Fantastic Soviet Republic" (R.S.F.S.R.), as we called it.

Depression engulfed me every time I went to the University. Entering the campus, one heard no more the sound of young voices and laughter. The place was dark. Lectures were given only in the evening. All lectures and seminars were held in the student's dormitory which was no longer crowded.

My classes in sociology at the University became the largest and most frequently attended in the whole institution, not because I was such a talented lecturer, but because sociology had now become such a vitally important subject. Not only the students, but the university clerks and the public attended my lectures. I knew that many Communist spies also attended and regularly reported my utterances to the Chekha. Very soon after my release from prison, Lunacharsky and Kristy—Commissaries of Public Instruction and Education—had offered me the position of Commissary of the Universities and Institutes of Petrograd. They thought Lenin's scheme to convert me and others into allies of the Communists—that is, to make us tools in their hands—a clever move. But if my colleagues and I were powerless to stop their physical and moral suffocation of the country, we had conscience enough not to encourage or to participate in their murderous activities.

In my lectures I never "played politics," but I did give scientific data, regardless of whether they supported Communist theories or not. Being a sociologist under such conditions was a damnable business, but I had to be honest. I can hardly describe the difficulties under which I continued my work, which I knew might any day cause my arrest. I lectured in the dark to an almost invisible audience. When I was obliged to consult my notes, I would ask: "Is anyone rich enough to loan me a candle end?" Usually someone produced a tiny inch of candle, which I blew out as quickly as possible; for the students, who took their notes in darkness, needed a little light whereby to study.

The faculty visited the University only for meetings and conferences. In our reading-room, as everywhere, desolation reigned. We had no new books or magazines, no scientific journals. Cut off from the whole world, we knew nothing of what our colleagues abroad were doing.

In Memoriam

This afternoon we buried the academician, Lappo-Danilevsky. When I visited him a week ago he looked like a living skeleton. Smiling feebly, he told me that, going to the Academy a few days before, he had fallen down and slightly injured his leg. Three days later I saw him in a hospital after he had undergone a surgical operation. Lying in his bed a dying man, he was reading *The Phenomenology of Spirit* by Hegel. "Never had time to study it attentively," he whispered, "begin now." The next day he died.

Yesterday Mrs. Darmalatov's beautiful daughter Vera threw herself out of the fifth-story window of our apartment. When we picked her up from the pavement, she was alive but unconscious. As she lay on the bed we could see no blood or bruises on her lovely body. Even her half-open, unseeing eyes were brilliant and unclouded. Two hours later she was dead. Vera was like a flower that could not live in this soil of cruelty and bestiality. She now lies on the table in the next room.

To die in Russia in these times is easy, but to be buried is very difficult. Four days elapsed, all of us standing hours in line, interviewing dozens of officials before we could get permission to bury Vera. Finally we swore to one commissary that unless he gave us a permit we would bring the body to his office. Tomorrow we shall bury her. Meanwhile we must carefully watch Mrs. Darmalatov. Crazed with grief, with nothing to look forward to but poverty, suffering, and memories of this horror, she runs about dumb and half-mad.

"*Ca ira*"* Some days ago Professor Khvostoff hanged himself. Yesterday Professor Inostrantzeff took potassium cyanide. So dies a notable philosopher and the most eminent geologist in Russia. During the last few weeks both he and his wife have been very ill. At last, unable to get food or medicine, unable even to call for assistance, they ended their own lives.

Professor Rosenblatt has just put an end to his life. "*Ca ira*" has a meaning somewhat different, I fear, from the old French Revolutionary song. Kapustin, Pokrovsky, Batushkoff, Kulisher, Ostrogorsky, Karpinsky, Arsenieff—one after another have died; and others are dying. Dying from typhus, influenza, pneumonia, and cholera, from starvation, and from all the seventy-seven plagues of Egypt. A friend one sees alive today is dead tomorrow. Our faculty meetings are now little more than solemn

* One of the popular mottoes of the great French Revolution, meaning "It will go on."

memorials to our colleagues. Closing one of these meetings, Rector Shimkevich addressed us with grim humor.

"Gentlemen," he said, "I beg you not to die so rapidly. In dying you find relief for yourselves, but you cause us a great deal of trouble. You know how difficult it is to get coffins for you; you know that there are no horses to transport your mortal remains to the cemetery, and you know how expensive it is to get graves for your eternal slumber. Please be considerate of your colleagues and try to live as long as you can."

To get coffins is indeed so difficult that most people simply wrap their dead in mats. Some rent coffins in which to carry bodies as far as the cemeteries.

In today's *Pravda*—we have only official newspapers now—an editorial appeared praising the creative energy of Communism. It referred to the decision of the government to build a crematorium, the largest in the world. The author is ignorant of the ironical significance of his article.

This afternoon Professor Laserson burst into my room in a state of almost insane agitation. "I can't, I can't endure this nightmare any longer," he wept. "My sister is dying, all our friends are dying. Around us we see only death, death, death. I cannot do anything. I read, but I do not understand what I am reading. There is no light—there is no end to these horrors!"

Even this triumph of natural death is not enough for the builders of the new society. The machine of the Red terror works incessantly. Every day and every night in Petrograd, Moscow, and all over the country, the mountain of the dead grows higher. Shchepkin and one hundred and fifty others, many professors among them, have just been executed in Moscow.

So many arrests are made daily that cloisters and schools are being transformed into prisons. When he gets up in the morning, no man or woman knows whether he will be free that night. When one leaves one's home, one never knows whether he will return. In forty-seven provinces of Soviet Russia the population has diminished by eleven million.

In the Home of the Czars

In the spring of 1920 we moved to Czarskoe Selo, once the residence of the czars, now the center of children's colonies. In the Agricultural Academy of Czarskoe Selo my wife and I both found work and, given two small rooms and a bit of land for a kitchen garden, we were much more comfortable than we had been in Petrograd. The beautiful parks of the old imperial town, if badly neglected and cut down, were still beautiful. The palaces, built according to Rastrelly's wonderful plans, still charmed our eyes and reminded my wife and me of the grandeur of our once great Russia. In free moments I wandered in the silent and desecrated parks, peaceful in spite of chopped down trees, scum-covered ponds, and obscene scrawls written on the arbors and bowers by Red soldiers. Everything there spoke of the long and glorious reign of the czars, and everything spoke also of the tragedy of the Revolution.

Not long after taking up residence in Czarskoe Selo, my *System of Sociology* was published after many delays. How I ever managed to write those two volumes I have often wondered.

Roses of authorship have their thorns, however. "What! Haven't you been shot yet?" exclaimed my friend Professor Radlov. "For certain pages of your *System*, page 142, for example, I think you deserve, under our admirable government, several executions. No one has published such an audacious criticism of the existing order as you have."

"Well," I answered, "since executions are the general rule, I would rather be shot for something than for nothing."

Neither did I object to denunciations which appeared in the Communist press: "The ideologist of counter-revolution"; "The leader of the most implacable professors and intellectuals"; "It is time to crush, once and forever, such persons"; "How long will the Chekha stand this man's activity"?

The Chekha did not intend to stand it very long. The ice beneath my feet became so thin that I did what many others did at that time. First, I neglected to register my address in

Czarskoe Selo, but continued to live there illegally. If my room in Petrograd were searched I would have time, being warned by friends, to disappear. With this necessity constantly before me, I provided for place into which to disappear.

In October, 1920, the "night visitors" went to my Petrograd address and demanded to see "Comrade" Sorokin. Truthfully, my friends told the men that I no longer lived there, and that they did not know where I was. When they asked for what crime I was wanted the men answered, "For banditry."

Next morning my students read the announcement: "On account of sudden illness, the lectures of Professor Sorokin are interrupted. Notice will be given of their resumption." Such announcements were so frequent that the students quite understood. For two weeks I peacefully reposed in the apartment of a friend, pursuing my studies. As soon as I "recovered my health" I went back to my lectures. But these sudden illnesses became more and more frequent between 1920 and 1922. After a public speech or the publication of an article, it became my habit never to spend the night in my own home. Always on going to bed I asked myself, "Will they come for me tonight?" I became accustomed to this, as man accustoms himself to anything.

The new commissary of the University, a freshman, Tsviback, deprived the Rector Professor Shimkevich, the most prominent zoologist in Russia, of all his seals and declared himself head of the University. In 1921-22 the Rector was dismissed and many of the professors discharged, banished, or executed. This policy of the government was a clear trial of the moral and social spirit of Russian scholars, and I can testify that most of them withstood every trial and temptation to which they were subjected. One of the greatest, I. P. Pavlov, showed to what heights moral and scientific ideals soared in Russia in those terrible days. As the two most outspoken men in our criticism of communism, Pavlov and I grew quite friendly during these years. Together we organized the Society for Objective Study of Human Behavior, Pavlov as honorary president, myself as active president. For no other reason than for foreign propaganda, the Soviet Government in 1921 issued a decree giving Pavlov special consideration, providing for the publication of all his works, and offering him a committee consisting of Maxim Gorky, Lunacharsky, and Kristy, to care for him and for his laboratory. Pavlov's answer to this decree was this declaration: "I am not a broker, and I do not sell my knowledge for your rations. The dogs in my laboratory may eat better food if you give it to them, but I will not accept any privilege or benefits from hands that are destroying Russian science and culture."

Such acts of heroism, such devotion to ideals in the face of all temptations have been everyday occurrences in Russia during the Soviet rule. Between the moral heroes and those men who have shown themselves cowards, there have been intermediate types, among them three or four scientists who, while hating communism, adopted a policy of *captatio benevolentiae*—flattery and servility to the ruling powers. The great majority of intellectuals have simply endured and, when endurance failed, died. Let anyone who seeks moral heroism turn his eyes to the thousands of people in Russia who, for years, from day to day, from night to night, despite persecution and temptation, have steadfastly replied to the Bolsheviki: "Man does not live by bread alone," and "Thou shalt worship the Lord thy God, and Him only shalt thou serve."

Expiation

"Can you, comrades, point to any other country in the world where the government gives to the working people food, clothing, lodging, and everything free of charge as we are doing in our Communist Russia?" So spoke Grishka (Gregory) the Third, otherwise Zinoviev (Apfelbaum), the Communist dictator of Petrograd, at a meeting of workmen early in 1921.

"I can!" cried a voice from the audience.

"Then, pray, do."

"In the old Czarist galleys food and clothes, lodging, and everything was free, just as in our communistic society. Only they were better," shouted the man.

"Good! Perfectly true," laughed the audience. Grishka tried to speak again, but he was interrupted.

"Sit down! We have heard enough, you fat devil!" And as the workers' patience, long suppressed, broke all restraints, Chekhists with revolvers surrounded Zinoviev. The shouts continued, personal insults were hurled, and Grishka the Third disappeared. Scenes like this were rapidly becoming more common.

By 1921 the destructive consequences of the Communist program became clear to even the dullest peasants. Their fields lay untilled and overgrown with weeds. The peasants had no seeds to sow and no incentive to industry. In the towns everything was slowing down to a dead halt. Nationalized factories, having no fuel, stopped operating. Railways broke down. Buildings fell in ruins. Schools had almost ceased to function. The deadly noose of communism was slowly choking the people to death. Stormy meetings and riots in factories and among peasants began to grow rapidly. Even in the Red Army desertion was increasing. The Russians in the Red Army several times refused to suppress demonstrations of the Russian people. In view of this, the Communist government organized a special International Army recruited out of the dregs of the population and well-paid murderers of German, Latvian, Bashkirian, Jewish, Hungarian, Tartar, and Russian origins. It was this International Army that killed many demonstrators in two revolts in Petrograd alone, in February, 1921. And it was this same army which saved the Communist government in the Kronstadt rebellion on February 27, 1921.

On February 27, we heard that the Kronstadt sailors, formerly ardent supporters of communism, had revolted. This turned out to be true, and had that revolt succeeded, had we had even one free newspaper to support their revolt, it would have been the end of the Soviet Government. We heard plainly the cannonade from Kronstadt, and plainly we saw the panic of the Government. Within twenty-four hours a proclamation was issued announcing the New Economic Policy (NEP).

According to the proclamation, requisitions from peasants were to be replaced by definite taxes; trade and commerce were to be re-established; many factories would be denationalized; people would be allowed to buy and sell food; special conferences of non-Communist workers would be organized to improve living standards. In this way communism was "castrated" and "NEP" was established. For three weeks we listened to the constant sound of guns, our hearts melting with joy in the hope that the sailors would win that life-and-death duel.

At that time both my wife and I were seized with pneumonia and placed in the hospital in Czarskoe Selo. In the same room lay five or six workmen, two Soviet clerks, and a university professor. *Boom! Boom!* echoed the sound of cannons from Kronstadt, and we whispered to ourselves: "Brave boys. God help them."

A week passed. The cannonade still went on—*Boom! Boom!* My wife and I progressed through the crisis of pneumonia and began to notice our surroundings, particularly the sound of guns. But on March 18 the firing died down and dead silence fell over Petrograd. Joyful excitement left the hearts of the people and fear took its place. The duel of Kronstadt was over. The Communists had conquered. Woe to the vanquished! For three days the town was at the absolute mercy of the Red troops. For three days the Lettish, Bashkirian, Hungarian, Tartar, Russian, and Jewish dregs of the International Army, unrestrained and mad with blood, lust, and alcohol, killed and violated the town's citizens.

In the days of their Communist madness those Kronstadt sailors had committed many crimes. They too had murdered and violated. But for what they had done they now expiated most horribly. The government, which had been raised to power principally through their support, had no mercy upon them. When the bloody feast in Kronstadt was finished, thousands of the "pride and glory" of the new regime were in prison or dead. This was true despite guarantees of the government that those who surrendered would be given immunity.

Three days after that, the people of Czarskoe Selo who lived near the Kazanskoe cemetery spent a sleepless night. Endless discharges of rifles were heard and seemed to strike the very heart of them. Five hundred sailors were shot that night near the cemetery.

New Butchery

The dreadful days of revenge passed. The machine of the Red terror still worked, but now it exterminated lives by tens and hundreds instead of by thousands and ten thousands. The New Economic Policy, forced on the Communists, began to have a revivifying effect on the country. As in a fairy tale, the dead land seemed to come to life. The limits of our freedom were narrow, it is true, but individual initiative and responsibility did assert themselves.

Little by little Petrograd began to assume the outward aspect of a European city. People were repairing their houses, taking some care of their dress and appearance. The marks of death and desolation which had lain on us like a pall for two years, by September, 1922, had almost been obliterated.

In the spiritual life of Russia there was a great revival. While all other buildings were left to decay, the churches were repaired. Religious services, little attended between 1917 and 1920, now became crowded.

The anniversary of the University's foundation was celebrated in a solemn and impressive meeting. About five thousand professors and students, besides those of the Institutes, were present at this meeting on February 3, 1922. After the former Rector Shimkevich delivered his address, I spoke. In my speech I pointed out the new guideposts which would be followed by the young generation. Individual freedom, individual initiative and responsibility, cooperation, creative love, respect for the liberty of others; reform instead of revolution; self-government instead of anarchy—these were now and should ever be our social ideals.

The next day the Communist papers attacked me furiously, but the only result was that my speech was broadcast over the country and received many plaudits. At that time attacks on the Communists had exactly that effect. Whatever their press condemned, the people praised. Whatever it praised, the people condemned. When Zinoviev and Lenin attacked me personally for my articles, their attacks greatly increased my popularity.

"Comrades, the hydra of counter-revolution is raising its heads again. Either these heads must be cut off or we shall be devoured by the monster." Thus spoke Zinoviev at a meeting of Communist officials soon after the great religious demonstration of May 2, 1921. "We must demonstrate that the machine of the Red Terror still exists and works efficiently," he concluded.

Very soon after this more than a hundred people, mostly scholars, writers, and priests, were arrested. A week or so later we read in *Pravda*:

"By order of the Petrograd Soviet the following persons were executed yesterday for participation in a counter-revolutionary plot:

"Tagantzeff, professor, for organization of the plot.

Mrs. Tagantzeff, his wife, for participation and for failing to denounce her husband.

"Lazarevsky, professor, pro-rector of Petrograd University, for drafting of a project for a new electoral law.

"Tikhvinsky, professor, for writing a report adversely describing the present state of the Soviet oil industry.

"Goumileff, writer and poet, for his monarchist opinions.

"Ukhtomsky, painter and scholar, for giving information about the museums.

"Gissetty and wife," and so on, more than fifty names, each with a short account of their "crimes." Some of these offenses were merely described as "counter-revolutionary." At the end was printed, "And other counter-revolutionaries."

Shot for adversely describing the state of the Soviet oil industry! The oil industry was indeed in a deplorable state, but Tikhvinsky's report had been written for the Soviet by the order of Lenin himself. Shot for giving information about the museums! Shot for writing a draft for a new electoral law!

Shot for his monarchist opinions! Neither the fact that Goumileff was one of the greatest poets in Russia nor his bravery in the war were enough to save him. In this "plot" were involved people who had never even known each other, and all of them had been denied an open trial.

"This proletarian justice once more shows our enemies our power," Grishka the Third declared in a speech. "Let them remember this lesson."

We remember.

S.O.S.

What we had feared most of all for Russia in 1921 happened. Looking over a map of the whole country, with provinces marked by harvests bad or totally lacking, we said: "Twenty-five million people, at least, are fated to die of starvation this winter unless the world comes to their aid."

We said this long before the government and Maxim Gorky issued their wild appeals to the nations of earth to help the starving masses. When the appalling famine of 1921 came, there was no remedy. No provinces had the necessary surplus of grain.

Having published my two volumes of *A System of Sociology*, I postponed the writing of the third volume in order to study at first hand phenomena typical of the Revolution. With my students and collaborators, and in close cooperation with the academicians I. Pavlov and V. Bekhterev, I began an investigation of the influence of hunger upon human behavior, social life, and social organization.

In the autumn of 1921, I, among many other professors, was forbidden to teach by the Soviet Government. Left with no work except research in the Institute of the Brain and in the Historical and Sociological Institute of the University, I felt myself comparatively free. I had studied city starvation, with myself as one of the subjects, and now I had an immense laboratory in the starving villages of Russia. In the winter of 1921 I started out for the famine districts of Samara and Saratov provinces to make a scientific investigation of mass starvation. I will acknowledge at once that I largely failed in this intention. I was able to make no experimental study, but I saw a famine; I know now what it means. What I learned in those awful provinces was far more than any scientific investigation could have given me. My nervous system, accustomed to many horrors in the years of the Revolution, broke down completely before the spectacle of the actual starvation of millions in my ravaged country. If I came out less an investigator, I do not think I came out less a man, less an enemy of any group of men capable of inflicting such suffering on the human race.

With one of the local teachers, my small group set out on foot from the last railroad station to visit the famished districts of Samara Province. We entered the village of N—— in the afternoon. The place was as though dead. Houses stood deserted and roofless, with gaps where windows and doors had been. The straw thatch of the houses had long since been torn away and eaten. There were no animals in the village, of course—no cattle, horses, sheep, goats, dogs, cats or even crows. All had been eaten. Dead silence lay over the snow-covered roads until, with a little creak, a sled came in sight, a sled drawn by two men and a woman and carrying a dead body. After drawing the sled a short distance, they stopped and fell exhausted on the snow. They looked at us dully as we approached, and with sick hearts we returned their gaze. I had seen starving faces in the cities, but such living skeletons as these three people I had never seen. In rags, shaking with cold, they were not white of visage, but blue, dark blue with yellow spots.

"Where are you taking him?" I asked, pointing to the dead body of the lad lying on the sled.

"To that corn-loft," answered the peasant, looking toward a low building. "There is plenty of corn there now."

The other man and woman tried to get up from the snow, but could not do so without our help. We offered to draw the sled, and with the three peasants went on to the corn-loft, the usual peasant grain receptacle, new and good. The strongest man, it appeared, was constable of the village, and he took out a key and unlocked the loft. There was plenty of corn there now, as he had said. Ten bodies, including three children, lay on the floor.

We carried the body in and laid it on the floor. The man and woman, parents of the lad, crossed themselves and silently went out. "Soon they will come here also," said the constable.

"How many have you brought here this last fortnight?" we asked.

"About ten or fifteen. Before that, more. Some ran away from the village."

"Where did they go to?"

"Where their eyes were looking." Then as he locked the door he whispered: "It is necessary to lock. . . . They steal."

"Steal . . . what?"

"Yes, to eat. That is what we have come to. In the village they guard the cemetery to keep bodies from being taken from the graves."

"Have any murders occurred for such a purpose?" I forced myself to ask.

"Not in our village, but in others, yes. A few days ago in the village of G— a mother killed her child, cut off his legs, cooked and ate them. That is what we have come to."

As he spoke, the clanging of the church bell broke the silence of the dying village. In the darkness of the forlorn and forsaken Russian wilds, this appeal to the world of the mad peasant ringing the bell wrung our hearts, reduced us to bitter weeping. *Ding-dong! Ding-dong!* Now quick and alarming like a firebell. *Ding-dong! Ding-dong!* Slow and mournful as a funeral knell. *Ding-dong!* For almost an hour it echoed in our brains, our hearts. Then dead silence fell again.

This S.O.S. of a mad peasant in the far interior of the land was heard. It crossed the ocean and beat on the hearts of the great American nation and brought relief that saved from cruel death at least ten million men, women, and children. God will forever remember that deed.

From the very beginning of the famine tens of thousands of

people were driven from their homes and went "where their eyes were looking." By the thousands they wandered; and, finding neither food nor work, they fell down and died.

In the next village, and the next, we saw the same awful picture. Death from starvation and its companion typhus.

"Cursed shalt thou be in the city, and cursed shalt thou be in the field.

"Cursed shall be the fruit of thy body, and the fruit of thy land, the increase of thy kine, and the flocks of thy sheep.

"The Lord shall send upon thee cursing, vexation, pestilence.

"And thou shalt eat the fruit of thine own body, the flesh of thy sons and of thy daughters."

This ancient curse filled my mind all during my wanderings and for days after I returned to Petrograd. Not much scientific knowledge did I gain in those twenty days I spent in the famine regions, but the memory of what I saw and heard there had made me absolutely fearless in denouncing the Revolution and the monsters who were devouring Russia. Many and great have been the sins of the Russian people, but in these years of famine, suffering, and death, the nation expiated, paid in full for all its offenses.

Banishment

In May, 1922, my book "The Influence of Hunger on Human Behavior, on Social Life and Social Organization" began to be printed. Before publication, many paragraphs, indeed whole chapters, were cut by the censors. The book as a whole was ruined, but what remained was better than nothing. The Soviets' "war on the ideological front" and terror were now being diffused with great energy. We all lived from hand to mouth, expecting some new blow each day.

Nevertheless, we were not entirely without hope. The country was showing unmistakable signs of regeneration. Under the ruins of our civilization, in the depths of the people's hearts and souls, something was stirring, the life and spirit of a new people. Whatever might happen to us, the rebirth of

Russia was a certainty. Time only was necessary for these new forces to grow strong enough to make themselves felt. We could wait, for the years had trained us in patience.

On August 10, 1922, I left Petrograd for a few days in Moscow. From the station I went directly to the apartment of Professor Kondratieff, who invited me to stay with him. We had breakfast and parted, arranging to meet at five o'clock in his apartment. Having attended to my business and visited friends, I returned to the apartment; but my friend was not at home. At six he had not come and I became a little uneasy. At seven a student came, asking for my friend's wife. I told him that neither she nor her husband were at home, and offered to take any message he cared to leave. The student looked at me fixedly and asked: "Who are you?" I introduced myself, and he said; "Professor, get out of this apartment. Your friend is under arrest and the Chekhists may be here any moment."

I took my bag and left, but I waited near the house until I saw my friend's wife approaching, and having agreed with her about our immediate plans, I went to the apartment of another friend. Alas, he too had been arrested. A few hours later we learned that professors Kizevetter and Frank, Berdyaeff and Yasinsky, Sofronoff and Ozeroff, Myakotin and Peshekhonoff, Osorgin and many others—prominent scientists and scholars, writers, and cooperative workers—about one hundred and fifty in all, had been arrested in a single day. Many students also had been taken. A big terror was evidently beginning and might be starting also in Petrograd. All doubt on this score was removed the following day when I read a telegram sent by my wife to a friend in Moscow. This telegram read: "Please detain my son. We have scarlet fever in our house."

We soon learned how timely was this warning for me to stay away from my Petrograd lodgings. In that city were arrested professors Lossky, Karsavin, Zubasheff, Lutokhin, Lapshin, Odintsoff, Selivanoff, Brutskus, Zamyatin, and others—about one hundred in all—along with many students. The

Chekhists had gone to my Petrograd address, and there in Mrs. Darmalatov's apartment, had found her second daughter Nadya, dying. Nadya's husband and the physician assured the Chekhists that I was not in the apartment, and they begged the men not to torment the dying woman with futile searching. The Chekhists went through all the rooms and, finding that I was not concealed there, they generously agreed to make no more noise and to leave no guard behind.

I remained comparatively safe in Moscow, for not very many people there knew me by sight. A week passed, and rumors about the arrested scholars and professors began to be circulated. It was said that they were not to be executed but banished. Soon in *Pravda* an article by Trotsky gave official authorization to these rumors.

The arrested people began to be released, the authorities warning them that they were to be banished. Each man had to sign two papers, one promising that in ten days he would leave the country and the other declaring that if he returned to Russia without permission of the Soviet Government he would be executed.

As soon as the fate of my arrested colleagues became known, I decided that my own banishment abroad was the best thing that could happen to me. I could do nothing more for my country, I was living illegally, and sooner or later I would certainly be arrested and probably shot.

It was a lovely September morning when I reached Czarskoe Selo. My wife was away from home, so I began to prepare my prison bag myself, packing it with food and linen and with two or three books with which to beguile the tedium of prison life. When my wife returned she tried at once to dissuade me from my purpose. She showed me copies of the *Petrograd Pravda* and *The Red Gazette* in which I was furiously assailed and threatened. On the way we met friends, who joined my wife in considering me quite mad to venture into Petrograd. "If Zinoviev and his crew do not shoot you at once," they said, "you will be banished to Siberia, and not to any foreign country."

Finally I agreed that it might be better for me to be arrested in Moscow, and the next morning I returned there. With my prison bag, I presented myself at the Chekha and after some time was admitted to the office of the official in charge of the affair of the banished scholars and scientists.

"My name is Sorokin," I said to him. "Your comrades in Petrograd want to arrest me but I was here in Moscow. I have come to you to know what you wish to do with me."

The Chekhist, a young man with the white face of a cocaine addict, waved his hand, saying, "We have plenty of people in Moscow we don't know what to do with. Go back to Petrograd and let the Chekha there decide your fate."

"Thank you," I said. "I will not go back to Petrograd. If you want to arrest me, here I am." After a moment's thought, he said, "Well, all arrested university people are to be banished abroad. Sign these two papers, and in ten days leave the territory of the R.S.F.S.R."

I signed willingly and asked where I was to apply for my passport. "In the Commissariat of Foreign Affairs," answered the pale young man. "I am just going to tell them about you."

"May I leave here?"

"Oh, certainly."

Going out of the Chekha office I sent a telegram to my wife to sell all our belongings and to join me in Moscow. There was nothing much except the remnants of my library to sell, therefore her task was light.

The process of getting passports and permissions was difficult and irritating. At the Commissariat of Foreign Affairs they told me that it would be five or six days before my passport would be ready.

Determined to get it sooner, I went to Karakhan, acting Minister of Foreign Affairs in the absence of Chicherin. Karakhan had been a friend from my student days, and I thought it might be amusing to see him now as a Bolshevist official. But when I offered my card to his secretary the fellow declared that Karakhan was busy and could not give me an audience. At that moment a man entered the room and greeted me. He was one of my old students from the Psycho-Neurological Institute. "What are you doing here?" I asked.

"Oh, I am head of the information and publicity department of the Ministry of Foreign Affairs," he answered proudly. "Have you read articles in the newspaper by Koltsoff? That is my pen name."

I said that I had read them, and he asked eagerly what I thought of them. "The same as of your Government," I replied. "Now this fellow here refuses to send my card in to His Excellency. Please make him do it."

They whispered for a moment and disappeared. Soon Karakhan appeared at the door, which was guarded by three Chekhists. "How do you do, Pitirim Alexandrovich," he said. "I am glad to see you. Come in."

The room was comfortably, even luxuriously, furnished, and Karakhan, once a lean, spare man, now looked well-fed and fat.

"Your Excellency," I said half-jokingly, "you know, of course, that I am exiled. Your subordinates refuse to give me a passport before three days, and that inconveniences me. Will you be so kind as to order them to have my passport ready by tomorrow morning?"

"With great pleasure," he answered, and over the telephone gave the order. "Tomorrow it will be ready for you," he announced, "and it will be given you free of any charge."

I thanked him, although it had never been my intention to pay for the passport. Not the next morning but the one after that the passport was ready. "Expulsé" was written on it in French. That same day I got Czechoslovakian, German, Lettish, and Lithuanian visas. I spent three days getting these cursed permits.

About the last visit I paid was to Communist leader Pyatakoff, a man with whom I had been friends in student days. I went to see him in behalf of a former comrade of us both, a man now in prison and seriously ill. Pyatakoff promised to do what he could, and after finishing that business, he told me he was about to write an article on my criticism of Bukharin's work *The Theory of Marxism.*

I said to him, "Pyatakoff, let me ask you, do you really believe that you are creating a communistic society?"

"Of course not," he replied frankly.

"You admit that your experiment has failed, and that you are building only a primitive bourgeois society. Why, then, are you banishing us?"

"You do not take into consideration," said the man, "that two processes are going on in Russia. One is the re-creation of a bourgeois society; the other is a process of the adaptation of the Soviet Government to it. The first process is going on faster than the second. This involves a danger to our existence. Our task is to delay the development of that first process, but you and the others who are to be exiled are accelerating it. That is why you are banished. Perhaps after two or three years we will invite you to come back."

"Thank you," I said. "I hope to return to my country—without your invitation."

On a gray afternoon, September 23, 1922, the first group of exiles gathered at the Moscow railway station. I carried our two valises into the Lettish diplomatic car. "*Omnia mea mecum porto,*" I could say of myself. In a pair of shoes sent me by a Czech scientist, a suit donated by the American Relief Administration, and with fifty rubles in my pocket, I left my native land. All my companions were in a similar plight, but none of us worried very much. In spite of prohibitions of the authorities, many friends and acquaintances came to see us off, with gifts of flowers, handclasps, and tears. We all devoured with our eyes their faces, the disappearing streets of Moscow, the last glimpse of the fatherland.

Next day we reached Sebage, the boundary line of Russia. Half an hour later we passed a Red flag—and Soviet Russia was behind us. That night, after five years, we lay down to sleep without asking ourselves the question, "Will they come tonight or not?"

A week later in Berlin I delivered my first lecture on the present conditions in Russia. It became clear that I had left none too soon, for the first letters that reached me said that "Our grandmother [the Chekha] is very sorry for having let you go without giving you her last and eternal blessing [execution]." In a Berlin newspaper, *Days*, I read that "At a meeting of the People's Commissaries in Moscow the head of the Chekha, Comrade Unshlikht, and Commissary of the Foreign Office Karakhan were censured by the other commissaries for having allowed Mrs. Kuskova and Professor Sorokin to go abroad." Simultaneously my book about famine was destroyed by the Soviet Government.

Whatever may happen in the future, I know that I have learned three things which will forever remain convictions of my heart as well as of my mind. Life, even the hardest life, is the most beautiful, wonderful, and miraculous treasure in the world. Fulfillment of duty is another beautiful thing, making life happy and giving to the soul the inconquerable force to sustain ideals—this is my second conviction. And my third is that cruelty, hatred, and injustice never can and never will be able to create a mental, moral, or material millenium.

So ends my *Leaves from a Russian Diary.*

CHAPTER TEN

Émigré

In Friendly Czechoslovakia

I was spared many hardships of the exile's *via dolorosa,* with its pains of violent uprooting, homelessness, nostalgia, its bewilderment, frustrations, and disillusionments. During the first few days of our stay in Berlin, my wife and I were exhilarated by our regained freedom and security. In the friendly circle of the Russian émigrés in Berlin, with their intense intellectual, artistic, and political activities, we felt revitalized and happy. We were not worried about the meagerness of our financial resources and the uncertainty of our future. After the "hell" in which we had existed in Communist Russia, everything appeared quite comfortable and certainly better than that Communist inferno. Lady-Fortune seemed to be smiling at us again.

On the fourth day of our stay in Berlin I received, through the Czechoslovakian embassy, an invitation from my friend Dr. Masaryk, then President of the Czechoslovakian Republic, to come to Prague as a guest of the Republic. The next evening I was dining with the President, Dr. Alice Masaryk, and Secretary of State Dr. Benesh, in the magnificent palace where President Masaryk lived. Despite his high position, this great man, scholar, and statesman remained as sincere and natural in his manners as he had been previously in the humble position of an émigré. During dinner we exchanged our views about the situation in Russia and then, over coffee, he smilingly asked me how much money I had. I answered that I still had a few thousand worthless German marks and a few rubles (which altogether amounted to about two dollars).

"Would you like to teach at our Charles University?" he asked.

"I don't think I am quite normal yet after living for several years in the bloody Russian madhouse. If it is possible I would like to have some time just to recover my mental sanity."

"Then we shall arrange a special scholarship for you as we have done for other Russian scholars."

In this gracious way the prosaic matter of our means of subsistence was quickly solved.

My wife and I rented a modest room in a house near Prague (Chernoshidze). After many years of precarious existence in Russia, we began to live a normal and orderly life of physical and mental recuperation and of enjoyable scientific and cultural activities. Besides walking, swimming, gardening, visiting historical places, and enjoying the beauties of the surrounding countryside, almost every day we commuted to Prague—Mrs. Sorokin to do her research in cytology in the university laboratories of Professor Nemez, and I to do some reading in the libraries of Prague; to deliver lectures; to attend the meetings of several committees to which I was elected; to discharge editorial duties of the journal *Peasants' Russia* which, together with Argunov, S. Maslow, and Boem, we had just started; to participate in convivial gatherings of friends; and, when invited, to attend dinner or lunch with Masaryk, Benesh, Kramarj, Klofach, and other Czech political and cultural leaders. During the nine months of my stay in Czechoslovakia we lived a good and fruitful life.

Because of the hospitality of the Czech government and people, Prague was then the center of concentration for notable Russian émigrés—among them eminent scholars and scientists, writers and artists, political and military leaders, clergy and students, not to mention the rank-and-file of the Russian refugees. With the help of the Czech leaders, the émigrés established in Prague a Russian university, several research centers, and literary, musical, theatrical, political, and other organizations. Thus an intense scientific, cultural, and political life went on in the vast colony of émigrés. Many of them still believed in the imminent collapse of the Communist regime and expected to return to the fatherland soon. Accordingly they were preoccupied almost exclusively with various political activities and plans for the future reconstruction of their native country.

For my part, I seriously doubted an early downfall of the Communist government and firmly believed that the future of Russia would be determined by the Russian people in the fatherland, not by the émigrés, no matter how high their mental and cultural qualifications. In accordance with these beliefs I devoted only a minor part of my time to political matters and no time at all to political squabbles among the exiles, and busied myself mainly with my resumed scientific studies. By intensive reading of recent sociological works by Western scholars, inaccessible to me during the years of the Revolution, I tried to bring up to date my knowledge of this sociological literature of the West. Then, when I was invited to give a series of public lectures in Prague, I wrote and then published these lectures in the form of a volume *The Contemporary State of Russia* (*Sovremennoie Sostoianiye Rossii*, Prague, 1922). While preparing my course of lectures for the students of the Russian University and for the Czech and the Carpatho-Russian teachers, I wrote and published another volume, *Essays in Social Pedagogy and Politics* (*Ocherki Sozialnoi Pedagogiki i Politiki*, Ujgored, 1923). As an editor and contributor to our journal *Peasants' Russia* (*Krestianskaiya Rossia*) I published several studies in rural sociology. These publications are the skeletons of theories later fully developed in the substantial volumes published during my professorship at Minnesota and Harvard universities.

My principal research, however, was in the field of the sociology of revolution. I succeeded in writing a preliminary draft of this study in Russian while in Prague. After my arrival in the United States it was published in an English translation under the title *The Sociology of Revolution* (Philadelphia and London, 1925).

This preoccupation with work prevented me from wasting

my time and energy in the sterile political disputes so common among the political refugees of all great revolutions. In subsequent years I often observed expectations, hopes, and bickerings quite similar to those of part of the Russian émigrés among Polish, Latvian, Lithuanian, Hungarian, German, Cuban, and other political refugees. Like the Russian "unadjusted" refugees, many of these recent émigrés have walked a *via crucis, via dolorosa* where their hopes faded and their expectations were shattered. Often embittered and disillusioned, these people lived painfully and died fruitlessly in a foreign country. They deserve our compassion and help in the crucial moments of their lives, but their unenviable fate should warn future émigrés not to build their lives upon hopeless political dreams and vain disputes. Without losing their individuality, the sooner they adjust themselves to their new country of residence and begin to unfold their creative potentialities, the better for them, their new land, and the old fatherland.

In Prague I became quite friendly with many outstanding Russian scholars—among them Peter Struve, N. Lossky, I. Lapshin, P. Novgorodzeff, E. Zubasheff—and with several eminent writers, poets, and musicians. There also I met such notable Czech sociologists as Dr. A Blaha and others. Over a glass of beer or a meal we used to discuss many a basic problem of philosophy, the social sciences, ethics, fine arts, politics, and economics. Almost all of these discussions tangibly enriched our understanding of these problems and of the many events of which we had been either observers or victims.

As a result of this creatively rich, exciting, but orderly life, my wife and I quickly recovered our physical and mental vigor and peace of mind. Some of our friends who had seen us before in Soviet Russia and then met us in Prague or after our arrival in the United States told us that we looked twenty years younger. These observations were correct: indeed we felt much younger than when we were in the Soviet Union.

Probably we would have settled in Czechoslovakia "permanently" as teachers in one of the Czech universities if I had not received invitations from two distinguished American sociologists, Edward C. Hayes of the University of Illinois and Edward A. Ross of the University of Wisconsin. They invited me to come to America to deliver a series of lectures on the Russian Revolution. These unexpected invitations radically changed the course of our subsequent life. For many years before, I had been greatly interested in the United States and had studied American social, economic, and political institutions and theories, American culture, literature, and the way of life. My Russian *Sistema Soziologii* shows that I also knew fairly well the works of the "patriarchs" of American sociology such as Lester Ward, Franklin Giddings, A. Small, and some of the younger generation of American sociologists and psychologists. I greatly admired the American people, democracy, and way of life. This admiration was seemingly so great that many of my friends and colleagues in Russia even nicknamed me "a Russian-American."

Besides this interest and admiration there was another reason for my acceptance of the invitations. Throughout my life I have preferred to stand on my own two feet in charting my life-course and in earning my living. This independent position appealed to me more than the position of an exile-scholar supported by a friendly government, no matter how generous this support was. For these reasons I accepted the offer of professors Hayes and Ross without hesitation. Though the stipulated honorarium for the lectures was modest, nevertheless it covered round-trip expenses to and from America if I traveled by tourist class on a cheap boat. If I could not secure a suitable position in the United States, I could always return to Czechoslovakia. Since the modest honorarium did not allow my wife to join me in this trip, we decided she would stay in Czechoslovakia until the question of my return or establishment in the United States was decided.

Without any difficulty I secured a Czechoslovakian passport which indicated my Russian nationality, American, Austrian, and Italian transit visas, and said good-bye to my Czech and Russian friends. In October, 1923, I took a train to Trieste where I booked tourist-class passage on a small Italian boat, the

Martha Washington. My series of lectures at the universities of Illinois and Wisconsin was scheduled for January and February, 1924. I started earlier because I wanted to improve my poor English during the two months or so before my lecturing began. In this way I resumed my lifelong role of a rolling stone, with its too familiar sad "departures" and uneasy "arrivals." In sociological terms, my "horizontal and vertical social mobility" was again suddenly accelerated. This time it carried me across the ocean and landed me on the shores of a great nation.

I enjoyed the long trip—the beautiful landscapes of Austria and Italy, the sunny Mediterranean, and the ever-changing Atlantic in its quiet and stormy moods. The slow rate of travel and frequent stops of our old *Martha Washington* at various ports of the Mediterranean gave me an opportunity to see Naples and Mt. Vesuvius; a magnificent eruption of Mt. Aetna; Patras in Greece; Almeria in Spain; Algiers in Algeria; and the famous rock of Gibraltar. To be sure the impressions they gave were superficial, but nevertheless quite fascinating and absorbing.

No less interesting were the passengers and the crew of the boat. They were mostly Slovenian and Italian immigrants to the United States, simple and good people in search of a better life in a new country.

Among the passengers there also happened to be a few Russian exiles and the American, Dr. Quayle, whom I had met in Prague. One of the Russian émigrés, a vivacious lady, made herself conspicuous by playing cards, frequenting the bar, and liberally flirting with the fellow passengers. "With this sort of conduct she is bound to have some trouble in the puritanical United States," I thought to myself. From reading some books on America I had got the notion that the American people were still at a puritan stage of their morals and mores. Fairly soon after my arrival in the States I discovered that my notion was incorrect and that—for good or ill—the puritanical stage had been superseded by that of much more liberal and elastic manners and morals. At the end of October, after sixteen days of travel, the *Martha Washington* arrived in Boston. Before the passengers were taken to New York, they had to stay for several hours in the Boston Custom House. Being hungry, I bought and tasted for the first time the renowned American mince pie. I liked it so much that I ate three pieces of it. This overindulgence was responsible for my avoidance of this pie for many years to come. The next morning we arrived in New York.

A New Crisis: Reintegration of my Weltanschauung

Before continuing my life story, perhaps at this point it is advisable to say a few words about a new crisis in, and reintegration of my philosophical and psycho-sociological views and value system. Already World War I had made some fissures in the positivistic, "scientific," and humanistic *Weltanschauung* I had held before the War. The Revolution of 1917 enormously enlarged these fissures and eventually shattered this world-outlook with its positivistic philosophy and sociology, its utilitarian system of values, and its conception of historical process as a progressive evolution toward an ever better man, society, and culture. Instead of increasingly enlightened, morally ennobled, aesthetically refined, and creatively developed humanity, these events unleashed in man "the worst of the beasts" and displayed on the historical stage—side by side with the noble, wise, and creative minority—a gigantic world of irrational human animals blindly murdering each other, indiscriminately destroying the great values, overthrowing the immortal achievements of genius, and glorifying vulgarity in its worst form. This unexpected world-wide explosion of the forces of death, bestiality, and ignorance in the supposedly civilized humanity of the twentieth century categorically contradicted all "sweet" theories of progressive evolution of man from ignorance to science and wisdom, from bestiality to noble morality, from barbarism to civilization, from the "theological" to the "positive" stage, from tyranny to freedom, from poverty and disease to unlimited prosperity and health, from ugliness to ever finer beauty, from the man-beast to the superman-god.

This decisive contradiction forced me, as it did many others, to sternly re-examine my prewar *Weltanschauung*. My personal experiences during the years 1914-22 powerfully reinforced the need for this re-examination. During these years I experienced and observed much too much of hate, hypocrisy, blindness, bestiality, and mass-murder to leave my "cheerful" views intact. It was these historical and "existential" conditions which started the weighing of my values and the reconstruction of my views and of my very self. This reconstruction took place slowly during five years in Communist Russia and then, after my banishment, in Europe and the United States. By the end of the 1920's this painfully blissful process was matured in its essential features. It resulted in what I now call the *integral system* of philosophy, sociology, psychology, ethics, and values. Some indications of it are already noticeable in my Russian *Sistema Soziologii* and in the works published in Czechoslovakia. They are more evident in my volumes published in America during the years 1924-29. In their mature form the basic principles of Integralism are systematically stated in my volumes published during the last three decades.

With my arrival in New York another chapter in my life closed and a new one opened.

PART FOUR

CHAPTER ELEVEN

First Steps in the New World

New York and Vassar College

It was a sunny October afternoon in 1923 when I stepped off the boat onto the shore of the American megalopolis. Carrying two fairly heavy suitcases filled mainly with manuscripts and books, I decided, for the sake of economy, to walk rather than to take a taxi to the office of the Russian Students' Relief adjacent to Grand Central Terminal. The buildings and canyons of the great city, the people, the traffic, and all the living scenery were so new, so absorbing and exciting, that I did not notice either my fatigue or perspiration until, after many inquiries as to how to get there, I finally reached the office of the Russian Students' Relief. There I found its secretary-manager, Mr. Alexis Wiren, and a few other employees. They all were exceedingly kind and helpful in many ways, from finding a cheap room for me in one of the rooming houses to giving me practical advice concerning the subways, inexpensive eating places, and other important "ways of life" in the bewildering city. They also informed of my arrival, Dr. B. A. Bakhmetiev, the Kerensky Government's ambassador to the United States (later a professor at Columbia University), and a few leaders of various Russian groups in New York. In the late afternoon Mr. Wiren "installed" me in the rooming house. Thus began my life in the New World.

Perhaps the most conspicuous feature of this life was a contrasting ambivalence. My very limited financial means and my reluctance to ask anyone for financial aid forced me to live among the poor people under very modest conditions. On the other hand, my aspirations and a little prestige I had among various Russians and a few Americans immediately brought me into contact with a number of intellectuals, politicians, artists, and cultural leaders of both nationalities, with their way of life quite different from that of my neighbors at the rooming house.

During the first few days of my stay in New York I met and lunched with Sir Paul Vinogradoff of Oxford, who had known me in Russia and who was now lecturing at Columbia University; I spent several evenings in the convivial company of the eminent artists of the Moscow Art Theater, who were then playing in New York. Then Ambassador Bakhmetiev arranged a dinner party in my honor at which I met Professor Giddings, Alexis Carroll, and several other American scholars. Bakhmetiev also introduced me to some influential Americans interested in the Russian Revolution and world politics. Soon the pre-revolutionary and post-revolutionary Russian groups invited me to give lectures on the Russian Revolution and, instead of an honorarium, presented me with a warm winter overcoat (which I needed badly in the cold New York weather). Among the Russian émigrés, I met Igor Sikorsky who at that time was trying to build—in a simple barn, with almost no capital—the predecessor of his subsequently famous clippers and helicopters. His position then was, in many respects, similar to mine; both of us were struggling against obstacles prior to realizing our aspirations. Eventually I was asked to write a few articles for Russian and American peroidicals for a small fee which partly covered my modest living expenses. The greater part of my time, however, I spent in learning English. For that purpose I attended daily all sorts of public lectures and meetings, sermons in various churches, and listened to and tried to speak English at every opportunity I had.

All this kept me vigorously active and hopeful that somehow, in this extraordinarily vital nation, I would be able to find an academic and creative position, to bring my wife here, and to settle down for the rest of my life.

These hopes were greatly encouraged by an unexpected invitation from the president of Vassar College, Henry Noble

MacCracken, to be a guest of Vassar for a few weeks, to study English there, and to prepare my lectures. I had met him previously at one of the dinners of President Masaryk of Czechoslovakia. President and Mrs. MacCracken knew well the difficult conditions of the Russian, Polish, and other intellectual émigrés and helped most generously many of them during the trying initial stages of their settling in the United States. When they learned of my arrival in New York, with utmost tact, understanding, and friendliness they invited me, in November, 1923, to come to Vassar, rented a room for me in a house in nearby Poughkeepsie, and placed at my disposal the facilities of the college library, lectures, dining room, and most congenial company of both professors and students. I could hardly have wished for anything better than this unexpected "bonanza" at that period of my life.* The some six weeks I spent at Vassar were indeed happy and fruitful ones. Each day I attended several classes, learned a great deal about the American academic way of life, worked over my forthcoming lectures at the universities of Illinois and Wisconsin, brought up-to-date my knowledge of American sociological literature, and fully enjoyed the friendly atmosphere of the college, the President's family, the professors and students.

At the end of my stay in this friendly society, I ventured to deliver my first lecture in English. My English was, of course, quite defective, but my Vassar friends encouragingly told me it was fairly good. Subsequently I witnessed the extraordinary tolerance of American audiences toward the atrocious English of many a foreign lecturer. I do not think such a sympathetic tolerance existed or exists in any other country. Toward the end of my stay at Vassar, through the

* Many years later I dedicated my *Power and Morality* to President and Mrs. Henry Noble MacCracken. In the Preface to this book I wrote: "Dedication of the book [to them] is a token of a deep appreciation of their generous help to me at a difficult period of my life, after my arrival in this country, in 1923." Their generous help was indeed the most important help I received at that time.

gracious efforts of President MacCracken and some professors, several lecturing engagements at various colleges and universities were arranged for the spring months of 1924. By about the same time I had almost finished my manuscript (in Russian) on the sociology of revolution, had arranged for its English translation for the Lippincott Sociological Series, edited by Professor Edward Cary Hayes, and had begun to work on my *Leaves from a Russian Diary* for E. P. Dutton & Company who had agreed to publish it. (Both of these books were issued at the end of 1924.)

After Christmas of 1923, I said a grateful "good-by" to my Vassar friends, received from them the humorous nickname of "an alumnus of Vassar," and departed to the University of Illinois, at Urbana, to deliver there my course of lectures on the Russian Revolution. On the way to Urbana I stopped over for two nights with Professor Samuel Harper of Chicago University, and besides his warm hospitality, I profited by his sound advice on a number of practical matters relating to lecturing and political activities.

At the Universities of Illinois and Wisconsin

Professor Edward Cary Hayes, chairman of the department of sociology at the University of Illinois, who had invited me to give lectures there, unfortunately passed away before I arrived in Urbana. His place was taken by Professor Edwin Sutherland who helped me to secure a room in the University Union and to arrange the dates and places of my lectures. Later on we met again as professors at the University of Minnesota and for a number of years maintained our friendship and cooperation in teaching and research there.

Despite my dreadful English, my lectures were fairly well attended, aroused considerable interest and conflicting reactions—favorable on the part of those who were opposed to communism and Soviet totalitarianism, and unfavorable on the part of those who sympathized with the Communist phase of the Russian Revolution. At that time a considerable number of American intellectuals in university circles idealized the Communist Revolution and viewed it as a sort of Don Quixote's beautiful Dulcinea, pure and free from all the defects of a prosaic girl of Toboso. Since in my lectures I particularly stressed the destructiveness, cruelty, and bestiality of the first five years of the Communist Revolution (outlined in the preceding chapters), such a contradiction of their image of revolutionary "Dulcinea" naturally aroused their bitter opposition to my lectures and to myself—opposition which lasted for several years and manifested itself in various efforts to discredit not only my lecturing and writing on the Russian Revolution but my academic activities and publications on other subjects. They tried to represent me as "one of those unscholarly political émigrés who learned nothing and forgot nothing." As my Russian volumes remained unknown to American scholars, this sort of campaign against me had considerable success until it provoked a vigorous opposition on the part of some eminent American sociologists such as Charles Ellwood, Charles H. Cooley, E. A. Ross, Franklin Giddings, and others, and until it was crushed under the weight of the world-wide prestige my subsequent volumes acquired.

I experienced these negative reactions to my lectures again at the University of Wisconsin where I moved after finishing my lecture course at the University of Illinois. At the University of Wisconsin, however, I found staunch defenders of my viewpoint in professors M. I. Rostovtzeff, E. A. Ross, John R. Commons, and other distinguished professors and administrators of the university. Though Professor Ross's viewpoint on the Russian Revolution differed from mine, this difference did not prevent him from respecting my views. With his usual fair-mindedness, his lack of dogmatism, and his understanding of the complexity of the Russian upheaval, he easily admitted a possibility of different interpretations of this momentous event. We both not only respected the differences in our views but in a sense deeply enjoyed them and found them mutually enlightening and stimulating. He not only defended the scientific legitimacy of my views against the denunciations of my critics, he also recommended me highly to several universities as a visiting or regular professor. So far as I know, his strong recommendations were largely responsible for the University of Minnesota's offer of a visiting professorship for the next summer session and, after that, for the next academic year. His fine personality, his friendship, and his generous help will be gratefully remembered to the end of my life.

Another joyfully important surprise at Madison was my meeting with Professor and Mrs. M. I. Rostovtzeff. As a student at the University of St. Petersburg, I had attended some of the lectures of this great historian and had studied some of his outstanding works. Then, during the years 1914-17, we frequently met at various political, literary, and educational organizations in St. Petersburg. Though we belonged to different political parties and had different backgrounds, these differences in no way diminished my deep respect and admiration for both of them. Both Rostovtzeffs were the finest representatives of Russian and world-culture at its best. They succeeded in leaving Russia three years before my exile. Several great universities of England and Europe eagerly offered professorships to the great historian. Over these offers he chose the offer of the University of Wisconsin, where in a short time he and his courses became deservedly famous and popular.

The Rostovtzeffs met and treated me with real warmth and friendly generosity. Being émigrés themselves, they perfectly understood my position and its difficulties. In the best possible way they helped me with their wise advice and sympathetic encouragement. During the month of my lectures at Madison, our lifelong friendship developed and matured. It continued up to the death of my noted friend and happily continues up to the present moment with Mrs. Rostovtzeff.* Both of them eventually became the god-parents of my two sons. This friendship has been one of the great joys in my family's life in the United States.

* She died on June 15, 1963, the day I was reading the proofs of this book.

Despite my defective English and the opposition of pro-Communist sympathizers, my lectures were quite favorably received by the non-Communist professors and students. As a result of this favorable impression, during my stay at Madison I received invitations from Professor Albion Small to give a talk at his seminar at the University of Chicago, from Professor Charles H. Cooley to give two lectures at the University of Michigan, from Professor F. S. Chapin to be visiting professor at the next summer session at the University of Minnesota, and from several civic organizations and public forums.

After completing my course of lectures at the universities of Wisconsin and Illinois, in March, 1924, I returned to New York. As I have never liked big cities, I rented a room in the house of my friend A. Wiren at Laurelton, Long Island. In this quiet suburb I settled down to give the finishing touches to my *Sociology of Revolution,* to finish writing *Leaves from a Russian Diary,* to write for the *Michigan Law Review* an article entitled "The New Soviet Codes and Soviet Justice" (published in the November, 1924 issue) and a few other papers for scientific journals and popular magazines. From this place I also made a few lecture trips to nearby universities and colleges (including Princeton).

Greatly encouraged by continued lecture invitations that secured my employment at least for several months, and having earned a modest sum to meet my fairly Spartan living expenses for at least half-a-year, I began to feel confident that I would eventually find a decent academic position in the United States and decided to settle permanently in this great country. I liked its vast spaces, the independence and vigor of its people, its way of life, and its cultural climate. Accordingly, I sent money and a message to my wife in Czechoslovakia to come and join me in America. At the end of March, 1924, I joyfully met her at the New York pier, and that evening, in a small company of our friends, we celebrated our reunion in the Wiren's house at Laurelton.

To sum up, in this difficult period of putting down roots

in the soil of a new country, I was spared many hardships of the *via dolorosa* usually traveled by the uprooted political émigré in his acclimatization to a new society, a new culture, and a new people. All in all my adjustment to the new conditions was fairly painless. Its comparative ease was largely due to the generous help of many mentioned (and unmentioned) friends; in part, to the Lady-Luck who continued to smile at me; and, perhaps, in part also to my own resourcefulness and efforts. When I look back at what I accomplished during the first six months of my life in the United States—I learned English sufficiently well to write and to lecture in that language, wrote my *Leaves from a Russian Diary,* completed my *Sociology of Revolution,* not to mention several scientific and popular papers, delivered two courses of lectures on the Russian Revolution and a number of lectures on several problems of sociology, and secured lecture-engagements for several months in advance, learned a great deal about the way of life, the mind and the heart of America—when I view these accomplishments now, through the tired eyes of a seventy-four-year-old man, I find them quite considerable. Certainly at my present age I would not be able to do so many things in such a short time. Obviously a person can do much more in his prime than he can in the late afternoon of his life. This, at least, is my only explanation for my accomplishments in that period.

CHAPTER TWELVE

Six Productive Years at the University of Minnesota

Summer of Probation

During the spring and summer of 1924 my wife Lena and I were both quite busy with our work. Being a plant cytologist, Lena was permitted to work in the plant cytology laboratory of Columbia University, while I, besides working on my two books, occasionally made a few lecture tours to various universities and organizations. Finally I went to the University of Minnesota to give my courses at its summer session. This engagement turned out to be very important in determining my activities for the next six years. As Professor F. S. Chapin, head of the sociology department there, later explained to me, my summer teaching session had been a sort of test of my professorial ability; if it happened to be satisfactory, the University intended to invite me as a visiting professor to replace Professor L. L. Bernard who was going on sabbatical leave the next year; if I had failed this test then the University would naturally have invited another man—a better scholar and teacher for that position. It seems I passed the test satisfactorily. One evidence which I still have of this success is the University of Minnesota seal, with appropriate poem, presented to me by the students of my courses at the end of the summer session. Here is the poem, which is self-explanatory:

DR. PITIRIM A. SOROKIN, AUGUST 27, 1924

We'd like to write a sonnet
  Or a pretty little rime
But we're worried about the meter
  And we might not keep the time;

So suppose we say quite simply
In a matter o-fact way
That we like Dr. Sorokin
Even better every day.
And we'd like to give a mem'ry
Of the days in Folwell hall
When we listened as his students
And enjoyed his lectures all.
We'd like to give the emblem
Of the Minnesota seal
And we hope to him it will express
The friendship that we feel.

Summer Classes in
The Sociology of Revolution
and Social Morphology–1924

Another more official proof that I had passed the test successfully was the University's offer at the end of the summer session of a visiting professorship for the next year. This offer established my title as full professor with a salary of $2,000 for the academic year (instead of the regular $4,000 salary of full professors of the University at that time). Like many other American universities, the University of Minnesota followed a bargaining policy of hiring its professors at as low salaries as possible. The administration of the University well realized my urgent need to secure an academic position in the United States and took this into consideration in making its offer. For my part, being comparatively free from the vice of attaching too great importance to pecuniary matters in human life, I gladly accepted the offer. After all, the limited salary was sufficient to meet my and Lena's modest living expenses, while the other conditions of the offer gave full opportunity for the development of my scientific work—the only thing that really counted in my opinion. So, with a light heart, I telegraphed Lena to come to Minneapolis; and after her arrival we rented a small but comfortable apartment near the University and thus started a new period in our life.

Years of Peaceful Life and Work—at Last!

After five trying years of the Revolution and two anxious years of political exile, the quiet and normal life at Minnesota seemed to us a real blessing. Being newcomers to this country, we could concentrate on our scientific and academic work undisturbed by political insecurity and by various non-academic distractions which are hardly avoidable for the "native-born" professors. At last we had real peace of mind and could devote ourselves to the work we wanted to do. It is true that my visiting professorship was only for one year, but somehow I felt quite certain of its renewal and eventually of its transformation into a permanent position. This expectation was quite correct; at the end of the first year, the University of Minnesota renewed my employment for another year with an increase of $100 in my salary; after that it offered me a permanent full professorship with the salary of $2,400, which was increased to $3,400 for the fourth year and to $4,000 for the fifth year. In the sixth year, after I had received an offer of full professorship at Harvard, Minnesota University was ready to increase my salary to the highest level of its professorial salaries. This highest salary, however, was still considerably lower than the salary offered by Harvard. For this and for other non-financial reasons, I accepted the Harvard offer; and, after six years of professorship at Minnesota, in 1930 I moved to the great university at Cambridge.

The six years at Minnesota were indeed happy years! Like new religious converts, we saw only the magnificent aspects of our new fatherland without noticing its uncomely features. Its federal, state, and municipal institutions appeared to us to be almost perfect. Its Constitution and Bill of Rights impressed us as magnificent realizations of the political and social ideals for which we had fought in Russia. We enjoyed in the deepest reaches of our selves the elating and inspiring grace of its encompassing freedom. This feeling of freedom was quite akin to the state of joy and sparkling vitality I used to experience in the moments of liberation from the Czarist and the Communist prisons.

No less wonderful did the people of all walks of life with whom we met, worked, and interacted appear to us. From the students and professors of the University and the neighbors in the apartment house where we lived, and extending to our grocery-man, mailman, the businessmen, community leaders, farmers, and other people with whom we came in contact—all were indeed friendly, honest, competent, reliable, fair, and pleasant to live and deal with. The "unseen wall" which separates the newcomer-immigrant from the native-born in many countries did not exist in our new country; we neither felt like strangers nor were we treated as such. We felt "at home" in this Minnesota community.

The wide open spaces of this state, its innumerable lakes, its prosperous farms and rolling fields, contributed their share to our enjoyment of life. They greatly enhanced the perhaps elementary but still most important form of freedom common to all living beings—the freedom from being cramped, fenced in, and enclosed within limited walls or narrow spaces which, both mentally and physically, hinder the freedom of spontaneous movements, actions, and aspirations. Probably because of the background of vast space and open skies of my early years, I have always felt cramped and somewhat imprisoned amidst the stone, brick, steel, and reinforced concrete buildings of big cities or thickly populated regions. When in later years I was forced by circumstances to live in densely populated cities and parts of Europe, I invariably experienced the sensation of being oppressed and restricted in the spontaneity of my actions and thence in unbounded flights of imagination. This feeling still remains with me and is probably the reason for my discomfort in, and dislike of, big urban and industrial centers. The vast spaces of Minnesota and the United States generally, their magnificent scenery of mountains, valleys, deserts, lakes, rivers, and sea-shores still unspoiled by industrial and urban civilization were and still are blessings of our life. "If we could not live in Russia we were lucky indeed in settling in the United States: no other country could have given us so much of this freedom as our new fatherland," so my wife and I congratulated each other.

In this happy state of mind we began our scientific and educational work in the Twin Cities. My wife decided to continue the graduate work which she had begun in Russia and to obtain a Ph.D. degree in botany from the University of Minnesota. Within one year she had successfully met all the requirements and received this degree in 1925. The University of Minnesota would have offered her a teaching and research position if there had been no legal provisions prohibiting employment of two or more members of the same family. For this reason she accepted the position of professor of botany at Hamlin University of St. Paul while she continued her research in the laboratories of the University of Minnesota.

At the University I established quite friendly relations with the administration, particularly with Vice President J. Lawrence, and deans G. S. Ford and H. Johnstone, the faculty, and the students. In the department of sociology its chairman, F. S. Chapin, and professors J. Finney, M. Elmer, M. Willey, and later E. Sutherland generously gave me their help any time I needed it. So also did the graduate and the undergraduate students. Despite my strongly accented speech, quite a considerable number of them registered in my courses and seminars. Soon I found myself surrounded by a warm fraternity of old and young companions in a common quest for a richer scientific knowledge and deeper understanding of human beings, their behavior, their social life and cultural processes.

My lifelong friendships and collaboration with many professors and students of the department of sociology and other divisions of the University were established during these years. There I had the delightful privilege of contributing a little to the growth of some of the graduate students into distinguished contemporary sociologists of America. T. Lynn Smith, N. Whetten, C. A. Anderson, Otis D. Duncan, P. Landis, F. Frey, E. Schuler, Ed. Taylor, C. and I. Taeubers, E. Monachesi, G. Vold, W. Lunden, E. Lott, G. Lundberg,

M. Elliott, H. Phelps, C. Hoffer, D. Thomas, R. Sletto, M. Tanquist, J. Markey, and others were for a long or short time members of this young sociological fraternity. Some of these young scholars came to Harvard after I moved to that university. If I was somewhat helpful to them in their scientific development, they were no less helpful to me in our common pursuit of knowledge and self-education. Among other things this common search resulted in the publication of several cooperative studies on monarchs and rulers, farmer and labor leaders, and the experimental study of the efficiency of work under various specified conditions—all of which were carried on in my seminars and courses.

Among the younger scholars in the department a particularly close friendship sprung up between myself and C. C. Zimmerman. Our collaboration produced, besides a few papers, our volume *Principles of Rural-Urban Sociology* and three substantial volumes of *A Systematic Source-Book in Rural Sociology,* commissioned through the initiative of C. J. Galpin by the United States Department of Agriculture. After I moved to Harvard, Professor Zimmerman followed me. At Harvard our friendship continued. At the present moment it is as warm as ever.

Among many friends outside of the University we particularly enjoyed the friendship of Mr. and Mrs. George Anderson (Dr. Anderson eventually became professor of Russian history at the University of Minnesota) and of Mr. and Mrs. John Lucey. Eventually both of the Luceys passed away, but these dear friends are still living in our memories as "the best Irish-Americans" we met in our lives.

It was only natural that under these conditions—normal for American scholars but exceptionally favorable for us after the years of revolution in Russia and of an émigré's way of life abroad—I earnestly devoted myself to research and writing. If I had something important to say and some capacity to do significant scientific work, now was the time to accomplish these tasks. Despite a heavy teaching load, the shortcomings of my English, modest financial remuneration, and a lack of funds for assistance in my research (the total sum of financial grants for my research during six years of my work at the University of Minnesota amounted to exactly $12.45, plus a few hundred dollars especially given by the U. S. Department of Agriculture for *A Source-Book in Rural Sociology*), there still was sufficient time left for creative scientific work, if one had the necessary enthusiasm and capacity to do it. Animated by enthusiasm, I did my best to achieve this purpose. During my six years at the University of Minnesota I published, besides many articles in American and foreign scientific journals, my substantial volumes: *Leaves from a Russian Diary* (1924), *The Sociology of Revolution* (1925), *Social Mobility* (1927), *Contemporary Sociological Theories* (1928), *Principles of Rural-Urban Sociology*, with C. C. Zimmerman as co-author (1929), and three big volumes of *A Systematic Source-Book in Rural Sociology*, with C. C. Zimmerman and C. J. Galpin as co-authors (1930-32). The last work was completed at Minnesota, although volumes two and three were published after my transfer to Harvard. Quantitatively, this output naturally required much time and energy to produce without secretarial or other forms of assistance. With the exception of certain chapters written by Zimmerman and Galpin in the volumes on rural sociology, everything in these volumes was researched and written by myself. Some of my distinguished friends, like Professor E. A. Ross, well understood this and cautioned me to relax the intensity of my work. In a letter written January 26, 1928, summing up his impressions of my *Contemporary Sociological Theories*, he wrote:

> I am simply amazed at the immense body of literature you have traveled over and at your skill in tearing the heart out of a book and expressing it in a page or two. . . . I feel certain that within two or three years you will have opportunity to occupy a high position in some one of our leading universities. Indeed it is quite possible that you will be hailed in a few years as the dominant spirit in American sociology. You

> can imagine my pride in mentioning that I enabled you to translate yourself from Europe to America. . . . Your book *Social Mobility* prompted me to create a new seminar on the subject.
> My only fear is lest you kill yourself with overwork. I am glad that you are "dreaming of summer and camping and forests."

So far as the quantity of my output for these six years was concerned, I was satisfied; I knew that it exceeded the lifetime productivity of the average sociologist—American or foreign.

As to the quality of my works, I was certain that they measured up to the average level of sociological works of that time, but I was not at all sure that they were better than the rank and file of current sociological books. However, this matter did not worry me much. I had done my best; the rest was in the hands of the gods. If my works were significant, they eventually would come into their own; if they were valueless, they did not deserve any recognition. In either case the results would be fair and square, though not equally pleasant to me. I simply assumed the position of curious observer of the life-course of my books—an attitude similar to that of parents in regard to their grown-up and married children: after their marriage it is up to them what they will make of their lives, a creative success or a dismal failure. After their publication it was up to my mental children either to slip into oblivion and die, unnoticed and unremembered, or to live a vigorous and meaningful life for some length of time.

The actual response of sociologists, intellectuals, and the general public to these volumes was on the whole considerably better than I had expected. Already the *Leaves from a Russian Diary* and the *Sociology of Revolution* were noticed and hotly commented upon, both positively and negatively, according to the ideological sympathies and vested interests of the readers, reviewers, and scholars. *Social Mobility*, *Contemporary Sociological Theories*, the *Principles*, and the

Source-Book in Rural Sociology were not only noticed but fairly definitely established my reputation as a leading contemporary sociologist. Eventually they have been translated into many foreign languages, have served as advanced texts in universities throughout the world, have been called the "pioneering" and "classic" works by many scholars, have produced quite a considerable literature—books, Ph.D. theses, scientific and popular articles—concerning the theories contained in these volumes, have given me honorary degrees and memberships in royal and national academies of arts and sciences; and some thirty-five years after their first publication they are still reissued, translated, and studied. In brief, they turned out to be real contributions to sociology and the psychosocial sciences. As such they have shown a greater vitality, longer lifespan, and more vigorous resistance to the obliterating effects of time than the rank and file of contemporary sociological works.

Of course, the professional and public appraisal of these volumes did not occur all at once. It has developed gradually over the course of years. The first reactions of my American colleagues and the press to *Mobility, Theories,* and the works in *Rural Sociology* were marked by these features: (1) the reaction was extraordinarily voluminous and intense on the part of my critics as well as my proponents; (2) the response of an overwhelming majority of eminent foreign and American sociologists, economists, and other scholars, including E. A. Ross, F. Giddings, Ch. H. Cooley, F. S. Chapin, Ch. Ellwood, C. Case, E. Sutherland, E. Huntington, M. Rostovetzeff, F. Taussig, T. Carver, R. B. Perry, A. Hansen, J. D. Black, and many others was enthusiastically positive. In their articles, reviews, and personal letters to me they appraised my volumes as great contributions to sociology and related sciences; (3) a small minority of American sociologists tried to undervalue my works as much as they could. As I learned later on, a part of this minority even started a deliberate campaign to "discredit Sorokin." I did not exactly know what the motives of these "campaigners" were. On the basis of fragmentary evidence I surmised that, besides an honest difference of opinion, "the campaigners" did not like the anti-Communistic activities I carried on at that time and my criticism of their pet theories and ideologies. In addition to this, they seemingly assumed that in some way I was responsible for the replacement of Professor L. L. Bernard in the department of sociology of the University of Minnesota, though as a matter of fact I had nothing to do with Bernard's "resignation" from the department in 1926-27. In these years these "detractors" seemingly viewed me as one of those Russian émigrés who had little relation to real scholarship and, as such, could and should be put in his proper place.

This whole situation was typically reflected in an incident which up to the present moment remains unknown to all except a few persons directly involved in it. One of the first "shots" fired by these critics was a review of my *Social Mobility* written by Andrew W. Lind in the *American Journal of Sociology* for March, 1928. The whole review consisted of only fifteen lines and conveyed the impression that my book did not amount to anything significant. Since it was one of the first reviews of my work published in an authoritative American journal of sociology, it naturally depressed me as a harbinger of my failure. Despite its unfairness, I decided, according to my principle, not to react to it in any way. After the first moments of depression, I acquiesced in the old adage *In captu, lectoris habent fata sua libelli* and in my "bullheaded" readiness to accept temporary defeat if the subsequent reactions to my book turned out to be similar to that of this review.

Fortunately for me, within the next few weeks a stream of letters from, and then reviews and articles by, eminent foreign and American sociologists gave quite a different, and most reassuring, evaluation of my book. Among these letters, especially encouraging was a short letter to me from Professor Charles H. Cooley, along with an enclosed copy of his letter to the editors of the *American Journal of Sociology*. These letters speak for themselves and need no comments from me:

April 20, 1928

Dear Professor Sorokin:

I have written a note to Professor Burgess protesting against the review of your book in the last number of the *American Journal of Sociology*. It occurs to me that you may be interested to see it and I accordingly enclose a copy.

Sincerely yours,

C. H. Cooley

Professor E. W. Burgess

April 20, 1928

Dear Professor Burgess:

I do not remember that I have often performed any functions as Advisory Councillor to the *Journal* but perhaps it may be one of them to express my present feeling that the review of Sorokin's *Social Mobility* in the March number is deplorable. Probably you think so too, and perhaps you have been unable to get a more competent or less indolent reviewer. As I have persistently declined to review books I perhaps ought not to complain. But men do write reviews, and if it is done at all it ought to be done considerately and fairly. Wouldn't it have been better to have had no review at all of *Social Mobility* than to inflict upon it so perfunctory, and hence so contemptuous, a notice? Surely the book is, for sheer weight of solid and intelligent scholarship, exercised upon a fundamental province of social theory, *comparable to the best work produced in this country or anywhere else*. How must the author feel when such a work is received in such a manner by the leading review in his field?

I would offer to write something corrective, but I have been unwell this spring and am getting ready to go away.

Sincerely yours,

C. H. Cooley

One of the results of this letter was another review of my book by Professor Rudolph Heberle, published in the *American Journal of Sociology,* July, 1928. This review was a lengthy one of more than six pages and appeared first in the review section. Its competence and positive evaluation was quite different from Lind's review. The editors of the *Journal* prefaced this new review with a footnote:

> A review of Sorokin's *Social Mobility* was published in the *American Journal of Sociology,* March, 1928. No complaint has come to the editors emanating from Professor Sorokin or anyone acting in his behalf, but a recent letter from a distinguished member of the American Sociological Society suggests that this review was wholly inadequate. In this opinion the editors of the *Journal* concur. It happens that Dr. R. Heberle has in preparation a book on the same general topic. At the suggestion of the editors, Dr. Heberle has written his own more adequate comment on Professor Sorokin's volume, as a supplement to, and in part as a correction of, the earlier review.

For me Cooley's letter was particularly significant because I had met this distinguished sociologist only once before and because his protest was done entirely on his own initiative without any request or complaint on my part. This incident and the prestige which the *Mobility* and the *Theories* rapidly acquired among American and foreign scholars restored my equanimity and self-confidence. These events also forced "the detractors" to relent in their clumsy attacks. Of course, honest criticism of my books and theories continued. As a matter of fact most of the reviews of my works, published in the *American Journal of Sociology, Social Forces,* and *American Sociological Review,* have been critical. But since they have been honest—sometimes competent, more often incompetent—criticisms, I did not mind them. On the contrary I enjoyed them much more than purely complimentary write-ups; if the criticism was stupid—as most of the criticisms have been—I was reinforced in the correctness of my theories; if it was competent I profited from it by correcting my errors. This explains why up to now I rarely read laudatory comments on my writings as carefully as I read sharply critical "raspberries" given to me and my "yarns." I have enjoyed the criticisms published in the above mentioned sociological journals for additional reasons indicated in my letter to the editor of the *American Journal of Sociology* (March, 1957, p. 515).

> The strongly disparaging character of the reviews is a good omen for my books because of a high correlation between the damning of my books by the reviewers of the *American Journal of Sociology* and their subsequent career. The more strongly they have been damned (and practically all my books were damned by your reviewers), the more significant and successful were my damned works, the more were they translated, and the more voluminous the scientific literature in the form of substantial articles, Ph.D. theses, and books about my books, the greater the space given them in various sociological lexicons and philosophical encyclopedias, and the more substantial the chapters in texts and monographs devoted to my theories and "emotional outbursts." Even more frequently my "yarns" have been appropriated by some of the damning reviewers a few years after publication of their reviews. . . .

In general I have welcomed this sharply divided reception of my books. To my observation this sort of reception has been typical for an overwhelming majority of the great works in science or philosophy, fine arts or religion, and in practically all creative fields. Only the works that offer nothing new and important, that do not challenge the prevalent ideas, styles, or standards—only such works, if their birth is noticed at all, receive a few complimentary notices and quickly pass into oblivion, with or without even short obituaries. "If I cannot imitate the great social thinkers in their great achievements, I am satisfied with resembling them in their small deeds." Such has been my attitude in these matters.

After the publication of *Social Mobility* and *Contemporary Sociological Theories* my name clearly appeared on the world's sociological map. The previous anxieties about my academic position largely subsided. Invigorated by the favorable reception of these works, I quietly continued my academic activities and began my studies in the field of rural sociology.

The intensive mental work described during these years should not give the impression that it endangered my health or brought me to the verge of nervous breakdown or prevented me and my wife from enjoying the fullness of life. Nothing of the kind. Though scientific and educational activities demanded the greater part of our time and energy, there still were time and vigor left for convivial gatherings with our friends, for philosophical, artistic, and cultural pursuits, and for simple enjoyment of such physical activities as camping, fishing, swimming, mountain climbing, playing handball, and others.

In company with the Chapins, the Zimmermans, and the Andersons, on the summer weekends we often went overnight to a beautiful spot on the St. Croix River to swim, sun, and sleep in the open around a bonfire under the stars. In the winter I regularly played handball with graduate students and professors. Many an evening I spent in the company of students, chatting spontaneously about anything which interested us. During longer weekends we undertook more extensive fishing-camping trips to the remote Minnesota lakes like Superior, Milacs, Woman Lake, the State Scenic Park, and other places.

One summer vacation, with the Zimmermans, we camped out all the way to the Black Hills and Bad Lands of the Dakotas, and to Yellowstone Park in Wyoming where we stayed in our tents for more than a week, fully enjoying the scenic beauty, the company of bears and other animals, hikes to interesting spots, swimming, and fishing.

Two other summers, with Professor MacClintock and his family, we drove to and stayed a month or so in the mountains of Colorado (elevation over 8,000 feet) camping in the open and never spending a night in either hotel or motel. There we climbed many a mountain, including Mount Elbert, the highest peak in Colorado.

These long camping trips are unforgettable! After intensive mental work for months, it was a real joy to climb into our second-hand, model-T Ford, and, forgetting all mental worries and enjoying a feeling of lighthearted freedom, to drive to magnificent ever-new places in the open air, under the sunny sky, amidst ever-changing scenery. At that time all these places were wilder, less commercialized and civilized than they are now. Though our old Ford was often "disorderly," and though many roads, especially in the Colorado mountains, were just dirt roads with hairpin turns quite close to precipices several thousand feet high, though now and then we experienced dangerous skids on these roads; though once in a while we were caught in violent storms and cloudbursts, or were marooned for several days by impassable roads—what of it? All these dangers and incidents only enhanced the intensity of our *élan vital* and joy of living. We drove wherever and for as long as we wanted, stopping at the chosen place. We fished, swam, boated, climbed mountains, and walked when and where we desired. We prepared our meals on a gas stove whenever we were inclined to eat. We slept in our tents and got up again according to our choice. Our whole way of living during these long trips was entirely free from the tyranny of the time-table with its minutely mapped activities, appointments, chores, and meetings: from 8:30 to 9:00, from 9:00 to 9:30, and so on for every twenty-four hours of our existence—a tyranny inevitable in our normal working periods of life. Besides this freedom from the tyranny of clock-time, during these trips we were also free from the shackles of many "civilized" but uselessly annoying conventions of the *comme il faut*, including artificial manners, proper apparel, and the like. This real freedom, the beauty of the magnificent scenery, the inexhaustible novelty of our physical activities, deep meditation and contemplation on the austere, resplendent peaks of the mountains or amidst the dreaming solitude of shining lakes, or listening to the poetic murmur of mountain streams and waterfalls—all these experiences were life at its fullest and best. Only the blissful moments of creative inspiration in mental work can rival and possibly surpass the joyful intensity of these experiences. No wonder, therefore, that a few days or weeks of these camping trips completely refreshed us, both physically and mentally. Their healing and invigorating effects prevented and eliminated the dangers of mental fatigue and nervous exhaustion and rendered any and all psychiatrists and "healers" unnecessary.

For six Minnesota years I did not spend a single day in the hospital and visited a doctor only few times. My "brother-body" and my mind behaved quite well in this sort of brimful living. The fullness of our lives was also greatly enriched by our cultural pursuits which reached far beyond the professional field of sociology and academic work. With vivid interest I continued to follow the developments of old and new currents in the fields of literature, philosophy, psychology, theoretical and practical economics and politics, ethics, law, and the fine arts. In this last field, besides reading, we attended many painting and sculpture exhibitions, plays and movies, symphonic concerts, and recitals of eminent artists.

At one such concert my subsequent lifelong friendship with the great conductor of the Boston Symphony Orchestra, Dr. Sergei Koussevitzky began. As a poor student in St. Petersburg I had often attended the magnificent concerts given by Koussevitzky's own orchestra. During Kerensky's regime we met once or twice as members of this government, in which Koussevitzky was in charge of the development and cultivation of musical art in all of Russia while I was the secretary to Prime Minister Kerensky. Since Koussevitzky's "escape" from Communist Russia in 1920, we had not met until this concert in the Minnesota University auditorium in 1929. After the concert I stepped into the reception room to congratulate the maestro on the splendid performance of the Boston orchestra. Our reunion was most cordial and joyful. We plunged into reminiscences of our Russian experience, informed each other about our post-Russian life, and exchanged views on the momentous problems of the present. It was a memorable reunion indeed! After my move to Harvard, it developed into a fine friendship between us and our families. For many years, until the death of our eminent friend, we enjoyed the ineffable grace of this friendship.

Of other memorable reunions in Minneapolis, that with my

closest old friend, Professor N. Kondratieff, must be mentioned. As a foremost agricultural economist and expert on business cycles, he was permitted by the Soviet Government to visit American universities and research institutions in his field. This task brought him to the University of Minnesota where he stayed with us for several days. It was a real joy for us to see him alive and well and to talk with him about our Russian friends, the economic and political conditions in Russia, and the basic problems of the world at large. Unfortunately this reunion was our last meeting. A few years after his return to Russia, he was accused by Stalin in 1931 of being the leading ideologist and planner of an anti-Communist reconstruction of Russian agriculture. As such, he was "purged," and disappeared. We heard rumors that he had been banished and had perished somewhere in Turkestan or Mongolia. But exactly how and where he perished we have never learned up to the present time. *Requiem eternam et lux perpetua* to you, our dearest friend!

This reunion with Kondratieff reminds me of my facetious recommendation to President Coffman that he invite Leon Trotsky to be speaker at the University convocation. About two years after my banishment from Russia, Trotsky was kicked out of Russia by Stalin and at that time was marooned on a Turkish island named Prinkipo, near Constantinople. "Although Trotsky banished me, since now we are both comrades in exile, I would be glad to introduce him to the convocation audience." For obvious reasons my ironic suggestion was declined.

And so we lived and worked in Minnesota. Having finished writing *Contemporary Sociological Theories,* I began, in cooperation with C. C. Zimmerman, my studies of the basic problems of rural sociology. Within one year we were able to round out these studies and to publish them in 1929 in the form of the volume *Principles of Rural-Urban Sociology.* Its reception was most gratifying. Among other positive results, publication of this volume brought to us an offer of the U. S. Department of Agriculture to undertake the preparation of a systematic manual and substantial source-book in rural sociology. The offer was initiated by a distinguished rural sociologist, Charles J. Galpin, then a chief of the Division of Farm Population and Rural Life of the U. S. Department of Agriculture. Even before the publication of the *Principles*, he had written letters expressing profound appreciation of my *Mobility* and *Theories*. Since the offer gave us an opportunity to expand, develop, and corroborate more fully the main ideas and generalizations of the *Principles*, and since Galpin himself wanted to cooperate with us in the undertaking, we accepted the offer and got busy with this task. Assisted by T. Lynn Smith, C. Taeuber, and other graduate students, we completed within some sixteen months the voluminous manuscript of *A Systematic Source-Book in Rural Sociology*. The University of Minnesota Press promptly published the first volume in 1930 and volumes two and three in 1931 and 1932, respectively.

Our collective preface to volume one states that "most of the introductions, selections, and systematization of the material and, in general, the greater part of the work of the *Source-Book* were done by Professor P. Sorokin. Without the encyclopedic knowledge of the literature of rural thought and of sociological theory that he brought to this task and his indefatigable attention to the details of arrangement and interpretation, the *Source-Book* would not have been thought possible at this time."

The preparation of these volumes in such a short time indeed required most strenuous work on my part. When the end was in view I felt somewhat fatigued, irritable, and increasingly impatient to finish the work as quickly as possible. With a deep sigh of relief, I sent the finished manuscript to the University of Minnesota Press, ebulliently welcomed my freedom from its pressure, and, to the content of my heart, did several things which I had wanted to do but could not until the work was completed.

Its completion freed me also for dreaming and turning over in my mind the topic of my next work. Somehow or other, this topic had already appeared in my mind in a vague form. It began increasingly to challenge my curiosity and imagination. Now, examining it more closely, I realized the tremendous difficulties involved in the serious study of the subject, the enormous amount of labor it required, and my limited capacity to cope adequately with such a gigantic problem. Despite these apprehensions, the challenge became so tantalizing that, after some hesitation, I accepted it. "Come what may, it is better to fail in the achievement of a great task than to be successful in the accomplishment of a pedestrian purpose"—such was the foolhardy motivation behind my decision. Having reached it, I started a leisurely preliminary exploration of the field of my topic. Some ten years later, in 1937-41, four volumes of my *Social and Cultural Dynamics* were born from this "reckless" decision.

Meanwhile the publication of the *Principles* and then of the first volume of the *Source-Book* notably enhanced my scientific prestige. The reception of these works was overwhelmingly enthusiastic. In reviews, articles, and personal letters they were acclaimed as "landmarks," as "great," "pioneering," and the like contributions to rural-urban sociology. Among many indications of this high evaluation there came to me two additional offers of full professorship from great state universities. Since, however, the University of Minnesota readily met the conditions of these offers and since my wife and I felt quite at home in this university, I declined these offers and remained at the University of Minnesota as one of its distinguished scholars. Quite content with our conditions, we expected to stay there until my retirement or death.

Invitation From Harvard

Soon, however, an unforeseen turn of Fortune's wheel abruptly ended this experience. In the spring of 1929 I received an invitation, from the Harvard University Department of Economics and the Committee on Sociology and Social Ethics, to visit Harvard and to deliver several lectures and seminar discussions on the topics of my choice. The invitation somewhat surprised me because I had never visited Harvard before and knew hardly any of its eminent scholars personally. Up to the time of this invitation my contacts with Harvard had been limited to receiving complimentary letters about my works from professors F. Taussig, T. Carver, and J. D. Black, and to reading quite favorable review-articles about my volumes in the Harvard *Quarterly Journal of Economics.* I naturally accepted the invitation and, in March, 1929, came to Harvard to fulfill my engagement. There I was treated with utmost cordiality and kindness by professors H. Burbank, F. Taussig, E. Gay, T. Carver, J. D. Black, R. B. Perry, C. Bullock, W. Hocking, R. Cabot, A. Whitehead, and many others. They honored me by attending my lectures, by discussing with me problems of common interest, and by organizing a special banquet to introduce me to many members of the faculty. I was also invited to lunch by the great president of Harvard, L. Lowell, and at his house met some of the members of the Harvard Corporation. Besides these senior members of Harvard, I also met a number of younger scholars —instructors, tutors, assistant professors, and graduate students —among these C. Joslyn and T. Parsons.

My lectures and seminar-sessions seemed to have gone well. At least many of the scholars heartily congratulated me on my performances. For my part I fully enjoyed my visit to Harvard. Its scholars and students, its atmosphere and mores, impressed me quite favorably. Toward the end of my visit this impression was somewhat complicated by a vague feeling that I had not been invited merely as a visiting lecturer but also as a possible "bridegroom" whom they wanted to look over carefully in regard to appearance, manners, values, personality, and academic performance. If this guess was correct, then Harvard certainly gave me a most thorough going over. Despite this feeling, no offer was made to me during this visit. Having finished my engagement, I said my grateful "good-bye" to new Harvard friends and returned to Minneapolis quite satisfied with my trip and with a generous check in my pocket.

After my return I put the finishing touches to the *Source-Book* and busied myself with writing a couple of papers. The ensuing summer vacation we spent camping in the Colorado mountains. Four weeks of rest fully restored my vigor and equanimity. From time to time during this camping trip, in between physical activities, I repeatedly indulged in spontaneous thoughts of the problems of my projected work. Completely refreshed, we returned to Minneapolis. There, with renewed energy, I promptly plunged myself into exploration of the field of the future *Dynamics*. This preliminary investigation clarified one thing for me; namely, if the projected work was to be done on the scale and depth at which it should be done, I could not accomplish it alone, without the substantial assistance of a number of eminent specialists in the historical and psychosocial sciences.

At the end of September, 1929, just when I was pondering how to secure this assistance (having no funds at my disposal to pay for it) a letter from President Lowell of Harvard reached me. In his kind letter this distinguished educator informed me that Harvard had decided to establish, for the first time in its history, a chair of sociology, and that their unanimous choice of a scholar for that chair was myself. The letter further specified the financial and other conditions of the offer, including my privilege to choose the department where I preferred to place my chair.

In my answer to President Lowell I wrote that the conditions offered were quite generous and acceptable to me. I added, however, that they would be still better if the new chair of sociology were promptly expanded into a full department of sociology. This desideratum was quickly approved, and on October 28, 1929, the "President and Fellows of Harvard College elected [me] Professor of Sociology to serve from September 1, 1930." "This election was duly confirmed by the Board of Overseers at their meeting of January 13, 1930."

It was further agreed that in December, 1929, I was to come to Harvard for a few days to arrange several details of my future activities there.

Thus in one month a significant change in my life was decided upon and eventually took place. With the exception of my feelings about the prospective "bridegroom," I had neither expected nor sought after any offer from this great university. "If your choice is wrong, the fault is entirely yours," I half-jokingly told President Lowell and Dean C. Moore during our meeting in December, 1929. Among other things, at this meeting President Lowell told me that Harvard had already decided to establish a chair of sociology some twenty-five years before. They had not done so until then because there was no sociologist worthy to fill the chair. Now, in their opinion, such a sociologist had appeared, and they had promptly made the decision. I was naturally elated by this turn in my life. After all, the appointment at Harvard was an impressive recognition of my humble achievements. It was recognized as such by the American press and by a stream of congratulatory letters from my friends, colleagues, and critics.

The administration and the Board of Regents of the University of Minnesota (whom I kept informed about the transaction with Harvard from its very beginning) offered me the highest conditions allowed by the legal regulations of Minnesota, but as these conditions were still notably below those of Harvard, they regretfully accepted my resignation "to take effect at the close of the academic year 1929-30" and "expressed their appreciation for the services which you have rendered the University of Minnesota" and their "best wishes for continued success in your new field of work." (Official letter of President L. D. Coffman, dated November 16, 1929.) Unofficially, President Coffman humorously remarked: "Here we take young calves and nurse and grow them into magnificent bulls; and then the big, bad wolf of Harvard comes and snatches them from us. There should be a law against this sort of predatory practice of Harvard."

This humorous criticism was factually correct: in the preceding three years Harvard had "snatched" from the University of Minnesota, Professors J. D. Black and N. S. D. Gras; and during the next few years after I left, it "snatched" professors C. C. Zimmerman, A. Hansen, and J. N. D. Bush. Harvard, however, could be fully excused for the policy of snatching since it has been practiced by all important universities and colleges in this country, including the University of Minnesota itself. Subsequent investigation has shown me that of the professorial ranks of our universities about forty per cent have been filled by "snatching" or "hiring professors from other universities and colleges, and only about sixty per cent have been filled by "inbreeding"—that is, by promotion from the lower ranks of instructors and assistant professors in each institution.

A multitude of small matters, together with inevitable distractions involved in my transference to Harvard, tangibly interfered with my work on the *Dynamics* in the months from October to the end of December, 1929. By the beginning of the new year (1930), however, these matters were arranged, the excitement subsided, and distractions abated. In January, 1930, I resumed my research and steadily continued it up to the beginning of August. In that month, having said goodbye to many friends in Minnesota, we drove for our vacation to the Lake of the Woods in Canada, hoping to catch some muskies there. We stayed for a few days on one of the islands of that lake, and, having no luck in our fishing, we were taken back in a small boat to the shore where we had left our car.

During this passage we were almost drowned. Shortly after we had started to cross the lake (there was a distance of some fifteen miles from the island to the shore), a violent storm burst. Within a few minutes it had churned the quiet water into a fury of whitecaps. Spray began to fill the boat, and huge waves threatened to overturn it at any moment. For a couple of hours we were in this dangerous plight. If our small outboard motor had stalled then, even for a short time, we would certainly have been lost in the frenzied waters. Fortunately the dear old motor unfailingly discharged its duty and brought us—wet but relieved—to land.

From the Lake of the Woods we started our unhurried drive to Cambridge, stopping for a day or two at various scenic and fishing spots in northern Minnesota, Wisconsin, and Michigan. Greatly refreshed and invigorated, we finally reached Cambridge at the end of August, 1930. Our arrival at Harvard closed an important period in my life and opened another.

Looking back over the Minnesota years, I find that they were indeed years of meaningful and creative life for Lena and myself. Being comparatively young and full of vitality, we had lived, worked, and enjoyed the plenitude of life at its noblest and best.

CHAPTER THIRTEEN

First Harvard Years

Establishment of the Harvard Department of Sociology

During the first few months of our life in Cambridge I had little time to work on the *Dynamics*. First, we had to find our living quarters, which we did by renting half of a comfortable two-family house on Washington Avenue. Then we had to "eat our way through Cambridge and Boston" at many lunches and dinners given by Harvard professors, "proper Bostonians," and by various dignitaries of both cities. I have never cared much for the "social life" of going from party to party; nevertheless, like all newcomers to Harvard, I had to go through this ritual to comply with the established mores. Then there was a multitude of small things—inevitable in settling in a new community—that had to be done to adjust ourselves to the new environment. These "extracurricular" activities consumed a considerable portion of my time.

The greater part of it, however, was taken up by my academic duties: preparation of lectures, learning the local rules and regulations, attendance of various committees, and particularly my chairmanship of the committee for the organization of the new department of sociology.

Before the department was organized, I placed my chair in the department of economics. I chose this department because its distinguished members—Taussig, Gay, Carver, Burbank, Bullock, Black, Crumm, and others—had played an important role in the establishment of the new department and in electing me first professor of sociology at Harvard; I respected them as eminent scholars and liked them as fine and congenial persons. I never regretted this choice: during the one year of my membership in the department of economics, I learned a great deal from its distinguished members and fully enjoyed their guidance, friendship, and cooperation.

At the very beginning of the academic year 1930-31, President Lowell appointed a special committee to organize the new department, with myself as chairman and as members professors R. Cabot, T. Carver, R. B. Perry, H. Burbank, A. Schlesinger, A. M. Tozzer, E. B. Wilson, J. Black, J. Ford, and G. Allport, who represented the departments of economics, history, psychology, anthropology, philosophy, and social ethics.

The diversity of the committee members' ideas of what sorts of courses and instruction the new department should give, made the tasks of the committee difficult to solve quickly. This inherent difficulty was increased by two conditions imposed upon the committee by the administration: first, it wanted to have a first-class department in regard to teaching staff, instruction, and research but it prescribed to recruit the staff exclusively from the faculty of Harvard, without any outside sociologists added to it. Since Harvard had almost no ex-officio sociologists, one could easily understand the difficulties in building a first-class department of sociology without sociologists, in the narrow sense of this term. The second condition was that the new department had to absorb and replace the existing department of social ethics. This condition naturally aroused the resistance of the vested interests in the department of social ethics. These interests could have seriously handicapped the work of the committee, if Dr. R. Cabot, chairman of the department of social ethics, had not wholeheartedly cooperated with the committee. His fairness and sincere participation in building the new department eliminated many difficulties created by other representatives of vested interests.

The wide diversity of the views of the members of the committee in regard to what the new department should be, and these two conditions threatened to lengthen the work of the committee for a fairly long time. Fortunately, the earnest desire of the committee to solve its task as quickly as possible, its spirit of reconciliation and mutual concessions, the considerable weight given by the members to my views and *desiderata*, and my position as a newcomer uninvolved up to this point in the wranglings of various Harvard cliques, allowed us to finish the work of the committee in a period of six or seven weeks. I did not get all that I wanted in regard to the structure of the new department, but still, under the circumstances, I got a great deal. Perhaps the greatest concession I had to make was my idea of the sociology department as a purely graduate department opened only to brilliant graduate students. I regarded and do regard sociology as the most complex of all the psychosocial disciplines. For financial and other practical reasons, even Harvard could not afford such an "exclusive" department. Therefore we agreed that the new department would have undergraduate and graduate divisions but that both would be open only to the upper ranks of students. As full-time members of the department—besides myself as its chairman—R. Cabot as full professor and J. Ford as associate professor, with C. Joslyn and T. Parsons as faculty instructors and P. Pigors and W. L. Warner as tutors were recommended. We also arranged that a number of courses and seminars given in other departments be open to sociology students, such as a criminology course given by S. Glueck in the Law School; courses of Taussig, Carver, Black, and Crumm in the department of economics; G. Allport's course in social psychology in the department of psychology; the statistics courses given in the department of economics and mathematics; courses in philosophy, history—including the history of religion—political science, anthropology, linguistics, literature, and the fine arts. In this way the hard core of basic sociological courses in the department was considerably increased and supplemented by courses and seminars offered by distinguished scholars in other departments.

In December, 1930, I submitted the committee's plan for the department to President Lowell. He and the administration approved it with the exception of one point: they refused to approve the appointment of Talcott Parsons as the department's faculty instructor. Somewhat surprised by this, I asked Professor Burbank, chairman of the department of economics (where Parsons was an instructor) what could be the reasons behind this refusal. The gist of Burbank's remarks was that Parsons seemed to be less interested in economics than in sociology, that possibly for this reason his work in the department of economics was not of the best quality, that he probably would do much better work in sociology than in economics, and that therefore the department of economics would be only too glad to transfer Parsons to the new department. My personal impressions of Parsons, formed from several meetings with him, were rather favorable. In our conversations he displayed a good analytical mind and a discriminating knowledge of the theories of Durkheim, Pareto, Weber, and other sociologists. Duly impressed, I strongly recommended Parson's appointment to the committee and obtained its approval of my recommendation.

In this frame of mind I told Burbank that we were quite willing to have Parsons in the new department and asked him, Taussig, Gay, Carver, and Perry to support the committee's recommendation of Parsons to President Lowell and the administration. I also asked the members of the committee to exert all their individual influence upon the administration in this matter. Backed by their support, I did my best to convince Mr. Lowell to change his negative decision to a positive one. After two talks with Lowell I finally obtained his approval of Parsons' appointment. With this point constructively solved, the constitution of the new department was promptly submitted by the administration to the Harvard faculty and was approved. At the end of the first semester of the academic year 1930-31, the department of sociology was duly established at Harvard, and with the beginning of the next academic year, 1931-32, it was open for business.

Thus, surprisingly for me, I happened to play an important role in the establishment of two departments of sociology: one at the University of Petrograd in 1919-20, the other at Harvard University in 1930-31. In later years I was invited to organize departments of sociology at the universities of Indonesia and at some universities in India and Latin America. Preoccupied with my studies and not being interested in administrative work, I declined these invitations.

I Resume Work on the Dynamics

By the end of the first semester at Harvard the work of organizing the new department was essentially completed. For the most part the time-consuming ritual of "eating our way through Cambridge" was also over. Completion of these tasks gave me more time to work on the *Dynamics* and to engage in extra-curricular activities.

My labor over the *Dynamics* was eventually assisted by financial grants from the Harvard Committee for Research in the Social Sciences. The grants, given for four years, amounted to some $10,000 for all four volumes of this work. This sum allowed me to obtain the urgently needed cooperation of eminent specialists in the history of painting, sculpture, architecture, music, literature, science, philosophy, economics, religion, ethics, law, wars, revolutions, and other important sociocultural processes. For a very modest honorarium these predominantly Russian specialists kindly agreed to do for me an enormous amount of spade-work, according to a schedule I prepared for each of them. (The names of these collaborators are given at the beginning of many chapters in the *Dynamics*.)

None of these experts was told for what purpose I needed the statistical tables and other material he agreed to prepare for me. Nor was any one of them informed of what sort of hypothesis or theory had to be tested by the systematic, largely quantitative data he was to compile according to my outline. I used this procedure of keeping them completely uninformed about my tentative hypothesis quite deliberately: I wanted from them a competent and complete series of relevant facts entirely uninfluenced by any sort of tentative theories I had in my own mind. This fact explains my intense excitement every time I received from each collaborator his tables and other summaries of empirical facts. Would these time-series and data corroborate my tentative hypothesis or would they contradict or be irrelevant to it?—that was the burning question in my mind each time I began to study the delivered material. Fortunately for me, almost all of the numerous materials confirmed my tentative hypothesis far more strongly than I had expected.

The deliveries of empirical materials continued for about four years and kept my excitement at a high pitch during this period. The total amount of empirical material delivered to me by my distinguished collaborators was enormous. In the *Dynamics* I used only the most important part of this material, but even that part—represented by hundreds of tables, each of which, in compressed form, summed up long-time series of many basic cultural processes—is so vast and systematic that it is certainly unexcelled and is hardly rivaled by any sociological work in the field of social and cultural systems, their fluctuations and changes.

This shows the utter lack of basis for some criticisms of the *Dynamics* which suggest that its main theories were dogmatically preconceived and that its empirical corroborations were but a subjectively arranged "window dressing." Of course, none of these critics did or could furnish any proof of their entirely dogmatic contentions. On my part, I have been quite amused and have wholeheartedly enjoyed these silly pronouncements. In P. Allen's volume *Pitirim A. Sorokin In Review*, one of my distinguished collaborators, Professor N. S. Timasheff, testifies that he, like other collaborators, did not know at all for what purposes I asked him to compile quantitative measurements of all the important internal upheavals in the history of Greece, Rome, Byzantium and the principal European countries (some 1,613 disturbances) and all the changes in regard to crime and severity of punishment in the main criminal codes of Europe, beginning with the Barbaric codes and ending with the latest Soviet, Fascist, and Nazi criminal codes.

Here I take the opportunity to express my deep indebtedness

to all the distinguished collaborators of the *Dynamics*: they fulfilled their tasks faithfully and competently. Without their enormous spade-work the empirical part of the *Dynamics* would have been much thinner, more casual, and less complete than the form in which it was published.

Beginning with the second semester of my first year at Harvard and for the next five years I devoted almost all my free time to this work. In this long labor there were, of course, many dark moments of feeling it a failure, of finding myself in a blind alley, of doubt as to the importance of the study and the advisability of its continuation. Sometimes these dark moments deteriorated into depression, irritability, and complete dissatisfaction with myself and my inability to do the work as it should be done. Fortunately, these dark periods were amply compensated by the moments of creative insight and fulfillment. These rare moments easily dispersed the "nights of the searching soul" and both together deepened and enriched the plenitude of my life-experience. After all, a touch of the tragic is quite necessary to protect our lives from clever but meaningless philistinism. The years spent over the *Dynamics* were spent well.

The Story of the Department

The academic year of 1931-32 was marked by the opening of the Department of Sociology. Though only the upper ranks of the undergraduates and highly selected and promising graduate students were permitted to concentrate in the department, their number in the first year of the department's functioning greatly exceeded our best expectations. Due to this careful selection, the percentage of students who graduated from the department with the *summa, magna,* and *cum laude* honors during the first years of the department's life, was exceptionally high. One of the results of this situation was that other departments began to protest against the department's privilege of taking only "the cream" of the students and leaving the less capable students to them. Since the protests were in a sense justified, especially from the standpoint of an "equalitarian democracy," this privilege was eventually abolished, and in subsequent years the department had to admit, as its majors, not only the upper but also the lower ranks of undergraduate students. In regard to graduate students, the severest selection continued to be practiced, at least to the end of my chairmanship in 1942. This selection, together with an influx of capable graduates from various universities attracted by Harvard's fame and, in a small degree by my own reputation (as the letters of several bright students testify), were responsible for an exceptionally high number of the younger leaders of American sociology who emerged from the Harvard Department of Sociology during the years of my chairmanship. And this occurred despite the fact that the staff of full-time members of the department was one of the smallest in the country: one full professor of sociology, myself (besides R. Cabot who continued his teaching in the field of social ethics and not in sociology), two associate professors, two faculty instructors, and some four to six teaching fellows.

When, in January, 1962, Charles and Zona Loomis' *Modern Social Theories* was published, in my letter to the authors I observed that practically all the sociologists whose theories are examined in the volume (Kingsley Davis, G. C. Homans, R. K. Merton, T. Parsons, R. Williams, and including Professor Loomis himself and W. E. Moore, the editor of the Van Nostrand series in sociology) were graduate students or an instructor (T. Parsons), or an associate (G. Homans), or a visiting lecturer (H. Becker) in the department during my chairmanship. To these names of the leading American sociologists I can add several others, such as professors C. A. Anderson, R. F. Bales, B. Barber, W. Bash, R. Bauer, C. Q. Berger, R. Bierstedt, G. Blackwell, R. Chamblis, A. Davis, N. Demerath, N. DeNood, J. Donovan, R. DuWors, J. B. Ford, R. Hanson, D. Hatch, H. Hitt, L. Haak, J. Fichter, W. Firey, H. Johnston, F. Klockhohn, J. B. Knox, M. Levy, V. Parenton, A. Pierce, B. Reed, J. and M. Riley, E. Schuler, T. Lynn Smith, C. Tilly,

E. A. Tiryakian, N. Whetten, Logan Wilson, and others who did their graduate work in the department during my chairmanship. If I did not contribute much to their growth except perhaps by furnishing a few seminal ideas, at least I did not hinder the development of their creative potentials. As founder and chairman of the departments of sociology at the universities of Leningrad and Harvard, I never pressed students to accept my personal theories uncritically but, rather, repeatedly advised them to follow the path of independent investigation and formulation of their own views regardless of their agreement or disagreement with my or any other conceptual schemes, methods, and conclusions. This attitude and policy have been fully justified by the subsequent development of these students, research-associates, and instructors into notable leaders of today's American sociology, psychosocial sciences, education, and other cultural activities.

The small size of the teaching staff of the department and the limited number of courses this staff was able to give in the first year prompted me to remedy this shortcoming by inviting several distinguished Harvard scholars to organize and to offer in the department some special lectures in the fields in which these scholars were eminent authorities. In this way, during the second and subsequent years of the activities of the department, its offerings were notably increased by courses and seminars on the Family, Rural Sociology, and Social Change given by C. C. Zimmerman after he was appointed an associate professor of sociology at Harvard; by the course on Sociology of Religion organized by Professor A. D. Nock and given for the department by several Harvard scholars of religion; by the course on Animal Sociology organized for the department by Professor W. M. Wheeler and given by several specialists in social life of different species; by the course in Sociology of Law given subsequently by Professor N. S. Timasheff, Dean Roscoe Pound, Dr. H. Kelsen, and Dr. G. D. Gurvitch; by the course in Criminology offered by Professor S. Glueck; by the course on Social Psychology offered by Professor G. Allport; and by a few other courses added in subsequent years. These regularly offered courses and seminars were subsequently increased by the offerings of the distinguished visiting professors invited for a semester or academic year or the summer session. During the years of my chairmanship we had as visiting professors such eminent scholars as Clarence Case, C. A. Ellwood, R. Park, E. Burgess, W. I. Thomas, F. S. Chapin, A. Kroeber, and H. Becker from American universities; Hans Kelsen, L. von Wiese, and R. Thurnwald from Austrian and German universities; and G. D. Gurvitch from the Sorbonne. These courses and seminars given by international leaders in their fields greatly enriched the offerings of the department and brought to them the superlative quality free from the defects of "too little" and "too much." Guided and trained by the full-time instructors and by these eminent scholars, the undergraduate majors as well as the graduate students could successfully pursue their training and research in sociology to the maximum of their abilities and inquiring minds.

In summary, within the first three years of the existence of the department, Harvard University was placed solidly on the world map of sociology and became about as important a center for that field as any other university.

The organization of the department having been accomplished and its satisfactory functioning secured, in the fourth year of my chairmanship I asked the administration to release me from the position and duties of chairman. I have never liked routine administrative work, nor do I particularly care about any administrative position. When my chairmanship was necessary for the establishment of a new department, whether at the University of Leningrad or at Harvard, I accepted it in the line of my duty to sociology and tried to discharge this duty as well as I could under the existing circumstances. But as soon as this task was accomplished, I was anxious to regain my freedom from boring administrative duties, in favor of the much more interesting and fruitful work of a scholar. Unfortunately my first request was denied by the administration. President Lowell simply told me that there was, as yet, no other scholar who could replace me in this position and that for a few more years I had to continue in the chairmanship of the department.

Some four or five years later I asked again to be relieved from this position and was again refused. Finally in 1942, for the third time, I went to President Conant with this request, but this time I took with me a copy of the recent faculty vote on this matter. According to this mandatory vote, chairmen in all departments of Harvard should be appointed only for three years—in exceptional circumstances, for five years—and under no conditions for a longer period. Showing a copy of the resolution to President Conant I said that I had already carried on the duties of chairman for more than twelve years and that morally and legally I was entitled to be freed from these duties—the more so since, while I was anxious to be rid of the chairmanship, some other members of the department were very eager to attain this position. To my great satisfaction, this time my request had to be, and was, granted. This ended my responsibility for the department and its future development. *Nunc dimittis. Feci quod potui, faciant meliora potentes*, I said to myself lightheartedly after the release from these duties.

So I am not responsible for whatever has happened to the department since, either for its merging with abnormal and social psychology and cultural anthropology to form a "Department of Social Relations," or for the drowning of sociology in an eclectic mass of the odds and ends of these disciplines, or for any other change that has occurred in this department since 1942. The Department of Social Relations has certainly expanded in its staff, budget, research funds, and self-advertising. But it has hardly produced as many distinguished sociologists as the Department of Sociology did during the twelve years from 1931 to 1942 under my chairmanship. I give anyone complete liberty to dismiss these remarks as the "biased grumblings of an old man." However, if such "interpreters" will check my grumbling observations they will probably find them fairly accurate.

CHAPTER FOURTEEN

Subsequent Years at Harvard

Two Great Events in Our Family Life

On the mantelpiece of my study at home are pictures of our sons and of our dearest friends. I would like to introduce them to my readers.

In our second and third years at Harvard our married life was blessed by the births of two sons: Peter in 1931 and Sergei in 1933. These happy events completed the fullness of our life. Their rearing and education imposed new burdens and anxieties upon us, especially upon their mother, but these were completely drowned in the ocean of pure joy the boys gave to us. Their nursing and continual care forced my wife temporarily to abandon her scientific work, which she gladly did without regret or hesitation.

Shaping our sons' physical, mental, moral, and creative personalities appeared to us as our paramount task at that period of our life. Although we gave them freedom to unfold their creative potentialities, at the same time we did not hesitate to discipline them for any mischief which they, as all children, happened to get into once in a while. In this sort of atmosphere they have grown as flowers—naturally, without particular crises or shocks. We asked our dear friends, Dr. and Mrs. Serge Koussevitzky and Professor and Mrs. Michael I. Rostovtzeff, to be their godparents. They gladly accepted. The name Peter for our older son was given in honor of my wife's father. When it came time to name our younger son, we, the Koussevitzkys, and the Rostovtzeffs decided that he should be named either Sergei or Michael in honor of one of his godfathers. Koussevitzky and Rostovtzeff drew straws and Koussevitzky won. Hence the name Sergei for our younger son.

(The dedication of my *Dynamics* reads: "To Peter and Sergei and their Godfathers and Godmothers: Serge A. and Natalia K. Koussevitzky, Michael I. and Sophia M. Rostovtzeff.")

Subsequently my sons had their training in Winchester public schools and their college educations at Harvard University. Both were graduated from these schools and Harvard with high honors, both did their graduate work at Harvard: Peter in the department of applied physics, Sergei at Harvard Medical School. Both received their doctor's degrees: Peter from the Department of Applied Physics at Harvard and Sergei from Harvard Medical School. Both selected scientific and academic careers: Peter as a research physicist with IBM and Sergei as instructor and research associate at Harvard Medical School. Both have already published a number of studies of some importance and both are doing their scientific work satisfactorily. I would not be surprised at their eventually becoming noted scientists in their special fields. Like most parents, my wife and I both are proud of our sons. A detail—when someone asks to talk to "Dr. Sorokin" on the telephone at our house we have to ask to which of the four Dr. Sorokins he or she wants to talk. Some of our friends say the Sorokin family is a miniature university, with its own mathematician-physicist, biologist-botanist, medical biologist, and—that interloper—a sociologist-psychologist-philosopher.

When our sons grew up and moved away, Mrs. Sorokin resumed her scientific work and is continuing it up to this time. Thus, among many blessings in my life, I have also been granted the grace of having two sons.

We Settle in Winchester

Among several changes in our life which Peter's birth occasioned, was our move from Cambridge to Winchester. I have never liked big cities and for this reason did not particularly enjoy Cambridge, which had grown to the size of a fairly big city. The birth of our first son made it advisable for us to buy our own house. During our walks in the Middlesex reservation we had visited Winchester and were favorably impressed by this residential town. Later we found there a house built for himself by an architect whose father was in the lumber business. Though the house was somewhat run-down, it was built very well and—more important—it was adjacent to the vast Middlesex reservation—some 40,000 acres of beautiful woods and lakes in which one could walk for hours undisturbed by automobiles or crowds. Only one short street led to the house and ended there.

These circumstances prompted us to buy the house and to move into it in February, 1932. We remodeled it and have lived there for the last thirty years. The hills and the cliffs around the house inspired me to develop by my own labors an azalea-rhododendron-lilac-rose-wisteria garden. To my surprise, it brought me a gold medal from the Massachusetts Horticultural Society and has been featured in full-page color photographs in the national magazines *Horticulture, House and Garden,* and others.

Working in the garden gave me all the exercise I needed, made unnecessary any psychiatrist for keeping the peace and integrity of my mind, and provided hours during which some fresh ideas have been born in my mind. So I strongly recommend that everybody develop his own garden and work in it as much as possible.

Good Friends and Worthy Opponents

Besides the pictures of my sons, on the mantel are pictures of my great teachers Leo Petrajitzky, M. Kovalevsky and E. de Roberty (whom I have mentioned before), and portraits of our dearest friends the Koussevitzkys and the Rostovtzeffs. Since our coming to Harvard until the death of both Koussevitzkys and both Rostovtzeffs, they were our closest and dearest friends. With Serge and Natalia Koussevitzky we met quite frequently, either at their or our house, and spent many a happy hour in convivial talks over a breakfast or dinner table. They used to invite us to the opening performances of new symphonies or concerts, and the maestro used my impressions as a touchstone of intelligent public reaction to each new piece of music.

From the time of our meeting in Minneapolis a deep sense of mutual congeniality had somehow sprung up between us and the Koussevitzkys and grew progressively until the passing away of our dearest friends. Both of them were remarkable persons. Serge was not only a great virtuoso of the double bass and one of the greatest conductors of a great orchestra but one of the finest men of culture at its noblest and best. Coming from a Jewish stratum of the Russian population, in his brilliant career he passed through the fiery ordeal of the most diverse experiences with all their pains and joys. His genius and these experiences enormously expanded his mental perspectives, enriched his emotional élan, steeled his will, and made of him not only a great musician but one of the remarkable men of our time. Better than most politicians, he grasped intuitively the political situations of the present age and the tragedy of today's humanity. Blessed with the grace of creativity, he enthusiastically welcomed and fostered it in all its forms, regardless of creed, race, political party, and other discriminating conditions.

In her own way Natalia Koussevitzky was also a distinguished person. A talented sculptor and one of the richest ladies of pre-revolutionary Russia, she had financed Koussevitzky's own orchestra—one of the very best in Russia. In my student days, whenever this orchestra visited St. Petersburg, I used to buy a cheap ticket for its renowned concerts. We spent many, many joyful days in the distinguished company of Serge and Natalia. We still have several photographs of our dear friends holding their godsons or taken in company with ourselves.

My wife and I visited the great maestro in the hospital when he became ill with leukemia. Together with Olga Koussevitzky, Serge's second wife whom he married after the death of his first wife, we witnessed the separation of the maestro's immortal soul from his body. His death created a vacuum in our life. Once a year or so, we visit the grave of our dear friends at Lenox, not far from the Tanglewood Music Center created by the maestro. We still enjoy the friendship of Olga Koussevitzky. Among other things, the maestro entrusted her with the supervision of the Koussevitzky Foundation and other funds for the financial support of talented young composers. Olga has been discharging this task faithfully and wisely. To this purpose she has dedicated her whole life.

Through Koussevitzky I met many eminent composers and musicians of our time. Association with them contributed to knowledge of contemporary music and its leading musicians. I am forced by our hurried world to limit my recollections of, and gratitude to, our dearest friends to these few lines.

I can also devote only a few lines of this fast-moving autobiography to the Rostovtzeffs. I have already mentioned that as a student, I attended some of the lectures of this great historian at the University of St. Petersburg. Then, in the years of World War I and at the beginning of the Russian Revolution, I met Professor and Mrs. Rostovtzeff personally in various political, scientific, and charitable organizations. I have mentioned also that soon after my arrival in this country I found them at the University of Wisconsin where they helped me with their advice and guidance. Subsequently they moved to Yale University, and a few years later we moved to Harvard. After settling in Cambridge, we visited them in New Haven and they visited us in Cambridge and Winchester.

It is impossible to describe in a few lines the deep affectionate ties, and the variety of common scientific, cultural, and political interests that vivified and intensified our friendship. It suffices to say that the hours spent with the Rostovtzeffs were always most happy, instructive, and enlightening hours for us. Both of them were intellectually, morally, and culturally the embodiment of the noblest and best of today's civilization. Their mental horizons were wide, their knowledge of the human universe and its history inexhaustible and deep, their value-system irreproachable, and their judgments about past and present events were almost always sound. Their warm and affectionate personalities, free from the empty artificialities of "civilization," their kindness and hospitality enormously increased the fascination and greatness of these two people. Their friendship has been indeed a real blessing for us.

Besides the Koussevitzkys and the Rostovtzeffs we enjoyed friendly relationships with many Harvard scholars such as Taussig, Carver, Gay, Black, Hansen, Whitehead, Schumpeter, Leontiev, Elisseieff, Nock, Allport, Whatmough, Hocking, and Sarton; and with several eminent scientists, among them Birkhoff, Huntington, Shapley, Wheeler, Henderson, Terzaghi, and others. Around a dinner table or at a cocktail party or at regular meetings of the "Now and Then Discussion Club," or at special conferences for discussion of divers important problems, we informally exchanged our views on various matters and our feelings of mutual sympathy and interest in each other's creative activities. At these informal meetings I learned many things which otherwise would have remained unlearned, especially in the branches of science quite remote from sociology and its related disciplines.

Eventually, side by side with these friendships arose opposition to my theories and to myself as a person belonging to a different clique from the opposing "cliques." At Harvard, as at any other institution, the professors, students, and members of the administration belonged to different ideological, political, philosophical, religious, artistic, ethical, and social "denominations." Each such "denomination," organized into its own club, association, or clique, tends naturally to acclaim all those who profess its credo and to criticize those who hold different, and especially opposite, views. If such signs of approval and disapproval are limited to a purely intellectual support of the congenial views and criticism of the opposite ideas, beliefs, and values, everyone profits from such an agreement or clash. I was not surprised by the opposition to my theories. As a sociologist-psychologist I realized only too well that many of my theories deviated greatly from and largely opposed many ideologies of certain Harvard professors and students. Politically, being in Henry Adams' definition "a conservative Christian anarchist," I did not join any of the existing parties (including the party of political anarchists) and was highly critical of the Republican as well as the Democratic, Communist, and Socialist parties and politicians. Among the students majoring in the Department of Sociology, Franklin D. Roosevelt, Jr. and John Roosevelt heard many of my criticisms of their father's policies, not to mention those of other political leaders. Although a religious man in my own way, I did not join any institutionalized religion. Neither did I share the enthusiasm of various sports-fans and devotees of passing social fads and fashions. In all these and other respects I was rather an independent nonconformist with my own theories, beliefs, standards, and values which I regard as truer, more universal, and more perennial than the transitory, local, and largely obsolescent values and ideologies of many of my colleagues and students.

Since I had been able to express my views with some clarity and success, it was only natural that opposition to them would emerge on the part of those whose philosophies were threatened by mine. As long as the clash of the *Weltanschauungen* was kept on a purely ideological level, without involving personal antagonisms—as fortunately it was—I heartily welcomed and enjoyed it. As a rule all nonconformist and pioneering ideas have always evoked some resistance and criticism, and since some of my theories have been assessed by several eminent scholars as being both nonconformist and pioneering, mild or violent opposition to them was to be expected. It has not disturbed me much. If the criticisms are stupid, they reinforce the soundness of my views. If they demonstrate my errors, they convince me to discard them. In both cases I have profited from the criticism and have seldom resented it.

The Completion of the Dynamics

And so for many Harvard years my life flowed along without violent storms and crises. Besides discharging my duties of professor and chairman, remaining happy in my family circle, enjoying my friendships and good relationships with my colleagues, students, and acquaintances, following as an observer the great historical events of our time, refreshing myself by gardening, music, fishing, boating, and struggling with "the jungle" around our summer place on Memphremagog Lake in Quebec, in most of my free time I continued to work on the *Dynamics*.

I usually did my work in the early morning hours before going to the University and in the evening hours, if the evening was free from various engagements and chores. Working steadily, I typed a first draft of each chapter and, after many corrections, retyped it two or three times until I was more or less satisfied with it. When a chapter reached this stage, with its tables checked and its diagrams drawn satisfactorily for printing purposes, the complete manuscript of each chapter was added to those of other chapters to be given eventually to a professional typist who would prepare the final version for the printer. Toward the end of 1935, the total manuscript with its tables and diagrams grew to the bulky extent of filling several cartons in my study. Glancing at these boxes now and then, I anxiously wondered whether I would find a publisher for this mass of "scrap-paper" which promised no particular profit and no large sales. "Who nowadays—when most people read only newspapers and popular magazines—would be interested in buying and reading several volumes of fairly dry stuff"? I thought. From time to time this anxiety somewhat troubled me but it did not impede my labors over the *Dynamics* because at the back of my mind persisted a firm belief that somehow the work would be published. This belief proved to be correct. Even before the manuscript of all four volumes of the *Dynamics* was finished, a representative of the American Book Company came to my house and offered me a contract for my work which his firm wanted to publish not so much for the sake of profit as for "prestige." In this way, without any effort on my part, the publisher appeared, the contract was signed, and the matter of publication was solved.

The more my work on the *Dynamics* progressed, the more

vigorously I redoubled my efforts to push it ahead as fast as I could and the more impatient I became to finish it as soon as possible. Finally, at the beginning of 1936, the manuscript of the first three volumes was completed. As these volumes represented a unity of their own partially independent from the fourth volume, the publisher and I decided to publish them without awaiting the completion of the last volume. In 1937 the first three volumes were published. Their publication temporarily relieved me from the heavy burden of labor, worry, depression, and irritation involved in their preparation. "I did my best to make them as good as possible. Now it is up to them either to die unnoticed or to grow up and have a vigorous life in the human universe," was my reaction to their publication.

Fortunately for me, their appearance was noticed, and noticed well, in practically all countries. Front-page articles and editorials in hundreds of papers and magazines of various countries, learned papers in scientific journals, special pamphlets devoted to them, an avalanche of letters to me from various readers, and other forms of voluminous public reaction marked their publication. Some of these reactions extolled the *Dynamics* as "the greatest work in sociology of the twentieth century"; others damned it as a total failure. This praise and damnation had one common feature, however: both were voluminous and emotionally charged. Whatever the vices and virtues of the *Dynamics,* it seems to have had something that strongly "hit" its proponents as well as its opponents. This "something" was enough to make me satisfied with it. I was content with the reception the work received. Like that of my previous works, it was similar to the reception given an overwhelming majority of the great works in the history of social thought. They also were enthusiastically praised as well as disdainfully condemned. If the *Dynamics* could not resemble them in their greatness, I was satisfied by its resemblance to the classical works in their minor characteristics. Among other things, this vast publicity was probably responsible for its fairly good sales. They were notably larger than we had expected.

As a relaxation from the strenuous labor over these volumes, I accepted an invitation from the University of California at Los Angeles for the summer session of 1937. We all were anxious to see the Western part of this country—its magnificent mountains, national parks, deserts, and canyons. So we shipped our car to Salt Lake City, traveled by train to this point, and from there, without hurry, we drove through the desert and stayed several days at the Grand Canyon, Bryce Canyon, and Zion Park, fully enjoying the marvelous scenery and our carefree nomadic life. In California, with the help of our good friend, Professor C. Panunzio, we rented a comfortable house at the Pacific Palisades, with a beautiful view of the ocean. From there I commuted five times a week to the university for my lectures and seminars, and for meetings with dignitaries of Los Angeles. Preceded by the extensive publicity which had heralded the *Dynamics*, I was treated as a sort of celebrity both in academic and other elite circles in the great city. The whole summer session was most pleasant, fruitful, and rejuvenating. When it was over we drove to San Francisco, visited the redwood forests and Yosemite Park. Then crossing the desert, we left our car at Salt Lake City from where it was shipped to Winchester. We took the train home. The whole trip was extremely refreshing for all of us.

A week or so after our return, I had to go to Paris to preside over the International Congress of Sociology there. As a vice president of the International Institute of Sociology I had attended the preceding Congress at Brussels in 1935; and now, as president, I went to Paris a couple of weeks before the Congress in order to brush up my rusty French so as to be able to regulate its proceedings. During these weeks I visited the important museums and historical points of Paris and met a number of eminent scholars and leaders in various fields. After the Congress ended, I returned to America through Germany. I stayed in Berlin for a few days, observed the Nazi regime in its prewar state, met several anti-Nazi German scholars, and returned to the United States on the German ship S. S. *Europa*. The trip was instructive and fruitful in many ways. Among other things, I observed many signs of the decadent, sensate culture of Europe. My trip confirmed the correctness of the *Dynamics*' diagnosis of a declining state of this culture. Impoverishment and exhaustion of its creative forces stared at me from many corners of this sensate civilization.

The California and European trips greatly reinvigorated me and dispelled my fatigue of labor over the *Dynamics*. Before starting work on the fourth volume, I decided to complete, in cooperation with Clarence Q. Berger (now vice president of Brandeis University) our research on how, in what kind of activities, and with what motives some one hundred white-collar unemployed spent each twenty-four hours of their time. The highly capable and vigorous help of Mr. Berger allowed us to complete this study within one year. In 1939 our monograph was published by Harvard University Press under the title *Time-Budgets of Human Behavior*. A volume of some importance for psychosocial scholars, for the public at large it probably was the most boring of all my boring works. In spite of this it received considerable publicity from papers and magazines. Of the popular articles about it, I still remember a long article in a Sunday edition of a Boston paper entitled "Nine Minutes for Necking." The columnist reported briefly how many minutes in each twenty-four hours the persons studied spent in various activities and then centered his article around our finding of an average of nine minutes spent in "necking and spooning activities." The columnist's introductory lines caught my attention. They ran something like this: "Professor Sorokin, who has an enviable reputation of having the best wine cellar among the Harvard faculty, . . ." I was quite flattered by this compliment, though it greatly exaggerated the virtues of my wine supply.

After completing this monograph, I resumed work on the fourth volume of *Dynamics*. I finished it in 1940, and in 1941 it was published. Its publication completed the big project vaguely conceived in 1929 in Minnesota. I was again free from a long servitude. I could again loaf to my heart's content and could freely plan my new works.

Some twenty-five years have now elapsed since the publication of the *Dynamics.* In our fast-living civilization few works survive such a period. Most texts and treatises in the psychosocial sciences die within a few months or years after their publication. Even most of the fictional and nonfictional bestsellers sink into oblivion in an average period of six months to one or two years. To my deep satisfaction, the *Dynamics,* in its various editions and translations, still lives a vigorous life, perhaps even more vigorous than during the first years of its existence.

Invited in 1941 to give Lowell lectures on *The Twilight of Sensate Culture,* I had to prepare these lectures in the form of a condensed and simplified version of the *Dynamics'* main theories. In 1941 these lectures (which according to the testimony of A. Lawrence Lowell, the trustee of the Lowell Institute, and W. H. Lawrence, its curator, attracted the biggest audience which progressively increased from lecture to lecture) were published under the title *The Crisis of Our Age.* Since its publication the book has had many reprints of its American editions; besides the English and New Zealand editions, it has been published in Portuguese, German, Dutch, Czech, Norwegian, Finnish, Spanish, and Japanese translations. A few additional translations of it are under way. In the form of this book the essentials of the *Dynamics'* theories have thus been widely diffused and have become known throughout the world. *The Crisis of Our Age* is still reissued, read, and discussed in American and foreign editions.

In 1956, when the *Dynamics'* four-volume edition was temporarily out of print, I was invited to prepare an abridged edition, which I did. In 1957 the American edition of this abridged one-volume version was published. In 1962 the two-volume abridged edition appeared in Spanish translation. Also in 1962 the set of all four volumes of this work was beautifully reissued in the United States. Spanish and Italian editions of these volumes are scheduled to be published in 1963-64.

Since its original publication up to the present time, a vast literature, both scientific and popular, has been published about the *Dynamics,* including hundreds of substantial scientific articles, thousands of popular write-ups, dozens of Ph.D. theses, and even eight substantial volumes by American, English, Belgian, Norwegian, and Chinese scholars. Furthermore, almost all competent recent texts in history of social theories, in theory of culture, in philosophy of history and social philosophy, in general sociology, and a number of texts and treatises in fine arts, psychology, political science, and philosophy have assigned a special chapter to the theories of the *Dynamics.* Series of lectures and seminars devoted to its study have taken place in many countries.

In brief, the work seems to have rooted itself quite deeply in the field of the psychosocial sciences, in contemporary culture and thinking. And what perhaps is still more important, its significance has not faded over the course of time; if anything, it has been growing and is growing. Among other "dividends" it brought me several honors such as membership in the Belgian and Roumanian Royal Academies of Arts and Sciences, the presidency of the International Institute and Congress of Sociology, of the International Society (and Congress) for Comparative Study of Civilizations, of the American Sociological Association, honorary membership in several American and foreign scientific societies, an honorary doctor's degree at the Mexican National University, and others. All in all I do not have any ground for complaint that this work has been neglected by the world: if anything, the world has paid far greater attention to it than I had expected.

Subsequent Activities and Publications

Since by my humorous definition a professor is a "mechanism processing air-waves and paper," I continued faithfully to discharge these professorial duties after the *Dynamics'* publication. The topics of my subsequent volumes were partly due to the catastrophe of World War II and other calamities which befell mankind in the 1940's, partly to my aspiration to round out my integral system of philosophy, sociology, and psychology—my integral *Weltanschauung* and system of values. Animated by these interests, I prepared and published in this period my volumes: *Man and Society in Calamity* (1942); *Sociocultural Causality, Space, Time* (1943); *Russia and the United States* (1944); *Society, Culture and Personality; Their Structure and Dynamics: A System of General Sociology* (1947); *S.O.S. The Meaning of Our Crisis* (1951), not to mention many papers published in scientific journals of various countries.

The explosion of World War II and of other catastrophes did not surprise me. Since the end of the 1920's in my lectures, then in my *Sociology of Revolution, Social Mobility,* and especially in the *Dynamics* I had predicted them in great detail and had repeatedly warned the foolishly gaudy, optimistic, and decadent sensate society of the West about the imminent wars, bloody revolutions, destruction, misery, and "liberation" in man of "the worst of the beasts." My diagnosis and warnings at that time were naturally only those of "a lonely voice crying in the wilderness." Many of my colleagues, students, and critics called these predictions "loony," "crazy," and "completely wrong." When World War II exploded, some of these critics apologized to me, "By gosh, how right you were!"

Despite the accuracy of my predictions these catastrophes depressed me greatly and deepened my "sense of the tragic in human life" which had already been implanted by my previous experiences. Giving some time and effort to an alleviation of the sufferings and of "the abomination of desolation" wrought by the War, I intentionally continued my research and writing as the best antidotes against my depressive moods. The war and other catastrophes prompted me to study the uniform effects of wars, famines, great epidemics, and bloody revolutions upon the mentality and behavior of the people involved, upon their economic, political, and family institutions, upon their social mobility, their moral, religious, and artistic life, and upon their creativity. The results of this study were published in my volume *Man and Society in Calamity*. By formulating the uniformities in all these fields, and among these "the law of religious and moral polarization," and "the uniformity of expansion of governmental regimentation in times of calamitous emergencies," I wanted to inform and to warn my fellow men what sort of changes in their own lives and in the life of their society they had to expect amidst the avalanche of catastrophes fallen upon the humanity in this century.

Unfortunately only a few of the rank and file heeded these warnings. The majority, led by ignorant politicians and the selfish "power-elite," have hardly paid any attention to them. They still carry on their hopelessly stupid policies; instead of decreasing the catastrophes they have increased them. Despite many millions of human lives lost in vain in the World Wars and in other wars and revolutions, famines, and epidemics; despite the gigantic waste of the natural resources and national wealth, these blind leaders of blind human sheep have not given the human race either lasting peace or real security or true freedom. Neither have they established a just, harmonious, and noble order in the human universe. Instead they have released the deadly forces of hate, mass murder, insanity, and tyranny, and have brought mankind to the verge of apocalyptic self-destruction.

The World War and its aftermath were also responsible for the writing and publication of my *Russia and the United States*. In this by no means exhaustive book I outlined the comparative similarities and differences between the peoples, social institutions, and cultures of the two nations; concisely traced their friendly relationships throughout the whole history of the existence of the United States; briefly sketched the mutually complimentary character of the two countries and the lack of serious conflict of their vital interests. My practical purpose in writing this book was to urge both countries and their leaders to continue their mutually beneficial cooperation and to warn of the dire consequences of any replacement of this cooperation by the policies of inimical conflict, "cold war" and "hot war." Though the book attracted considerable attention and has been published in British, Japanese, and Portuguese editions, my advice and warning have been largely ignored, especially by the politicians and the "power-elites" of both countries. Animated by their "tribal" interests, scarcely understood by themselves, they started their fatal conflict as soon as the fragile armistice was signed. Since their unholy beginnings, the suicidal policies of both countries, and subsequently of both blocks of nations, have grown in their deadliness, destructiveness, and catastrophic results to the extent now of threatening the very survival of the entire human race. Universal incineration is pending now upon every human being and may explode at any moment.

In all of human history there has hardly been such a deadly critical period for the survival of man, such an epidemic of insanity among the masses and particularly among the power-elites, and such a liberation in man of "the worst of beasts," as we have now. "Man the Killer, Man the Destroyer has become the Death of Man's Body; the Death of Man's Spirit; the Death of Man's Culture; and the Death of Man's Beautiful Dreams. *Agnus Dei qui tollis peccata mundi miserere nobis! Dona nobis pacem!*"

Thus paying tribute to the catastrophes of our time, in my more quiet moods I continued to work over my integral system of sociology and its basic categories. The results of this work were published in the form of the volumes *Sociocultural Causality, Space, Time* and *Society, Culture and Personality: Their Structure and Dynamics, A System of General Sociology.* Neither of these volumes was intended as a text for undergraduate students but were monographs for scholars in these fields. As such, they have tangibly influenced the advanced psychosocial thought of our time and are still performing this function *crescendo* rather than *diminuendo. Society, Culture and Personality* has also been published in Spanish, Portuguese, Japanese, and Hindi translations. The American edition of both works, after being out of print for a few years, was reissued in 1962. They are now possibly reaching a larger circle of the rank and file of sociologists of various countries than they had before.

I was glad to have these works published. Even while I was working on *Society, Culture and Personality* the relentless occurrence of calamities and the highly critical situation of mankind persistently disturbed me and seriously interfered with the book's completion.

The pressure of these crises grew so strong that it prompted me to decide in 1945 that, after the completion of the treatise, I would devote all my free time to the investigation of the means of preventing the imminent annihilation of the human race and of ways out of the deadly crisis. Applied to mankind, the old adage *Primo vivere, deinde philosophare* may explain the reason for my decision.

Motivated by it, I rushed the completion of my work and then began to orient myself in the little-explored field of these problems. This preliminary orientation led me to the establishment of the *Harvard Research Center in Creative Altruism* and to the new phase of my studies described in the next chapter.

PART FIVE

CHAPTER FIFTEEN

The Harvard Research Center in Creative Altruism

Establishment of the Center

This is not the place to explain in detail how and why preliminary investigation led me to concentrate my research on the nature, the ways, and the power of unselfish, creative love. It suffices to say that this concentration was but a logical result of the theories expostulated in my *Dynamics* concerning the nature of the present crisis—its causes, consequences, and the ways to overcome it. Perhaps the following excerpts from my Report on the Studies of the *Harvard Research Center in Creative Altruism,* and from my address at the Eighteenth International Congress of Sociology in 1958, *The Mysterious Energy of Love,* may partly explain my concentration on this problem and its connection with the *Dynamics'* diagnosis and prognosis.

> At the basis of the Center's establishment there were two main assumptions already vindicated by the minimum necessary evidence. The first of these assumptions is that none of the prevalent prescriptions against international and civil wars and other forms of interhuman bloody strife can eliminate or notably decrease these conflicts. By these popular prescriptions I mean, first, elimination of wars and strife by political changes, especially by democratic political transformations. Tomorrow the whole world could become democratic, and yet wars and bloody strife would not be eliminated because democracies happen to be no less belligerent and strife-infected than autocracies. Still less pacification can be expected from autocracies. Neither the United Nations nor the World Government can give a lasting internal and international peace if the establishment of these bodies is not reinforced by notable altruization of persons, groups, institutions, and culture.

The same goes for education in its present form as a panacea against war and bloody strife. Tomorrow all grown-up persons in the world could become Ph.D.'s, and yet this enormous progress in education would not eliminate wars and bloody conflicts. Since the tenth century on up to the present century education has made enormous progress—the number of schools of all kinds, the per cent of literacy, the number of scientific discoveries and inventions have greatly and almost systematically increased—and yet international wars, bloody revolutions, and grave forms of crime have not decreased at all. On the contrary, in the most scientific and most educated twentieth century they have reached an unrivaled height and have made this century the bloodiest among all the preceding twenty-five centuries of Graeco-Roman and European history.

The same goes for religious changes, if by religion is meant a purely ideological belief in God or in the credo of any of the great religions. One of the evidences for that is given by our investigation of 73 Boston converts "brought to Jesus" by two popular evangelical preachers. Of these 73 converts only one changed his overt behavior in an altruistic direction after his conversion. Thirty-seven converts slightly changed their speech reactions; after their conversion they began to repeat more frequently the words, "Our Lord Jesus Christ" and similar utterances, but their overt behavior did not change tangibly. The remaining converts changed neither their actions nor their speech-reactions. If by religious revival and "moral rearmament" are meant this sort of ideological and speech-reactional transformation, it would not bring peace or decrease inter-human strife, because it represents mainly a cheap self-gratification for psychoneurotics and sham-religious persons.

The same goes for Communist, Socialist, or Capitalist economic remedies, for scientific, artistic, legal, or other ways of establishing and maintaining lasting peace in the human universe when these are not backed by increased altruization of persons and groups. In my *Reconstruction of Humanity* (1948) I have given the minimum of evidence to substantiate these statements. This assumption positively signifies that without a notable increase of unselfish, creative love (as ideally formulated in the *Sermon on the Mount*) in overt behavior, in overt interindividual and intergroup relationships, in social institutions and culture, there is no chance for a lasting peace and for interhuman harmony, internal or external. This, then, was our first assumption, already vindicated to a considerable degree by the existing body of inductive evidence.

Our second assumption was that this unselfish, creative love, about which we still know very little, potentially represents a tremendous power—the veritable *mysterium tremendum et fascinosum*—provided we know how to produce it in abundance, how to accumulate it, and how to use it; in other words, if we know how to transform individuals and groups into more altruistic and creative beings who feel, think, and behave as real members of mankind united into one intensely solidary family. Viewed in this light, love appears to be one of the highest energies, which contains in itself enormous creative and therapeutic possibilities.

With these hypotheses the Center started to investigate scientifically this unknown or little known energy. At the start we were quite aware of the gigantic disparity between our limited capacities and meager material resources, on the one hand, and the tremendous difficulty of the problem, on the other. We did not and do not expect to contribute more than the proverbial drop in a bucket. But, since governments, big foundations, and better brains seem to be absorbed mainly in the promotion of wars and in the invention of increasingly destructive means for the extermination of man by man, someone, somehow, and sometime had to engage in the study of the phenomena of unselfish love, no matter how inadequate his capabilities or how low the esteem of his colleagues for his engaging in such a "foolish research project."

In recent decades science has opened several new fields to its exploration and use. The probings into the subatomic world and the harnessing of atomic energy are but two examples of these ventures. Perhaps the latest realm to be explored is the mysterious domain of altruistic love. Though now in its infancy, its scientific study is likely to become a most important area for future research: the topic of unselfish love has already been placed on today's agenda of history and is about to become its main business.

Before the First World War and the later catastrophes of our time science largely shunned this field. The phenomena of altruistic love were thought to belong to religion and ethics rather than to science. They were considered good topics for preaching but not for research and teaching.

The explosion of the gigantic disasters after 1914 and the

imminent danger of a new suicidal war have now radically changed the situation. These calamities have given impetus to the scientific study of unselfish love. They have also led to basic revisions of many theories until now regarded as scientific, and especially those which dealt with the causes and means of prevention of wars, revolutions, and crime.

These excerpts may help to explain why my preliminary orientation in these problems led me to the study of "the mysterious energy of creative, unselfish love" and, eventually, to the establishment of this Harvard Research Center in Creative Altruism.

The Instrumental Role of Eli Lilly

When I began these studies I expected to carry them on entirely by my own efforts, without any research staff or financial assistance, as I did practically all my research and publications at the University of Minnesota and, except for the *Dynamics,* during the Harvard years of my life. For several reasons I was reluctant to apply for a financial grant for my research to any foundation, government, or even university. I seem to belong to the "lone wolf" variety of scholars who, if need be, can do their work alone without a staff of research assistants or funds. On a small scale and with some reservations I can repeat what Albert Einstein said of himself: "I am a horse for a single harness, not cut out for tandem or teamwork; for well I know that in order to attain any definite goal, it is imperative that *one* person should do the thinking and commanding." Of course, if and when some funds or a team of co-workers and assistants had been available, I would have been glad to have such help as I had had in producing the *Dynamics.* Knowing, however, the prevailing policy of large foundations to give financial support mainly—and often exclusively—to large, collective research projects tailored to the vested interests of the contributing foundation, government, or university; and knowing also the kind of people in these institutions who actually decide the matter of financial grants, I was certain that if I applied for financial support of my research on "creative, unselfish love" my application would be voted down and my project assessed as "a totally foolish project." Knowing well the kind of research particularly favored by these institutions, I frequently warned young scholars who planned to apply for financial support of their truly important research projects not to expect favorable reactions on the part of these institutions in regard to their applications: "If Plato's *Republic* had never been written and you were the person who had first written the greater part of it and then applied for a grant for its completion, I am sure your *Republic* project would be refused a grant as a grossly unscientific speculation." In addition, being naturally "bullheaded," I valued my independence and freedom of thought too highly to adapt my studies to the questionable interests of the managers of these institutions.

Furthermore, I had proved to myself and to others that I could produce something significant—and certainly more important than the bulk of studies lavishly supported by these institutions—with almost no financial help or staff of research assistants. It was precisely on the basis of this personal experience, supported by the similar experience of many great creators—scientists, philosophers, scholars, writers, artists, founders of great religions and systems of ethics—whose achievements were unaided by funds or staffs of assistants, that I often reminded my colleagues who were anxious to obtain such help that the correlation between the amount of money spent for a research project and the significance of the results produced is very low, often even negative. This attitude also explains my highly critical position in regard to the prevailing policies of foundations, government agencies, and learned institutions: many millions of dollars granted by them for support of their pet projects, especially in the psychosocial sciences, have been largely wasted. So far they have produced very few significant works in the fields of these related disciplines.

In this frame of mind I decided to embark upon my "foolish project" as soon as *Society, Culture and Personality* was finished. But before its completion, one day in the winter of 1946 I received a letter which, without any solicitation on my part, eventually offered me a considerable sum for assistantship in my "foolish research" and, through the fund, the cooperation of a number of eminent and younger scientists and scholars. The author of this letter wrote me that, on the basis of reading my works, he thought that I was one of the few scholars who could fruitfully study the problems of the moral and mental regeneration of today's confused and largely demoralized humanity and that, on his part, he would be glad to assist such a research financially, beginning with a sum of twenty thousand dollars which he would send to me as soon as I accepted his offer. In his letter he did not use the terms "altruism" or "creative, unselfish love," but the meaning of the problems he wished me to investigate was almost identical with the problems I had already decided to study. The letter was signed "Eli Lilly."

At that time I did not know who Eli Lilly was, and therefore asked my secretary, "Who is this unusual man who, sight unseen, is offering me quite a big sum of money for assistantship in my research"?

"Oh! Eli Lilly is the head of the biggest drug corporation, president of Lilly Endowment, and one of the philanthropists and eminent business leaders of this country."

This information assured me that the surprising offer was real. Made by an eminent person, it required thoughtful consideration from me. Being "super-Scotch" and highly responsible for money not my own, I consulted President of Harvard James Conant and some of my colleagues before answering the offer. They all told me that, of course, I should accept the offer; and President Conant suggested that I advise Mr. Lilly to make his grant of twenty thousand dollars to Harvard University (for tax exemption purposes) and not to me directly. Although formally granted to Harvard, actually this sum would be entirely at my disposal to be used for assistantship in my research. I followed this advice, informed Mr. Lilly that I was gratefully accepting his generous offer, and asked him to turn his grant over formally to Harvard University. A few days later I received Mr. Lilly's check for twenty thousand dollars which I promptly forwarded to the treasurer of Harvard to open a special account for assistantship in my studies.

In this way a substantial fund for support of my "foolish research project" fell into my hands, without any demands for it or annoyances of red tape on my part. There was something "providential" about this help arriving at the very moment when I needed it. Throughout my life I have often experienced this sort of "luck" from unanticipated sources in the moments of my urgent, sometimes even desperate need. In this sense I can repeat Gandhi's remark: "When every hope is gone I find that help arrives somehow, from I know not where."

Having completed my *Society, Culture and Personality,* I began to orient myself in the vast and almost entirely unexplored field of the phenomena of altruistic, creative love. An "inventory" of the existing knowledge in this field showed that this gigantic problem had been largely neglected by modern science. While many a modern sociologist and psychologist viewed the phenomena of hatred, crime, war, and mental disorders as legitimate objects for scientific study, they quite illogically stigmatized as theological preaching or non-scientific speculation any investigation of the phenomena of love, friendship, heroic deeds, and creative genius. This patently unscientific position of many of my colleagues is merely a manifestation of the prevalent concentration on the negative, pathological, and subhuman phenomena typical of the disintegrating phase of our sensate culture.

Ignoring this sensate "idiosyncrasy" I steadily carried on my explorations in this field during 1946 and 1947. The result was my volume *Reconstruction of Humanity,* published in 1948. (It had already appeared in German, Norwegian, Japanese, Spanish, and Hindi translations, and was issued in special English and Indian editions.) In this work I systematically investigated the prevalent methods of preventing war and bloody interhuman strifes; demonstrated the inadequacy of these prescriptions; outlined the main defects of the existing sensate social institutions and of the prevalent type of personality, culture, and values; delineated a comprehensive plan of what and how these should be reconstructed to establish a new, nobler, and better peaceful order in the human universe; and particularly stressed the all-important role of unselfish, creative love in this reconstruction. The book was published in March, 1948.

In April I had a telephone call from Mr. Lilly who had come to Boston. He expressed a desire to meet me personally and invited me to lunch with him. I gladly accepted the invitation because I wanted very much to meet the distinguished benefactor of my studies. So we met. His sincerity, wisdom, common sense, and kindness impressed me most favorably. During the lunch I informed him that from his fund of twenty thousand dollars I had spent some $248 to prepare the *Reconstruction of Humanity* and that, at this rate of spending, his twenty thousand dollars would assist my research for many years. "Can't you put more steam into this business?" was his reaction. I said that I could, but that in that case I would need millions of dollars to gather together the best brains and heroic moral leaders and to put them to full-time work on this paramount contemporary problem. If the governments, foundations, and leaders really understood the critical situation mankind is in they would have undertaken this task long ago. Instead, shortsighted governments and power-elites were feverishly busy preparing for a new world catastrophe by lavishly spending billions of dollars for destructive purposes, wasting natural resources, and callously sacrificing daily the lives of "expendable" human beings. Mr. Lilly said that he could not give me millions but that the Lilly Endowment and he could offer for my pilot studies an additional one hundred thousand dollars for five years—twenty thousand dollars per year. Frankly, I was astounded by the generosity of his offer.

"It is such an enormous amount of money that before giving you any answer I should like to consult the administration of the

University and my colleagues. Give me a couple of days for this consultation. Just now I am simply afraid to shoulder the great responsibility of a fruitful use of this huge grant."

Mr. Lilly well understood my hesitation and agreed to wait for my decision in this matter. President Conant and my friends definitely advised me to accept the generous offer. In addition, President Conant suggested the establishment of a special Harvard Research Center in this field.

"I know that this fund is offered for financial help in your research. But suppose that I resigned and a new president replaced me. He might not know this, and for this reason you might have some trouble in your use of this grant. Therefore, why not establish a special Harvard Research Center? We will appoint you its director with complete control of this fund. Only your signature will count for the treasurer and comptroller of Harvard. You can use it for research assistantship as you find best."

I accepted this suggestion, informed Mr. Lilly about it, soon received his check for a one hundred thousand-dollar grant to Harvard University, transferred it to the treasurer of Harvard, and in February, 1949, the Harvard Research Center in Creative Altruism was formally established, with myself as its director, my time being divided equally between the Center and professorial duties at Harvard.

In this way Eli Lilly and the Lilly Endowment were instrumental in the establishment of the Center and its subsequent research. They never interfered in any way with the activities of the Center except by giving hearty encouragement, and when, some ten years later, the fund was about exhausted, by granting an additional twenty-five thousand dollars for continuation of its work; for publication of the Proceedings of the First International Congress for Comparative Study of Civilizations at Salzburg in 1961, of which I happened to be president; and for a part-time secretarial assistantship in my writing and world-wide correspondence.

During these years, through correspondence and another personal meeting, I learned to know Eli Lilly much better than I had at our first meeting. I learned that he has been a noted leader of American industry; a generous benefactor of religious, scientific, artistic, and other institutions and cultural activities; a recipient of many honorary degrees from learned institutions; president of the Indiana Historical Society; an eminent scholar and author of several important works like *Prehistoric Antiquities of Indiana, Little Church on the Circle, Schliemann in Indianapolis,* and others; organizer of an experimental farm for crossing and breeding a better variety of cattle and agricultural plants; preserver and curator of the old historical buildings in Indiana; and an artist and refined cabinet-maker—to mention only a few of his many-sided activities and talents.

Still more remarkable has been his warm sincerity. Despite his most eminent position and the heavy burden of his important duties, he found time, for instance, to meet me personally at the Indianapolis airport and then, during the two days of my stay at his beautiful mansion in Indianapolis, to give me many hours of his time. His and Mrs. Lilly's hospitality was truly overpowering. I mention this episode because it exemplifies these characteristics of Eli Lilly and Mrs. Lilly; for, after all, there are few, if any, among such outstanding leaders of this country, who would be willing to waste so much of their valuable time and energy, as the Lillys did, just for an ordinary professor helped by their grants in his research. I consider myself fortunate indeed to enjoy the privilege of their friendship, trust, and generosity. In the early afternoon of my life this privilege has been one of the most significant events of my life-experience. If, in so-called capitalist society, there were more "capitalists" like Eli Lilly, there would be no need for the appearance of powerful anti-capitalist movements! These few lines give an idea of the providential role which Eli Lilly, Mrs. Lilly, and also Mr. and Mrs. Josiah Kirby Lilly and Josiah Kirby Lilly III, have played in the establishment of the Research Center and in the development of its studies.

The Work of the Research Center

As to the research of the Center, the following excerpts from my report *Studies of the Harvard Research Center in Creative Altruism,* give an idea of the nature of our investigations.

During the years of the Center's existence our studies have had two phases, or two main topics. Our first step consisted in delineating and formulating a working definition of unselfish, creative love and in finding out what was the state of this problem in contemporary science. These studies were published in a *Symposium* volume, *Explorations in Altruistic Love and Behavior* (1950), and in my volumes, *Reconstruction of Humanity,* and *Altruistic Love* (1950). The *Symposium* attempts to give a delineation of the main aspects, forms, and dimensions of love, and of the place of this problem in contemporary science and philosophy. It opens with my study of a multi-dimensional universe of love in its physical, religious-ontological, biological, ethical, psychological and sociological aspects, subdividing each aspect into two forms: love as *eros* and as *agape.* Concentrating on empirical, psychosocial love, the study reduces observable and partly measurable aspects of empirical love to five "dimensions": the intensity of love, its extensity, its duration, its purity, and its adequacy; and then explores the uniformities in the relationships, covariations, and correlations of these "dimensions" with one another. It also outlines the problems of production, accumulation, and distribution of love-energy.

Subsequent chapters of the *Symposium* deal with a mathematical theory of egoism and altruism (N. Rashevsky); with biological foundations and factors of cooperation, conflict, and creativity (M. Ashley Montagu, Trigant Burrow, Therésè Brosse); with a psychological approach to the study of love and hate (G. W. Allport); with scientific, philosophical, and social foundations for altruism (F. S. C. Northrop, L. Dechesne); with altruism in the psychotherapeutic relationship and interactions in the mental hospital (M. Greenblatt, H. Hichborn, R. W. Hyde); with altruism among college students and nursery-school children (P. Sorokin, D. Cove); parapsychological (extrasensory) perception and friendly relationships (J. B. Rhine, S. D. Kahn); tangible positive relationships, with electroencephalographic aspects of normal, homicidal, and friendly personalities (M. Greenblatt, B. Sittinger);

with the techniques of emotional integration (Swami Akhilananda); and with the problems of labor harmony (G. K. Zipf).

My volume, *Altruistic Love,* is an unpretentious preliminary study of some of the tangible characteristics of all the Christian saints (some 4,600 about whom the necessary data are available), and of some five hundred living American "good neighbors." It is the first "census" of all the Christian saints, their age and sex composition, their marital and family status, their parental families, their occupational, economic, and social positions, their education and school intelligence, their longevity and health, their ways to sainthood, their rural-urban and national distribution, their political ideologies and group-affiliations, and so on. Side by side with this census, the study also investigates the changes in all these characteristics which saints as a group have undergone during the twenty centuries of Christianity.

Of several results of this census, one or two can be mentioned here. First, the extraordinary longevity and vigorous health of the saints is remarkable. In spite of the ascetic mode of living followed by a great number of saints, along with unhygienic conditions and frequent physical self-torture including some 37 per cent of premature deaths of these saints through martyrdom, their average life-span turns out to be far longer than that of their contemporaries and even somewhat longer than the longevity of contemporary Americans or Europeans. Second, the proportion of women saints grows fairly steadily as we pass from the first to the twentieth century. While the proportion of saints from the royalty, the nobility, and, later on, from the bourgeoisie has been steadily decreasing, the proportion of the saints from the lower and poorer classes has been rising during the last few centuries. These changes reflect respective changes in the social organization of the Christian societies: growing equalization of the status of women with that of men, declining importance of royalty and aristocracy, then bourgeoisie and rich strata. Finally, after the seventeenth century, "the production" of saints declines sharply and reaches almost a zero-line at the end of the nineteenth and the beginning of the twentieth century.

Along somewhat similar lines, five hundred living American altruists are studied. All in all the study gives some concrete material about the biological, mental, and social "make-up" of both saintly and secular altruists contrasted with the "make-up" of criminals, aggressively selfish, and subhuman types of individuals.

In this first, orientative phase we have also had to make some studies of the problem of the power of love. Since we assumed that love was power, we had to test this assumption. Our investigations of this problem have been carried along diverse lines and by different methods, beginning with a mere collection of the existing historical and individual facts recording this power, and ending with semi-experimental and experimental testing of the hypothesis on students at Harvard and Radcliffe College, on the patients of the Boston Psychopathic Hospital, and on several groups of mutually antagonistic persons. These studies (published in my volume *The Ways and Power of Love; Types, Factors, and Techniques of Moral Transformation,* 1954) uncovered a sufficient body of evidence to show that unselfish, creative love is power which, when used wisely: (1) can stop aggressive interindividual and intergroup attacks, (2) can transform inimical relationships into amicable ones; we further discovered (3) that love begets love, and hate generates hate, (4) that love can tangibly influence international policy and pacify international conflicts. In addition to these effects, an unselfish and wise (adequate) love manifests itself, (5) as a life-giving force, necessary for physical, mental, and moral health; (6) that altruistic persons live longer than egoistic individuals; (7) that children deprived of love tend to become morally and socially defective; (8) that love is a powerful antidote against criminal, morbid, and suicidal tendencies, against hate, fear, and psychoneuroses; (9) that love performs important cognitive and aesthetic functions; (10) that it is the loftiest and most effective educational force for enlightenment and moral ennoblement of humanity; (11) that it is the heart and soul of freedom and of all the principal moral and religious values; (12) that its minimum is absolutely necessary for the enduring existence of any society, and especially, for a harmonious social order and creative progress; (13) finally, that at the present catastrophic moment of human history an increased "production, accumulation, and circulation of love-energy," or a notable altruization of persons and groups, institutions, and culture—especially an extension of unselfish love of everyone on everyone in mankind—is a necessary condition for the prevention of new wars and for the alleviation of enormously increased interindividual and intergroup strife.

With a notable increase of our knowledge of love, its potentialities can be used to serve mankind in immeasurably greater proportions.

Having thus validated, to a tangible extent, the assumptions of the first phase of our studies, we have passed to the second phase of our research. In this stage we have concentrated on the investigation of the effective techniques and factors of altruistic formation and transformation. We have analyzed and, when possible, tested the efficacy of various methods of altruistic education of human beings and groups experimentally, beginning with the ancient techniques of Yogas, Buddhism, Zen-Buddhism, Sufism, and somatophysic techniques of Orthodox Christianity (the studies of R. Godel, J. H. Masui, A. Migot, P. Masson-Oursel, M. Eliade, G. E. Monod-Herzen, A. Bloom, E. Dermenghem, R. Kita, K. Nagaya, H. Benoit, P. Marinier, published in the *Symposium: Forms and Techniques* of *Altruistic and Spiritual Growth,* 1954); the techniques invented by the founders of great religions and monastic orders—Oriental and Occidental (the techniques of St. Basil the Great, St. Benedict, St. Francis of Assisi, St. Bernard, St. John Climacus, John Cassian, St. François de Sales, Ignatius Loyola, and others, published in my volume *The Ways and Power of Love*); then the techniques of the eminent secular educators, such as Comenius, Pestalozzi, Montessori, Froebel and others; and ending with the techniques known to contemporary education, psychology, psychiatry, sociology, religious, moral, and civic trainings and the techniques used in such contemporary Christian altruistic communities as the Society of Brothers in Paraguay, and as the Mennonite, Hutterite, and Quaker communities in the United States (studies of E. C. H. Arnold, C. Krahn, J. W. Fretz, R. Kleider in the *Symposium: Forms and Techniques* mentioned above, and my studies in *The Ways and Power of Love*).

A careful analysis of the ancient techniques of Yoga, Buddhism, and the monastic orders has been made because of the unexcelled—possibly even unrivaled—ingenuity, subtlety, and efficacy of these techniques. The known and unknown inventors of these techniques perhaps knew more about the effective methods of moral transformation of man than we know at the present time. They certainly have been successful moral educators of humanity.

As indicated, we did not limit our study of these techniques to a mere theoretical analysis, but wherever possible have tried to test them empirically and experimentally. Do these techniques work? Are they effective, and under what social and cultural conditions? The following examples give an idea of this experimental testing. One of the steps in Raja-Yoga techniques is *pranayama,* or training in voluntary control of respiration. It is paralleled by training in voluntary "suspension" of heart activity. It is a well-known fact that the real Yogi can voluntarily "suspend" or reduce his heart and breathing activities to an almost intangible degree for hours, days, and weeks. Eminent specialists, cooperating with the Center, tested in the light of modern science the authenticity, the mechanism, and the therapeutic consequences of voluntary regulation of respiration. Other eminent cardiologists of the Center made objective, instrumental—cardiographic, encephalographic, girographic etc.—investigations on the suspension of heart activity by the Yogi, as well as instrumental recordings of all the important changes in the functions of important organs of the human organism that occur when a person concentrates and deconcentrates his thought; when he experiences hate and love; when the Yogi reaches the state of *samadhi;* and so on (the studies of W. Bischler, F. P. Jones, Therese Brosse, J. S. Bockoven and M. Greenblatt, in the *Symposium*: *Forms and Techniques*).

Further on, to test the efficacy of the "techniques of good deeds" we chose five pairs of students. The partners of each pair hated each other. We set for ourselves the task of changing (within a period of three months) these hateful relationships into amicable ones by the technique of "good deeds." We convinced one partner of each pair to try to exhibit friendly actions (invitations to lunch, to movies, to dances, etc.) toward his disliked partner, and then we observed what changes, if any, the repeated good deeds produced in both partners. To make a long story short, we changed four pairs into friends and one into indifferent partners. A similar experimental transformation from inimical to amicable relationships between the nurses and patients of the Boston Psychopathic Hospital was made by the method of good deeds, and had similar success (studies of J. M. Thompson, R. W. Hyde, H. M. Kandler in the *Symposium*: *Forms and Techniques*). These examples give a notion of our experimental testing of the various techniques studied. Similar analyses and testing of various techniques for reducing group prejudice, of group therapy techniques for altruization of "the hardened prisoners" in the Iowa penitentiary and for making friends among the students of Harvard and Radcliffe, of "the psychodramatic production techniques," have been done for the Center by G. W. Allport, P. Sorokin, J. L. Moreno, W. A. Lunden, B. Davis, A. Miller (their studies are published in the *Symposium*: *Forms and Techniques*). F. S. C. Northrop and M. Engelson investigated the kind of international law and the new Declaration of the Rights of Man and Citizen necessary for the realization of altruistic values in mankind.

All in all some thirty different techniques for the altruistic transformation of persons and groups have been analyzed, and several of these have been experimentally tested.

In trying to unravel the mystery of the how and why of altruistic transformation, we have also made a detailed analysis of the process of altruization in the lives of the great apostles of unselfish love, Buddha, Jesus, St. Francis of Assisi, Gandhi, and many others. Since they succeeded in becoming the living incarnation of love, they evidently had successfully solved the problem. How did they solve it? What techniques, what factors, and what sociocultural conditions were involved? These "case studies" formed a large slice of our research. Here again we have tried to be as empirical, experimental, and scientific as possible. These detailed case studies yielded several results. First of all, there seem to be *three types of altruists*: (*a*) "fortunate" altruists, who since their childhood display a well-integrated set of egos, values, and social affiliations centered around the values of love and supreme "self," and who, like grass, quietly and gracefully grow in their altruistic creativity without any catastrophe or sharp conversion. Albert Schweitzer, John Woolman, Benjamin Franklin, Dr. T. Haas, and many others exemplify this type; (b) "catastrophic" and "late" altruists whose life is sharply divided into two periods—pre-altruistic, preceding their transformation, and altruistic, following the total transformation of their personalities, prepared for by a disintegration of their egos, values, and group affiliations, and precipitated by catastrophic (sickness, death of their beloved, etc.) and other events in their lives. The process of transformation of such persons is ordinarily very difficult and painful, and it lasts from a few months to several years. During this period the respective persons have to perform the difficult operation of a basic rearrangement of their egos, values, and group affiliations. When this operation is completed and well interiorized, a new altruistic personality emerges and develops to the end of its life. Buddha, St. Francis of Assisi, Brother Joseph, Ignatius Loyola, St. Augustine, St. Paul, Simone Weil, and others exemplify this type. (*c*) Finally, the intermediary type is marked by some of the traits of the fortunate and the late-catastrophic types. St. Theodosius, St. Basil the Great, Gandhi, St. Theresa, Sri Ramakrishna, and others, are examples of this type.

Second, these investigations led to confirmation of the *law of polarization* previously formulated in my volume *Man and Society in Calamity* (1941). Contrary to the Freudian claim that calamity and frustration uniformly generate aggression, and contrary to the old claim, reiterated recently by Toynbee, that "we learn by suffering," and that frustration and catastrophes lead uniformly to the moral and spiritual ennoblement of human beings, the law of polarization states that, depending upon the type of personality, frustration and misfortunes are reacted to and overcome on one hand by an increased creative effort (deafness of Beethoven, blindness of Milton, etc.), and by altruistic transformation (St. Francis of Assisi, Ignatius Loyola, etc.—positive polarization), and on the other by suicide, mental disorder, brutalization, increase of selfishness, dumb submissiveness, and cynical sensualism (negative polarization). The same polarization occurs on a mass scale when catastrophes and frustrations fall upon a large collectivity. Some of its members become more aggressive, brutal, sensual (*carpe diem*), mentally and morally disintegrated, while the other part of the collectivity becomes more religious, moral, altruistic, saintly, as shown also by our "catastrophic altruists." This law also explains why the periods of catastrophe are marked by disintegration of the value-system of a given society, on one hand, and, on the other, by a creative reintegration of a new value-system, especially of religious and ethical values. As a rule all great religious and moral systems have emerged and have been ennobled in catastrophic periods of a given society, be it ancient Egypt, China, India, Israel, the Graeco-Roman or the Western nations. A vast body of other empirical evidence well supports the validity of the law of polarization (roughly outlined here and more precisely analyzed in my *The Ways and Power of Love*).

The third result of these studies has been a revision of the prevalent theories of personality-structure and personality-integration. Investigation of the undertaken tasks made the current theories entirely untenable. The first blunder of these theories is found in their merging into the category of the "unconscious" or "subconscious" (E. von Hartmann, P. Janet, S. Freud, and others) of two radically different "energies" of man: the *biologically unconscious* that lies below the level of the conscious state of mind and the *supraconscious* ("genius," "creative élan," the *nous* of the Greeks, the "pneuma" of the Church Fathers, etc.) that lies above the level of any conscious or rational thought or "energy." The "depth psychology" of the prevalent theories is, in fact, quite shallow. It either flattens the mental structure almost exclusively to the level of the unconscious or subconscious id, with a sort of epiphenomenal vague, and ineffective ego and superego (S. Freud), or just depicts it as a "two-story building"—the unconscious (subconscious), and the conscious (rational). Instead of these utterly inadequate theories we have been forced—by logical and factual reasons—to construct a fourfold framework of personality-structure: (1) the biologically unconscious (subconscious); (2) the biologically conscious; (3) the socioculturally conscious; and (4) the supraconscious. The unconscious and the supraconscious mental levels are devoid of any consciousness of ego, while the socioculturally conscious level has as many different egos as there are groups with which the individual is associated (ego of his family, ego of his occupational group, egos of his political party, religious group, nationality, state, economic group, and other organizations in which he holds a membership.) If the groups with which the individual is affiliated are in harmonious relationship with one another and "dictate" to him similar ideas, beliefs, tastes, values, and imperatives of conduct, all the egos and values of the individual will also be in harmony with each other, merging together into one integrated ego and one main system of values. As a result, such an individual will have peace of mind, strong convictions, an unclouded conscience, and a consistent conduct. If the groups of the individual's affiliation are mutually contradictory in their values and in their demands on the individual, his egos and values, representing these groups, will also be at war with one another; the individual will become a house divided against itself, devoid of peace of mind, of consistency of thought and conduct, suffering from incessant inner conflicts, dissatisfied and psychoneurotic. Indeed a large part of neuroses are due to these inner tensions and wars of the egos—the results of unfortunate affiliations of the individual with mutually contradictory groups. This last hypothesis has been tested in various ways by us and by other psychiatrists and is becoming increasingly accepted. This pluralistic theory of the ego as a microcosm reflecting the macrocosm of group affiliations of a person explains why the fortunate altruists, since early childhood placed amidst harmonious and altruistic group-affiliations (beginning with a good family) have a harmonious set of egos, values, and actions, and therefore in their altruistic growth do not need to pass through painful crises accompanying rearrangement of their ego, values, and group-affiliations; and why the persons (catastrophic altruists) who happened to be affiliated with mutually discordant groups and having, therefore, a set of discordant egos, values, and actions are forced to pass through the painful process of their disintegration and reintegration, if they do not commit suicide or become mentally ill or regress to the state of a brutal, passive, or decadently sensual human animal.

Finally, as to the supraconscious in man, we collected and analyzed a considerable body of empirical evidence showing its reality, its creative functioning in men of genius, and some of its characteristics. Though this evidence is still meager, it is just about sufficient to establish the reality of this highest form of man's creative energy. It seems to be the main source (working in cooperation with rational thought) of all the greatest creative achievements in all fields of culture, from science and the fine arts to religion and ethics. It is also a condition necessary for becoming a genius of altruistic love.

Among other tests of this hypothesis of the supraconscious, T. Brosse carried on its experimental-instrumental verification (cardiographic, encephalographic, girographic, etc.). Her pioneer study instrumentally confirmed the tangible effects of the supraconscious upon the activities of heart, lungs, and other organs of some 213 persons experimented upon. (Brosse's study is published in the *Symposium: Forms and Techniques;* the theory of personality-structure and of the supraconscious is published in my *The Ways and Power of Love.*)

All in all the process of a real altruistic transformation for persons who were not altruistic in their early lives (the catastrophic and late altruists), is a very difficult and painful process usually taking a fairly long time and hardly ever occurring suddenly. This explains why almost all momentary religious or moral "conversions" are superficial, and why today's "religious revival," so widely advertized in the United States and elsewhere, is a mere surface-ripple which barely touches the deeper currents of the social life and the moral conditions of nations and of mankind.

A profound comprehension of the nature and workings of unselfish, creative love is impossible without an adequate knowledge of the society, culture, and value-system in which the human beings involved live and act. This explains why, besides investigating the basic problems of altruism, we had also to study the structure and the historical dynamics of sociocultural and value-systems. In addition to the attention given it in my previous works: *Social and Cultural Dynamics; Society, Culture and Personality; Social Mobility; Crisis of Our Age,* I had to return to a study of certain aspects of these problems. The results of these reinvestigations were published in the form of my volumes: *Social Philosophies of An Age of Crisis* (1950); *Fads and Foibles in Modern Sociology and Related Sciences* (1956); *American Sex Revolution* (1956); and *Power and Morality* (1959).

Here is a summary list of the Center's publications with their translations into foreign languages.

P. A. Sorokin, *Reconstruction of Humanity* (1948), German, Norwegian, Japanese, Indian, Spanish, and Hindustani editions (1952, 1953, 1951, 1958, 1959); P. A. Sorokin (editor) *Explorations in Altruistic Love and Behavior: A Symposium* (1950); P. A. Sorokin, *Altruistic Love: A Study of American Good Neighbors and Christian Saints* (1950); P. A. Sorokin, *Social Philosophies of An Age of Crisis; Danilevsky, Spengler, Toynbee, Northrop, Kroeber, Schweitzer, Berdyaev, Schubart, and others* (1950), German, British, Spanish, and Hindi editions (1953, 1954, 1964); P. A. Sorokin, *S.O.S.: The Meaning of Our Crisis* (1951); P. A. Sorokin (editor) *Forms and Techniques of Altruistic and Spiritual Growth: A Symposium* (1954); P. A. Sorokin, *The Ways and Power of Love: Types, Factors, and Techniques of Moral Transformation* (1954); P. Sorokin, *Fads and Foibles in Modern Sociology and Related Sciences* (1956), Spanish, British, French, and Italian editions (1958, 1959, 1963); P. Sorokin, *American Sex Revolution: Manifestations and Consequences* (1956), Japanese, Spanish, Portuguese, and Indian editions (1957, 1958, 1959); abridged, one-volume edition of P. A. Sorokin's *Social and Cultural Dynamics* (1957), Spanish two-volume edition, 1962; *Power and Morality* (1959), Japanese, Indian, and, in part, French editions, 1960, 1962, 1963.

This sketch gives an idea of the studies of the Research Center. Its publications have attracted world-wide attention; have already been published in twenty foreign translations; have produced a considerable literature in the forms of articles, Ph.D. theses, and books about these books; and have engendered the establishment of somewhat similar research centers in various countries and the Research Society in Creative Altruism in this country. The establishment and incorporation of this Society (different from the Center) was originated by the initiative group at a meeting held on October 29, 1955. Invited by me, the group consisted of the following persons: Swami Akhilananda, M. Arnold, Dean E. F. Bowditch, Dean W. Clark, Senator R. E. Flanders, Rev. D. Howlett, Dr. F. L. Kunz, Dr. H. Margenau, Chancellor D. Marsh, Dr. A. H. Maslow, Dr. F. S. C. Northrop, Dr I. I. Sikorsky, Dr. J. H. Shrader, and Dr. R. Ulich. After my introductory statement the group unanimously voted to establish and incorporate the Research Society in Creative Altruism. This was done. After many committee meetings the Society organized the Conference on New Knowledge in Human Values, October 4-5, at the Kresge Auditorium of Massachusetts Institute of Technology. It was attended by several hundred scientists and scholars. The Proceedings of the Conference were published in a symposium volume *New Knowledge in Human Values*, edited by A. H. Maslow (1959). It contains the papers read at the Conference by G. W. Allport, L. von Bertalanffy, J. Bronowski, T. Dobzhansky, E. Fromm, K. Goldstein, R. S. Hartman, G. Kepes, D. Lee, H. Margenau, P. Sorokin, D. T.

Zuzuki, P. T. Tillich, and W. A. Weisskopf. These scholars summarize the existing knowledge in the field of human values.

Despite the brilliant success of the Conference and excellent plans for the development of research and educational activities of the Society, for several reasons—mainly because of lack of necessary funds—it could not realize these plans and, after a few years of quiet existence, died. The prevalent world-wide climate of bloody belligerency and interhuman strife, with their individual and tribal egoisms, turned out to be exceedingly unfavorable for the cultivation of the garden of an unselfish, creative love.

As to the Research Center, in a reduced form it continues to exist. My retirement as Emeritus from Harvard at the end of 1959, and the near-exhaustion of the fund for its research forced me, first to reduce its research to my own studies, which I carry on without any remuneration, and second, to transfer the Research Center from Harvard to the American Academy of Arts and Sciences with which the Center is now affiliated. Since the modest remaining fund of the Center only permits the employment of a part-time secretary (eighty dollars a month) and payment of the Center's mailing expenses, it cannot engage any other scholar in specific research for the Center, even for a semi-nominal remuneration. This explains why its research was greatly curtailed.

For the last two years, I have been able to devote only part of my time to the projected substantial volume *Sociology of Moral Phenomena and Values.* I hope to complete it as my last work in this field before senility or death strikes. The rest of my time I now give to a study of sociological problems only indirectly related to the problems of creative, unselfish love. I have devoted some ten years of my life to the study of the "mysterious energy of love." This study has seemingly added something to the extant knowledge of this energy. If the results are more modest than I might have wished, my excuse can be expressed by an old adage *Feci quod potui faciant meliora potentes.**

* I did what I could, let those more capable do better.

CHAPTER SIXTEEN

Activities of an Emeritus

Freedom Begins With Retirement

The concentration of my activities at the Research Center from 1949 to 1959 did not prevent me from engaging in other activities outside of the Center. From 1949 to 1955 I continued to give one half of my time to courses and seminars at Harvard; once in a while, though rarely, I attended national and international scientific meetings. Of many invitations to lecture received from American and foreign universities and from the governments of India, Indonesia, and West Germany, I accepted only very few. Two of these shall be mentioned here.

In April, 1950, I gave the Cole lectures on "Recent Philosophies of History" at Vanderbilt University on the occasion of its seventy-fifth anniversary. In an enlarged version these lectures were published in 1950 under the title *Social Philosophies of an Age of Crisis.* In 1955 I gave a series of lectures and seminars at the summer session of the University of Oregon. This engagement furnished us with an opportunity to drive across the continent and back and to see the marvelous scenery of the northern part of the United States, Canada, and of the states of Oregon and Washington. My wife, Sergei, and myself (Peter was busy with his Ph.D. thesis and could not join us on this trip)—fully enjoyed the journey across the continent, many local trips to the beautiful spots of these states, fishing in their lakes, not to mention the friendly company of professors, students, and other Oregonians and Washingtonians. The whole trip, as usual, greatly refreshed all of us. Driving home we crossed the northern part of Minnesota where my wife and I used to camp and fish during our Minnesota years. With a sense of disillusionment we observed how heavily commercialized this region had become and how much of its natural beauty had vanished during the twenty-five years since our last visit to these places. My "agricultural and pastoral soul" was so painfully impressed by this "progress of civilization" that we hurriedly crossed the region without any desire to return to it in the future.

During the same period, 1949-55, I continued to observe carefully the unfolding drama of human history, and, in accordance with its changing acts, to make the necessary adjustments in my appraisal of these events. These changes, however, were concerned less with the substance of my already matured, integral philosophy and my interpretation of the basic trends of our time, than with some of their secondary characteristics.

In January of 1955 I reached the age of sixty-six, which is the usual retirement age of Harvard professors. About that time, President Pusey came to my office and kindly inquired what my plans and wishes in this matter were. Did I want to be retired at the age of sixty-six, or did I prefer to continue my professorial duties up to the age of seventy—a privilege granted by Harvard to some of its distinguished professors? I thanked him for offering me this privilege and asked him to retire me from all professorial duties at Harvard at the age of sixty-six, leaving me, however, as director of the Harvard Research Center in Creative Altruism up to the age of seventy. I explained that, after teaching at various universities for more than forty years, I was somewhat tired of routine professorial duties and preferred to be free from their burden in order to devote the remaining part of my active life to a study of the problems which interested me and to the "life, liberty, and the pursuit of happiness" of a free man. All my wishes were approved by the Harvard Corporation, including my desire to remain director of the Research Center.

So at the age of sixty-six I became largely free from the tyranny of prescribed lectures, conferences, and committees, and from the many rules and regulations imposed by universities upon the life and work of their professors. Although in theory I gave half my time to the Center, in fact I had complete liberty to use this time as I pleased. In this arrangement I remained up to December 31, 1959, when, at the age of seventy plus, I became an Emeritus retired from all my duties to Harvard.

My reaction to this event was, on the whole, positive; nevertheless it did have some pensive notes. Retirement reminded me of the fact that the morning and the noon of my life were over and that it was now entering its late afternoon, to end eventually in the darkness of death. Since, however, after the death sentence passed upon me in 1918, the awareness of mortality had become habitual with me, this mood was neither depressive nor debilitating. Like elegiac music in some minor key, it was rather light, sweet, and consoling. After all, the thirty years of my association with the great university had been enjoyable and fruitful; during this period I had served the university and mankind as well as I could, and in turn they had effectively helped me to unfold my modest creativity. Of course, in these thirty years of my work for and in the university there had been painful and disheartening moments, but they were lost in the ocean of joyful experiences.

My retirement by no means marked either the termination or the relaxation of my scientific and cultural activity or any curtailment of my freedom of choice in the lines of my study, recreation, and conduct. On the contrary, in all these respects I was now freer than before. My "brother-body" was still in fairly good shape and my mind was still not notably enfeebled by the infirmities of old age. The retirement from Harvard likewise did not seriously interfere with my activities because, having been a "rolling stone" throughout my life, I have never invested my whole personality in any one institution and can do my work under varying conditions and in different institutional settings. I have observed many a professor for whom retirement really meant the end of scientific and educational activities, the dead end of creative life. In my case, fortunately, this melancholy rule did not apply. I still felt capable of continuing my work as before. As yet the miasma of senility had not taken possession of me, and if death were to come to end my existence, I preferred to die with my boots on—alive and active up to the last moment.

"Relaxed" Activities of an Emeritus: More Publications

In this frame of mind, after my semi-retirement from all routine professorial duties at the age of sixty-six, I steadily continued my scientific, educational, cultural, and recreational activities. The main change consisted in my decision not to undertake any more vast research projects which, like the *Dynamics,* would require many years and sizable funds for their completion. Though physically and mentally I was still in good shape for my chronological age, nevertheless I could not expect that this health would persist for many years and that the inevitable infirmities of old age would not eventually creep into my body and mind.

In accordance with this decision, my studies done in the years of 1956-59 were published in the form of several papers and volumes: *Fads and Foibles in Modern Sociology and Related Sciences* (1956), *American Sex Revolution* (1956), and *Power and Morality* (1959). *Fads and Foibles* offers a serious criticism of some of the fashionable currents of thought and research in recent American sociology, psychology, and psychiatry, such as unwarranted claims for making new discoveries which in fact were discovered long ago; "obtuse jargon and sham-scientific slang"; "sham-operationalism," and "testomania" (the fad of intelligence, projective, and other mechanical tests); "quantophrenia" and "the cult of 'social physics' and 'mental mechanics' "; the pseudo-experimental studies of "the small groups"; and the "obsolescent philosophy and theory of cognition" of these fashionable currents. My criticisms were naturally unpleasant for the partisans of these pseudo-scientific fads. But I could not avoid this unpleasantness if I wanted to fulfill the main duty of a scholar to tell the truth as he sees it, regardless of its pleasant or painful character. With all my vices I have seldom violated this duty, even under danger of being arrested or severely punished for my faithfulness to it. Instead of adjusting my views to the vested interests of any person or group I have steadfastly tried to follow the venerable old motto *Amicus Plato sed veritas amicissima.* No wonder, therefore, that this loyalty to *veritas* has at times aroused antagonistic feelings toward me on the part of some of the criticized individuals and groups.

Despite this "backwash," the criticisms of the *Fads and Foibles* have not been wholly ineffective. They seem to have tangibly influenced a number of American and foreign sociologists, psychologists, and psychiatrists. A few years later, in a somewhat simplified form, most of my criticisms were reiterated by C. Wright Mills in his book *Sociological Imagination.* In his personal letter to me, written soon after publication of my volume, he expressed his high evaluation and essential agreement with most of my conclusions. (For one reason or another, he did not mention my volume at all in his book, which in fact was noted and adversely commented upon by the reviewer of Mills's book in the *London Times Literary Supplement.*) Since its original publication in 1956, *Fads and Foibles* has already appeared in French, Spanish, and Italian translations, and a couple of additional translations are underway.

As to the *American Sex Revolution* and *Power and Morality,* both of these books were intentionally written in a semi-popular form accessible to the intelligent lay reader. In *American Sex Revolution* I tried to show the dangerous consequences of sex obsession and sex anarchy which have flooded American life, culture, and values in the last few decades.

In accordance with this objective, the book sums up the main manifestations of this obsession and anarchy and their destructive effects upon the physical, mental, moral, and social well-being of individuals and nations infected with these sex maladies. The book has been widely read, discussed, approved, and criticized in this country and—in its Swedish, Spanish, Portuguese, Japanese, and Indian editions—in other nations.

The main objectives and conclusions of my *Power and Morality,* written with Professor W. Lunden, can be seen from the following quotation from the opening pages of the book:

The well-being and survival of the human race are today largely determined by a mere handful of the top rulers of the great nuclear powers. In the hollows of their hands they hold monopolistic control of unprecedented deadly weapons. Upon their wisdom or stupidity largely depends mankind's fate—lasting peace or suicidal war. Never before in history has the life or death of so many depended upon so very few! . . .

This dangerous situation naturally raises the momentous questions of our time: Can we entrust the fateful decision of war or peace—and through that the "life, liberty and pursuit of happiness" of hundreds of millions of human beings—to the few magnates of this power? Do they have the wisdom of the serpent and the innocence of the dove necessary to lead us to a lasting peace and magnificent future?

For our part we are inclined to answer these questions in the words of the Psalmist: "Put not your trust in princes (and rulers) . . . in whom there is no help." . . . The gigantic task of peacefully resolving the tremendous difficulties of the present cannot be entrusted to the existing governments. . . . Being still mainly "tribal governments of politicians, by politicians and for politicians," today's ruling groups do not display the minimum of intellectual, moral, and social qualifications necessary for a successful solution of these tremendous tasks.

In the first place, throughout history the moral integrity of powerful governments has been—and still is—too low and their criminality too great to entrust to them the life and well-being of mankind. Secondly, a fruitful solution of these problems far exceeds the creative ability of the existing governments. Thirdly, a constructive realization of human aspirations demands: (*a*) a replacement of these "governments of politicians" by the "governments of scientists, saints, and sages"; (*b*) an establishment of certain conditions, such as universal and total disarmament which can automatically prevent misuse and abuse of power by each and every government; (*c*) a replacement of the largely obsolescent political ideologies and tattered values by new ones; and finally, (*d*) the spontaneous mobilization and inspired cooperation of all creative forces of humanity—its best minds, purest hearts, and highest consciences—for building a nobler and better order in the human universe.

Subsequent chapters of the book give a development and corroboration of these propositions, particularly the thesis concerning the mentality and criminality of rulers. The essential characteristics of these are summed up in the following generalizations.

1.) When the morality and mentality of rulers and the ruled are measured by the same moral and mental yardstick (and not by a double standard), then the rulers' morality and mind appear to be marked by a greater mental and moral schizophrenia than the morality and mentality of the ruled populations.

2.) The ruling groups contain a larger proportion of the extreme mental types of the gifted and the mentally-sick than the rank and file of the ruled populations. The ruling strata have a larger proportion of domineering, aggressive, highly selfish, bold, and adventurous persons, men harsh and insensitive to other human beings, hypocrites, liars, and cynical manipulators, than the strata of the ruled populations.

3.) The moral behavior of ruling groups tends to be more criminal and submoral than that of the ruled strata of the same society.

4.) The greater, more absolute, and coercive the power of rulers, political leaders, and big executives of business, labor, and other organizations, the more corrupt and criminal such ruling groups and executives tend to be.

5.) With a progressive limitation of their power, criminality of the rulers and executives tends to decrease qualitatively (by becoming less grave and murderous) and quantitatively (by decreasing the rate of criminal actions).

These propositions concern not only autocratic but also democratic rulers, with the difference indicated in points four and five. Each of these somewhat abstract generalizations acquires its full significance only when it is demonstrated by relevant concrete examples. For instance, proposition number three becomes strikingly important when one learns that from 20 to 90 per cent of the kings of England, France, Austria, Russia, Iran, Byzantium, Turkey, Germany, Italy, the Roman Empire, Japan, the Arabian dynasties, and the Inca kings have been guilty of committing the gravest forms of murder—patricide, matricide, fratricide, uxorcide, etc., while the murder rates for the ruled population fluctuate between 0.0008 and 0.2 per cent. In other words, the autocratic rulers' rate of criminality is many, many times higher than that of their ruled populations.

An interesting anecdote may be mentioned here. I sent complimentary copies of this book to President Eisenhower, Secretary of State Herter, Premier Khrushchev, and a few senators and congressmen of the United States. Somewhat surprisingly for me, I received complimentary thanks from all of them. Their secretaries evidently did not read the book and acknowledged its receipt automatically, without realization of the book's highly "subversive" character. Like most my books, *Power and Morality* has appeared in an Indian paperback edition and in Japanese and French (abridged) translations.

Since the publication of *Power and Morality*, my book productivity has somewhat subsided. Only two "light" volumes have been published in the period of 1959-63. One is a Spanish volume *Convergencia de Estados Unidos y la U.R.S.S.*, published in Mexico in 1961. It is a Spanish translation of my two addresses (the other address being *A Quest for an Integral System of Sociology*) given at the plenary sessions of the 19th International Congress of Sociology at Mexico City, in 1960. The other light volume is this *Autobiography*, written largely for my own amusement and curiosity.

This decreased book productivity has been partly due to the slower tempo of my work at the septegenarian age—I find that at my present age I cannot work as fast as I used to in my younger years; and in part it has been due to my increased activities along somewhat different lines.

Participation in Scientific Conferences

Since retirement I have been prompted to write a larger number of substantial papers for various national and international scientifc conferences than I had before. With rare exceptions, I have been as reluctant to attend these congresses and meetings as ever, but for one reason or another, after my retirement a number of scientific organizations began so insistently to press participation in their meetings upon me that in several cases I simply could not decline their urgent and repeated invitations. Thus, for instance, I had decided not to attend the 18th International Congress of Sociology at Nürnberg, in 1958. Accordingly I informed the Committee of the Congress. The result was a series of letters and telegrams from the President of the Congress, the Nürnberg Organizational Committee, and from many European, Asiatic, and American sociologists—all of whom insisted that my participation in the Congress was urgently necessary. Besides this insistence the Committee of the Congress assured me that all my traveling and living expenses would be fully paid. Finally when, some four days before the Congress, I tried to argue that in so short a time I could not secure my passport and get a smallpox innoculation and airplane ticket, Professor Zimmerman, at the Committee's request, successfully arranged all these things for me. Under these circumstances I could no longer refuse to attend the Congress. As a result, on the eve of the Congress I found myself flying to Nürnberg on a Pan-American plane in company with C. C. Zimmerman. Dr. A. J. Toynbee happened to be on the same plane. An informal chat with this distinguished scholar greatly enlivened the boring hours of flight from Boston to London where he left the plane. At Nürnberg airport, we were met by the members of the local organizational committee and were driven to the hotel where rooms were reserved for us. In this easy way I found myself in postwar Europe which I had not visited before.

It goes without saying that the seven days of the Congress were most enjoyable, absorbingly interesting, and fruitful. The hospitality of the distinguished German scholars, members of the Nürnberg Organizational Committee: professors, Hans Freyer; K. V. Müller; H. G. Rasch, the Rector of the *Nürnberg Hochschule fur Wirtschafts-und Sozialwissenschaften,* Dr. F. W. Schoberth, of the municipal authorities of Nürnberg and of the Bavarian and the Federal governments of Germany, was overwhelming. The attention paid me by the members of the Congress was so unexpected that I jokingly remarked to my colleagues that it made me dizzy and that I would now think much more highly of myself than I had before the Congress. There I met many sociologists and scholars from various countries and had an opportunity to become acquainted with the younger generation of European, Latin American, and Asiatic sociologists.

Besides taking active part in the discussions of the Congress I was asked to give two addresses at its plenary sessions. As I had not expected to attend the Congress at all, I had not brought any paper for delivery there. Fortunately for me, at home before the Congress I had written drafts of two papers for publication. I delivered the gists of these drafts extemporaneously in my addresses. Later on, after my return home, I finished the drafts and they were published in their final form in the *Akten des XVIII Internationalen Soziologenkongresses,* Vol. I, under the titles: "The Mysterious Energy of Love" and "Three Basic Trends of Our Time." Since then these essays have been republished in English in several American and in translations in foreign scientific journals and semi-popular publications.

After the formal adjournment of the Congress, on the eve of my departure for home, I spent a delightful evening in the distinguished company of the members of the Nürnberg Organizational Committee, the rector of the Hochschule, the eminent members of the Congress and their wives. As a crowning token of their hospitality that evening they presented me with a bottle of refined wine, the "Heilig Geist Spital, No. 5," to take home. With this gift, I returned home, greatly refreshed and encouraged by the richness and fruitfulness of my experiences at the Congress.

A similar story was repeated with my attendance of the 19th International Congress of Sociology at Mexico City, in September, 1960, and of the Annual Meeting of the American Sociological Association in New York immediately preceding the Congress. I did not plan to attend either of these meetings but eventually I had to yield to the pressure of these organizations. The president of the American Sociological Association, the late Professor Howard Becker, and the chairman of the section of Sociological Theory, Professor R. Chambliss, repeatedly asked me to deliver the main address at the Centenary Celebration of Herbert Spencer to be held at the meeting of the Association. They even shifted the day of this commemoration from August 30th to August 29th to enable me to fly to the opening of the International Congress of Sociology at Mexico City from September 1 to 8, 1960. Thus insistently pressed, I finally accepted the invitation, and on August 29th delivered my address, "Variations on the Spencerian Theme of Militant and Industrial Types of Society." My fame or, perhaps, notoriety seemed already to have become so conspicuous that my speech attracted the biggest audience of the Association and was responded to by thunderous applause and many congratulations.

The next morning I flew to Mexico City with my wife.

One interesting aftermath of this address deserves to be noted here. Since my delivery of it was a sort of "command performance" insisted upon by the president of the Sociological Association and since it had a most enthusiastic reception, I felt obliged to submit it for publication to the *American Sociological Review,* the official organ of the Association. I did so, without any eagerness or enthusiasm, because of my previous, rather unfriendly relationship with the editors of the *Review.* A few weeks later I received a letter from the editor of the *Review,* Dr. Harry Alpert, dated October 31, 1960, in which he wrote:

> I find it my unpleasant duty to inform you that it is not possible for us to accept your paper for publication in the *American Sociological Review.* . . . Your manuscript is being returned under separate cover.
>
> Sincerely yours,
> HARRY ALPERT

I was neither surprised nor even irritated by this letter. When I humorously mentioned this fact to some of my scholar friends, they asked me "Who is this Alpert?"

"As an office administrator he has been doing well. Now he is a dean of the graduate school of Oregon University. As a scholar he is just a third-class sociologist, who, so far as I know, wrote only one poor book about Durkheim."

"Then how did he dare reject your paper?"

"For the same reason for which the papers of incomparably greater scholars than I happen to be rejected by midgety editors. Don't you know," I added facetiously, "that Leibnitz's nurse and servant never understood why so many important people, even royalty, paid such great respect to their seemingly plain master? Don't you know also that the ways of clerical administrators are inscrutable?"

Of course, my paper was not particularly important, but certainly it was at least as good as the rank and file of papers published in the *Review*. Since several American and foreign journals had already offered to publish the paper before, I sent it to *Social Science* where it was published in the next issue; since then it has been republished in translations in European, Latin-American and Asian scientific journals. So much for this humorous incident.

My wife and I fully enjoyed our attendance of the conference at Mexico City. The hospitality of the Mexican scholars, of the government, and of the Mexican people toward the congress and toward us was even more overwhelming than that of the Nürnberg Congress. The attention paid me by the congress was again quite extraordinary, far greater than I deserved or expected. My two addresses, mentioned before, attracted the biggest audience and were received enthusiastically.

When I had finished my address on *Mutual Convergence of the United States and U.S.S.R. to the Mixed Sociocultural Type*, among many members of the Congress who congratulated me on the address was Dr. Adolf Grabowsky, the editor of an important German political science journal, *Zeitschrift für Politik.* He asked me for a carbon copy of my address to be promptly translated into German and published in the *Zeitschrift* in its next December issue, 1960. Then the editors of the *Mémoires* of the Congress and the Mexican Organizational Committee informed me that it would be published not only in its English text but also in a Spanish translation made by the president of the Committee, Dr. Carlos A. Echanove T. Dr. Echanove also arranged for Spanish editions of both my addresses in the form of the above-mentioned volume *Convergencia.* Subsequently the *Mutual Convergence* was published not only in the *Mémoires du XIXe Congrès International de Sociologie,* Vol. III, and in German and Spanish editions, but was republished in English by the *International Journal of Comparative Sociology,* and in a Russian magazine, *Nezavisimaya Rossia,* issued in New York City.

At the Congress I met many Latin-American and foreign sociologists. Among them I was particularly gratified to meet personally Dr. Lucio Mendieta y Nuñez, director of the Mexican Institute of Social Research, editor of the *Revista Mexicana de Sociologia,* and a most eminent Latin-American sociologist. I corresponded with him for many years before and was indebted to him for the Spanish translation of my *Social Mobility* (and now for starting the translation of all four volumes of the *Dynamics*), and for accepting in my behalf the honorary doctor's degree granted to me by the National University of Mexico at its four hundredth anniversary in 1952. (I was not able to attend personally the ceremony which conferred this honor upon me.)

The eight days spent in Mexico gave us an opportunity to see several historical places in and near Mexico City, to lecture at the National University of Mexico, and to enjoy the hospitality of several embassies of foreign governments. In other words, again I was glad I had attended the Congress and had not persevered in my reluctance to do so.

Somewhat different were the conditions of my attendance of the *First Synopsiskongress of the International Society for Comparative Study of Civilizations* at Salzburg in October,

1961. A group of distinguished European scholars met and organized this society in 1960. I was neither invited to nor did I participate in this meeting. I learned about the establishment of the Society from the letter of its secretary-general, Dr. Othmar Anderle.

He informed me that the founding group had unanimously elected me the first president of the Society and hoped I would accept this office. As an inducement to my acceptance the letter stressed that the presidency would impose almost no burdensome duties upon me. I accepted the honor with the clear reservation that no work should be expected from me, not even attendance of the meetings of the Society. But when its first international *Synopsiskongress* was announced and I informed the Committee that I would not be able to attend it, the usual stream of letters and telegrams urging me to come to the Congress followed. As usual, my reluctance was overcome and on October 7, 1961, I was met at Munich airport by Dr. Anderle, driven by him to Salzburg, and left at the hotel where a comfortable room was reserved for me.

Unlike many other conferences, we ruled out reading long papers and used all the sessions for face to face discussions between the scholarly members of the Congress. During the seven days of the Congress, in its two daily sessions, the basic problems of the main topic of the Congress "The Problems of Civilization" (*Die Problematik der Hochkulturen*) were thoroughly discussed by historians, sociologists, philosophers of history, archeologists, anthropologists, biologists, psychologists, philosophers, and scholars of religion, law, and fine arts. The discussions were carried on in German, English, and French with simultaneous translation into these languages. All statements were tape-recorded in order to be transcribed later on, edited, and published in the *Proceedings of the Congress* (at the moment of writing these lines, the volume of the *Proceedings* is already prepared and will be published in 1963). Its publication has been greatly assisted by Eli Lilly who generously granted five thousand dollars for this purpose.

We did not regret the replacement of lengthy papers by

discussions. This procedure greatly enlivened each session, largely eliminated the boredom of listening to long papers, gave the opportunity to active participation to all members of the Congress, and yielded a better knowledge of the problems of civilizations than could be given by a mere reading of a limited number of papers. No wonder, therefore, that the proceedings of the Congress were widely reported by the European press, radio, and television. *The New York Times* also published a report of a clash of Toynbee's and my views on the Russian and the German civilizations with those of some of the German historians.

Here again the hospitality of the city of Salzburg, of the governments of Salzburg Province, and of Austria was most generous. The beauty of Salzburg and its surroundings, the historical places, including the Mozart museum and the fortress of the city, the excellent food, beer, and wine of its restaurants, and the peaceful atmosphere of neutral Austria, greatly increased the enjoyment of the members of the Congress.

As president of the Congress I again received attention far greater than I deserved. Of other "high spots" of the Congress I must mention my meeting there with Dr. and Mrs. Toynbee. Our rooms happened to be adjacent in the same hotel. Every day we had breakfast, lunch, and dinner together. In the discussions of the Congress Toynbee's views happened to be similar to my notions on almost all the problems discussed. This association with the Toynbees greatly increased my respect and admiration for them. Their sincerity, integrity, and kindness, their simplicity and freedom from false pretenses, not to mention the outstanding creativity of that outstanding scholar, were most impressive. They exemplified the perennial and universal values of human culture at its best.

Somewhat physically tired but mentally and morally refreshed, on October 16 I was back in Winchester.

Finally my participation in the simultaneous meetings of the Fifth International Congress of Sociological Associations, of the annual meetings of the American Sociological Association, and of the Catholic Sociological Society at Washington, from August 30 to September 5, 1962, was deliberate on my part, and was decided without particular promptings by these societies apart from their invitations to deliver my papers at each of these meetings.

A few months before these meetings, I received an invitation from the Austrian Government to give a lecture at the International Diplomatic Seminar (July 31 to August 10, at Salzburg, 1962) on "What Modern Sociology Can Teach the Modern Diplomats." Then there arrived invitations from the three mentioned scientific societies scheduled to meet at Washington, from August 29 to September 8, 1962; from September 12 to 18 was scheduled the Twentieth International Congress of Sociology at Cordoba, Argentina, which I was expected to attend as nominated and voted president-elect of the next Congress; from September 24 to 30 I had to attend, as president, a tentatively scheduled Second Congress of the International Society for the Comparative Study of Civilizations at Salzburg.

"If I were to attend all these meetings I would certainly be dead at the end of September, if not earlier," I said to myself, and decided to attend only the Washington meetings. However tempting was participation in the International Diplomatic Seminar (ordinarily addressed only by the heads of governments, foreign ministers, and eminent diplomats), in the 20th International Congress of Sociology, and in the Second International Congress at Salzburg, I simply could not attend all of them. Subsequently, with regrets and apologies I informed the Austrian Ambassador at Washington of my inability to accept the privilege of addressing the Seminar; asked the Committee of the 20th Sociological Congress to cancel my nomination and election to the next presidency of the Congress, and two weeks later informed it of my non-attendance of the Congress. If I had remained a president-elect I would have been obliged to attend the Congress; after cancelling my nomination and election, I was free not to attend it. As to the participation in the Second Congress at Salzburg, as its president, I suggested that the Committee postpone the Second Congress to September, 1964. This suggestion was approved by the Committee and the Second Congress is now to take place at Salzburg, from September 22-30, 1964. (Later on, due to the unstable political conditions in Argentina, the 20th Congress of Sociology was also postponed for one year.)

In accordance with my decision, in the spring and the summer months of 1962 I prepared my papers for all three meetings at Washington. A substantial paper for the Fifth World Congress of Sociology, "The Theses on the Role of Historical Method in the Social Sciences," was published in the *Transactions of the Fifth World Congress of Sociology*, Vol. I, even before the Congress took place. The paper for the American Sociological Association, "Practical Influence of 'Impractical' Generalizing Sociological Theories," was contracted for publication by *Sociology and Social Research* before the meeting, and was published in its October, 1962, issue. Likewise the paper for the American Catholic Sociological Society, "Remarks on P. T. de Chardin's *The Phenomenon of Man*," was published in the *American Catholic Sociological Review* (Winter, 1962).

When driving to the Washington meetings my wife and I stopped overnight with our son Peter, the physicist, at Ossining, near the IBM main laboratories. We fully enjoyed our visit with him and with Dr. B. Dunham who lived in the same house. Next morning we continued our drive and arrived in Washington in the early afternoon.

At the Shoreham Hotel—headquarters of the meetings—I met many of my previous students who were now distinguished scholars and leaders in education, government, and business, and other sociologists. From morning to evening of each day they wanted to talk with me about various matters, invited us to join them at cocktails, breakfast, or dinner. The delegations of Chinese, Japanese, Indian, and Latin-American sociologists wanted to consult me about divers scientific and other problems. For the first time among foreign sociologists, we met a delegation of Soviet, Polish, and Czech sociologists. They were anxious to meet us and we were no less interested to meet them. So we saw each other several times at the Congress; and, later on, five of them dined with us in our home at Winchester. Our meetings were friendly and our talks quite frank.

"Though our views differ from yours on many points, nevertheless we regard you as a great living sociologist. Many of us carefully study your works and duly appreciate them. We are even proud of your achievements because we consider you a Russian sociologist. You must visit Russia. You can be sure you will be heartily welcomed there." Such was the gist of their views and attitude toward me.

I have had similar reactions from other Russian scholars and scientists whom I have met at Harvard and in our home during the last two years. Quite a change! Until recent years my works were prohibited in Russia, and contact with me was forbidden to all Russian scholars, scientists, and artists. Now, they told me, my main works could be found in the university and national libraries of Russia, although they are still accessible only to the Communists and to professors and graduate students. When, half-humorously, I mentioned that not one of my volumes, which have been translated into all the European and the main Asiatic languages, has had the fortune to be translated into Russian, they advised me not to be surprised if in the near future one or more of my books were published in Russian translation in Soviet Russia. With mutual hope of closer association and cooperation in the future, we concluded our friendly meetings.

As to my addresses to all three societies, they went with the usual success, attracting large audiences, being received favorably, arousing plenty of discussion (some of which, with my *Replies,* were later published), and bringing me many a hearty congratulation from sociologists. I was particularly pleased to deliver my paper for the American Sociological Society in the section presided over by one of my previous students and collaborators, Professor R. Merton of Columbia, and discussed by another of my students, Professor W. Moore of Princeton, and by my old friend Professor T. Abel of Hunter College. It was a real pleasure for me to see these old students of mine grown into eminent leaders of the younger generation of American sociologists.

I had the same pleasure, and for the same reason, in lunching with Dr. and Mrs. Logan Wilson, now Chairman, of American Council on Education, and in meeting and talking with other students, now distinguished professors and expert advisers with the American government, like professors J. B. Ford, C. Loomis, E. Schuler, B. Barber, R. Bierstedt, J. Fichter, Dr. Porter, and many others. No less of a pleasure for me was my meeting at the Congress with Professor H. Zetterberg of Columbia University, who was responsible, as the head of the Bedminster Press, for reissuing all four volumes of my *Dynamics,* and also lunch with my old friends, professors Mendieta and Recasens-Siches of Mexico.

Three additional surprises came to me at the Congress. Dr. S. del Campo Urbano of Spain brought me the first copy of the Spanish edition of my *Dynamics,* hurriedly bound for that purpose by the order of my old, distinguished friend, Professor Manuel Fraga Iribarne of Madrid University, director of the Spanish *Instituto de Studios Politicos,* and recently appointed Minister of Culture in the Spanish government. Another surprise was a letter from Porter Sargent, the publisher of *Power and Morality,* with a copy of the contract which he had just signed with a Japanese publisher for the Japanese edition of this book. The third surprise was a copy of a new Chinese edition of my *Contemporary Sociological Theories* in Formosa, brought me by the delegation of the Formosan Chinese sociologists.

We fully enjoyed the five days of our participation in the Washington meetings and returned home physically fatigued but mentally refreshed.

These examples of my post-retirement participation in various scientific meetings show that in my emeritus-life these activities have not in the least subsided.* Since participation in these meetings involved preparation of a fairly substantial paper for delivery, the number of such papers delivered and published in my retirement period has increased rather than decreased.

In a word, as an Emeritus, I have been busier with this sort of activity than I was in my pre-retirement period. This "business" is exactly what I want to have to the end of my life, provided it does not mean the business of Lao-Tze's famous statement that "Doing nothing is better than to be busy doing nothing." I hope I have not been busy doing nothing.

Itinerant Lecturer

Another line of activity which has somewhat increased during my post-retirement period is my itinerant lecturing at various universities and learned institutions. Even before retirement I used to receive a considerable number of such invitations, not only from American and foreign universities but also from the governments of India and West Germany. With very rare exceptions, I ordinarily declined almost all such offers. The main reason for this practice was simple: working and writing quietly at home, through my publications and their translations I was reaching much larger selective audiences than I could by moving from place to place and repeating my lectures at various universities.

After my retirement, for some reason, the offers for permanent professorship, of annual or semester lectureship, and for one or more lectures notably increased. One of the first invitations was that of the Indonesian Government and Jogjakarta University to come to Indonesia for two years as a professor and as organizer of the departments of sociology in the universities of this nation. With my thanks and apology,

* On April 7, 1963, I attended the annual meeting of the Eastern Sociological Society in New York to receive the Society's reward of merit; and while reading these proofs I was informed I was named as president-elect of the American Sociological Association.

I declined this as well as many subsequent offers of professorship or lectureship that have continued to come in ever-increasing numbers during the post-retirement years. I have accepted only a few invitations for short-time lecture engagements lasting from one day to one month. The main reason for my decline of numerous and sometimes munificent invitations has been the same as mentioned before. In contrast to long engagements, a few lectures delivered from time to time break long periods of study and writing at home, give a chance to visit many universities and to meet many professors and students, to have a vacation in the balmy climate of Florida, California, or Texas with expenses paid, to enjoy the excitement of addressing responsive audiences, to see old friends, and—last but not least—to replenish the modestly comfortable, but not too affluent means of subsistence of a retired professor. Thus motivated, in the post-retirement years I have given one or more lectures in many universities and colleges: These include practically all the New England universities and colleges, twelve colleges and universities in California (in a three-week period), ten in Georgia, eight in Virginia, six lecture courses at St. Louis, Buffalo, and Purdue universities, a series of lectures in three seasons at the University of Florida, and then one or two lectures at the universities of Princeton, Pennsylvania, Cornell, Michigan State, Wayne State, Syracuse, George Washington, and others—not to mention the lectures given at various religious and cultural organizations.

Due to efficient arrangement of my lectures and to excellent organization of the transportation from college to college by the inter-university centers or by the administrations of the universities involved, I was able to deliver ten lectures—one in each of ten Georgia universities in five days, eight lectures in eight colleges of Virginia in four days, and so on. With such compact arrangements, these itinerant lectures did not take much time or energy. I accepted longer three-week or one-month engagements only at the colleges and universities of Florida, California, and Texas. These engagements were a sort of vacation in the balmy climates of these states during one of the rough winter months in Massachusetts.

So arranged, my itinerant lectureship has been truly enjoyable, exciting, and refreshing. Everywhere my wife and I have been received most cordially; everywhere my lectures have attracted big audiences and have been a notable event in the daily, routine life of the universities and colleges visited. The administration, professors, and students have always done their best to make our visits both comfortable and entertaining.

At the University of Florida, President J. W. Reitz and Mrs. Reitz invited us to stay in their beautiful mansion and, later on, in a delightful apartment for the guests of honor of the University. My previous student and now the leading rural sociologist and Latin-American expert, Professor T. Lynn Smith, and his wife did their best to make our stay at the University of Florida invigorating and exciting. Among other things, T. Lynn took us fishing several times in the tropical rivers, the Mexican Gulf, and the Atlantic Ocean. We visited many historical and scenic spots of Florida. Warm hospitality was shown us by other professors, students, and the leading citizens of Gainesville.

Similar treatment was rendered to us by San Fernando Valley State College—our headquarters during my lecture engagement in California, and by other universities and colleges of this state. Professor J. B. Ford, also one of my previous students, and Mrs. Ford, turned my lecture-engagement in California into a series of convivial parties in between my lectures and conferences. President R. Prator, deans D. T. Oviatt and L. Wolfson, and professors and students of San Fernando Valley State College crowned their extraordinary hospitality by elevating me to the rank of an alumnus of the college. Similar hospitality was proffered us by the University of California at Santa Barbara, Redlands University, California Institute of Technology, the State College of the City of Los Angeles, and other universities.

Besides the academic institutions, several artistic, religious, and cultural organizations invited us for lunch and dinner conferences. Among many distinguished persons met there, I particularly enjoyed a long visit with Aldous Huxley and meetings with Professor and Mrs. Charles MacIntosh, who generously helped the Center for Creative Altruism by their sizable contributions and advice. Along with several interviews with the press, radio, and television, these various activities excitingly filled every day of our stay in California from morning to evening.

In previous years I had lectured twice at the Yale Divinity School and Sociology Club. In 1959 I was invited for a three-day visit to Yale University by the Fellows of Pierson College. The master of that college, professor and eminent composer Quincy Porter, wrote to me: "Each year we invite a man who is distinguished in one or another field to come and live in the College for three days. The idea is for him to be available for informative talks with our young men and to participate in one or two seminars with them. In the past we have had such people as Archibald MacLeish, James Reston, and Professor I. A. Richards of Harvard."

The three days I lived in Pierson College were not only delightful but feverishly busy from early morning to late evening. The demand for informal talks, extemporaneous remarks at various classes and seminars of the University, and for convivial chats at lunch or dinner, over a glass of beer, or at a cocktail party, was so great that at the end of my engagement I was almost exhausted physically. Despite this fatigue these three days were memorable days for me, immensely enjoyable and fruitful. The hospitality of Professor Porter and the Fellows of Pierson College, especially Professor Wells, was overwhelming.

From New Haven we drove to Washington where, invited by Secretary of Labor J. Mitchell, I was scheduled to have a lunch conference with him and assistant secretaries of the Labor Department, and after lunch to give a lecture to one hundred top officials of the Department.

Next day at noon, I was met in the offices of the Secretary by an assistant secretary, George Cabot Lodge. He welcomed me and told me that during his Harvard years he had taken two of my courses. I expressed my sympathy for his wasted time in these courses.

"No, your courses happened to be the most important of all the courses I had at Harvard."

I looked at him whimsically and said, "I see that despite your young age you have already learned the art of diplomatic flattery."

"Not at all, I meant what I said."

While we were engaged in this chat, Secretary Mitchell came in and we moved to the room where an excellent lunch was prepared for us. Unfortunately, I hardly had a chance to enjoy it: the Secretary and the assistant secretaries began to bombard me with so many questions that, in answering their highly thoughtful inquiries I did not have time to eat lunch. After this lunch conference we moved to a lecture hall in the Department building. There I delivered my lecture and answered the questions of the members of the highly selected audience. The engagement was quite rewarding. Mr. Mitchell, his assistant secretaries, and the selected audience greatly impressed me. They displayed a dedication to their tasks, most searching intelligence, and competence in their work.

From Washington we drove to Princeton where I was scheduled to give a lecture to Princeton sociologists, social scientists, and graduate students. We stayed overnight there in the comfortable house of Professor Wilbert Moore, one of my previous students and now chairman of the Department of Sociology at Princeton. He and Mrs. Moore extended to us their warmest hospitality and care. At a cocktail party in their home I was welcomed by my previous students, professors M. Levy and E. Tiryakian, and met then and there at the dinner party a number of other scholars and graduate students of Princeton. After dinner I delivered my lecture. The lively discussion which followed continued far into the night. Next morning we drove home. Exhilarated by the whole lecture-tour, we eagerly resumed our labors and habitual way of life.

Of other lecture engagements two episodes deserve to be mentioned here. My lecture at the University of Pennsylvania was given in the big lecture hall of the new physics building. At the bottom of the amphitheatre where I stood lecturing there was a long laboratory desk with several faucets built into it. The audience overflowingly filled the big hall—a feature which had become typical of my itinerant lectures. Before the lecture, in a company of scholars, we had a convivial dinner in the house of our old friend, Professor Dorothy Thomas. In an exuberant spirit of after-dinner "spirits," I started and continued my lecture until I reached a point where I was criticizing Sigmund Freud's theories. Just at that moment, an explosively hissing sound began to come from one of the faucets. "Be quiet, Sigmund! Shut up your neurotic *libido!*" I retorted. By a long, hearty laugh, the audience seconded my admonition to the Freudian ghost. In my exhilarated mood it seems I had inadvertently touched a part of the faucet that released compressed air. "The ghost of Freud" cheerfully amused the audience as well as myself.

The other episode occurred at a dinner party preceding my lecture at Mary Washington College in Fredericksburg, Virginia. At dinner I was seated beside Professor Philip J. Allen, whom I met there for the first time. During our chat, among other things, he mentioned his plan to start a series of volumes about well-known living sociologists and asked me what I thought of it. As a matter of courtesy I naturally approved of it, provided it could be carried out. At this point the matter was dropped and went out of my mind. One can imagine my surprise at Allen's letter received several months later! In that letter, Professor Allen informed me that he had proceeded with his plan, had decided to devote the first volume of his series to Sorokin, had already received several articles from distinguished scholars for the volume, and expected to have other essays during the next few months.

To make a long story short, Allen's volume, consisting of essays devoted to analysis, evaluation, and criticism of my various theories by some twenty distinguished European, American, and Asiatic scholars, with my substantial "Reply," was published in February, 1963, by the Duke University Press under the title *Pitirim A. Sorokin in Review.* Thus, out of a few seemingly casual remarks at a dinner party, that substantial volume was born through the initiative and labors of Professor Allen. This sort of "surprise" has happened to me several times in my life.

This sketch gives an idea of my post-retirement activities as itinerant professor. Though the accepted lecture engagements represent only a small fraction of the lectures I have been invited to give, still they show that I have not quite retired as yet from this sort of activity. And, what perhaps is still more symptomatic, the invitations continue to come in ever-increasing numbers. Only in 1962 I declined some thirty invitations from American and foreign universities. This naturally heartens me, as indeed it would almost any septegenarian Emeritus.

My present itinerancy reminds me of that of my boyhood years when for a few years I was an itinerant artisan going from village to village designing ikons, silvering the objects of religious ritual, and painting church buildings, schools, and peasant houses. I enjoyed the itinerancy of the spring of my life and I enjoy no less the itinerancy of its late autumn. After all, the role of rolling stone has its own fascination.

"The Wasting of Good Paper Still Goes On As Usual"

This phrase is my customary answer to the inquiries of what I have been doing and writing in recent years. Though since 1959 I have published only two "light volumes (mentioned before), nevertheless the total output of my papers published in the years 1960-62 has been quite considerable. If published in book form, as I hope they will be, these papers would easily make a substantial volume of *Essays in Integral*

*Sociology, Psychology, and Philosophy.** If to these papers various "Replies," "Prefaces," "Forewords," "Reviews," and especially the reissues and translations of my volumes are added, then quantitatively my total book output during these years can well satisfy almost any scholar in the psychosocial sciences. Roughly, some fourteen substantial papers (already translated into two or three foreign languages) were published during this period; new editions of the four volumes of the *Dynamics*, of *Society, Culture and Personality*, and of *Social Philosophies of An Age of Crisis* have been issued; and some eleven additional translations of my published volumes, bringing the total number of translations of my books to some forty-two, with more underway. Considering that all these translations have been undertaken entirely by foreign scientific institutions, scholars, and publishers, without any help from the American government, foundations, universities, or other agencies, this record appears to me significant and reassuring. Furthermore, many of my lectures have been recorded live by universities and two of these were recorded and issued for educational and commercial uses by the Campus Library. This output shows that the "wasting of good paper goes on as usual."

As usual, the "wasting of good paper about my wasted paper" also continues on the part of scientific institutions, other scholars, and private publishers of many countries. Besides hundreds of popular write-ups in newspapers and magazines, dozens of scientific articles, Ph.D. theses, and books about my books continue to be published. In February-March, 1963, two substantial volumes devoted to the dissection of my theories were published.†

Therefore I scarcely have reason to complain of being "a forgotten man" or a "has-been scholar." If anything, the world seems to be paying my "yarns" attention far beyond their merit.

* Some of these essays will appear in the volume, *Basic Trends of Our Time*, to be published by College and University Press in 1964.

† P. Allen *P. A. Sorokin in Review* and E. Tiryakian, *Essays in Honor of P. A. Sorokin.*

Together with my outlined participation in scientific meetings and itinerant lectureship, this paper-wasting of mine and of other people keeps me creatively alive and kicking.

World-Wide Correspondence: Visits from Abroad

Three or four days a week my morning hours are spent answering letters from all corners of the world and from people in all walks of life. I usually dictate my answers to my part-time secretary, Miss R. Leydon. She takes them down in shorthand and then types them. If I had to write the answers myself, the correspondence would take most of my time. The letters and inquiries range all the way from the "crackpot" and foolish up to the highly important ones written by eminent thinkers, inventors, writers, artists, statesmen, and businessmen, religious, moral, and cultural leaders. I do not answer stupid and pointless letters. Of the thoughtful letters I try to answer as many as I can. Their increased number, however, takes more and more of my time. This time would be still greater if I were to read numerous papers, pamphlets, and books sent to me by their authors or publishers with requests to give my reactions to them. Slightly blurred vision and the strained state of my eyes give me a sufficient excuse for declining these requests with the exception of a few important ones.

Despite these drawbacks, this correspondence helps me keep in touch with the important currents of modern thought and deep "undertows" of historical processes. In its give-and-take the correspondence has often been a fruitful dialogue with my numerous correspondents. This "keeping in touch" is helped also by discussions with many a distinguished person—American and foreign—who now and then visits me at my home. The time spent exchanging views with these visitors has been quite rewarding and more enlightening than my attendance of many public discussions by mediocre, frequently doubtful, "experts" of various forums, and especially by radio and television "educational" shows.

"Loafing"

The activities I have described should not give a false impression of my being too busy to loaf and indulge in recreational pleasures. As a matter of fact I have been a chronic loafer and an enthusiast of *dolce far niente* all my life. This is the other side of the Taoist precept that "doing nothing is better than to be busy doing nothing." Almost daily I spend a couple of afternoon hours in my favorite ways of "doing nothing" mentally: working in my garden, cutting the lawn, struggling with the jungle around my summer cottage, walking, swimming, fishing, and climbing mountains. To the consternation of my wife, I still climb tall trees if there is need of cutting their branches—still dig, plant, and transplant heavy bushes, chop big trees, shovel snow, and do other kinds of physical work.

Quite frequently I also loaf by meditating on a beautiful sunset or sunrise, whitecaps or the stillness of dreaming waters, the fireworks of a thunderstorm or the "deafening silence" of a starry night. At our summer place each season, I enjoy friendship with various animals living in nearby woods: porcupines, raccoons, deer, and other creatures. A porcupine lived under the floor of our kitchen for several years. Every day a raccoon comes for his meal and then loafs on the veranda of our cottage. Poor fellow! last winter he seems to have gotten in a trap and lost one of his legs. When we arrived at our summer place the next spring, he came, looking shabby and emaciated. By the end of the summer, however, thanks to good meals, he had recovered his good looks and was getting along all right on his three legs.

As to my indoor recreation, besides a good novel, music is my main hobby. I have a good library of records. It contains practically all the important compositions of great music I like, beginning with the Gregorian chants and ending with the masterpieces of the present century.

A few years ago at Christmas, my sons presented me with a good radio-phonograph set. I listen to musical *chef-d'oeuvres* not only in moments of rest but quite regularly during my study and writing. Before starting work, I usually put on my phonograph several records of duos, trios, quartets, quintets, or piano masterpieces—not too loud and not too dissonant—and then effortlessly listen to their beauty while I am working over my problems. Going to bed, I turn on my bedside radio and listen to classical masterpieces broadcast by hi-fi stations until I fall asleep. When the Koussevitzkys were alive and we were younger, we used to attend the concerts of the Boston Symphony Orchestra regularly; now, with the Koussevitzkys gone and ourselves older, we satisfy our musical needs at home without wasting the time to drive to Boston or Cambridge; this way we can arrange the program of records best suited to our mood at a given moment.

In music, as in the other fine arts, my taste is broad but conservative. I enjoy great music of the centuries from the fourteenth to the beginning of the twentieth, but I do not care much about modern music. With a few exceptions I find it disorderly and cacophonic rather than beautiful. It says nothing either to my heart or to my soul. As a sociologist, from time to time I have to listen to it as a mirror of the present confusion of minds, anarchy of standards, of social antagonisms, and "cultural atonalities." As for so-called popular music—jazz, crooning, etc.—I simply cannot stand its vulgarity, monotony, and ugliness. Again as a sociologist, I have to follow it from time to time, but otherwise I am deeply sorry for the inventors of various musical instruments so horribly misused by the performers and broadcaster of this cacophony of sounds. I have the same regret and sympathy for the inventors of radio and television. Little did they think that their inventions would be used to broadcast precious vacuities, ugly atrocities, and vulgar shows. My use of these marvelous instruments is limited to listening to shallow "news in depth," to watching documentary telecasts of current events, animal life, nature's scenery, travelogues, and good plays.

For similar reasons I do not regularly read popular magazines or best-sellers. My mental equipment does not allow me to enjoy this "intellectual chewing gum." Instead of filling my mind with this "exhaust of sensate civilization" I prefer to stock it with the immortal values of human culture. In all frankness, I am fed up with the prevailing cult of ugliness and accentuation of the negative in the modern arts. No less tired am I of our creatively "being busy doing nothing." Our cultural activities seem largely to consist of monotonous transfusions of "a glittering vacuum into a glamorized emptiness," and vice versa. Blessed are those who can enjoy these operations. I am too old for these "cultural pleasures" and "civilized recreations." Leaving to everyone the freedom to be as crazy as he pleases, for my part I decisively prefer my old fashioned ways of loafing and recreation. They have tremendously enriched my life, its vigor, zest, and beauty.

Life Clouds

This chapter sketches my way of life as an Emeritus. On the whole this life is still worth living. Of course, as any human life, it has its own sorrows, infirmities, and disillusionments. I had a full share of these "tragic fall-outs" in my early life. I have also had "dark clouds" in my later years. If in this travelogue I passed by these "clouds" in silence, the reason for the omissions is well expressed by a Russian proverb, "Keep your troubles to yourself." To this reason I can add a philosophical consolation: Like sky-clouds, our life-clouds come and go. If they do not by their "tragic fall-outs" impair our physical, mental, and moral integrity, they enrich rather than impoverish the meaningfulness of human life. A merely "fine and dandy" life, untouched by the sense of the tragic, is a shallow life. With this consolation I end this chapter.

CHAPTER SEVENTEEN

Reflections on the Journey

The travelogue of my journey will conclude with a few observations. I am glad I have had the great privilege of making this journey and am deeply grateful to the forces that made it possible. I value this blessing so highly that, to repeat Benjamin Franklin's expression, I would not mind living its second edition—revised and corrected, if possible. . . .

As I write these lines, in the human world around me the deadliest storm is raging. The very destiny of mankind is being weighed in the balance of life and death. The forces of the dying sensate order are furiously destroying everything that stands in their way. In the name of "God," "progress," "civilization," "communism," "democracy," "freedom," "capitalism," "the dignity of Man," and other shibboleths they are uprooting these very values, murdering millions of human beings, threatening man's very survival and tending to turn this beautiful planet into an "abomination of desolation."

From a strictly selfish standpoint, I am neither frightened nor surprised by the deadly tornado. The worst it can do to me is to spoil and shorten the last leg of my journey. Beyond this damage it cannot hurt me in any serious way. For a person of my age it does not make a great deal of difference whether he lives for a few more years amidst the growing infirmities of my "brother-body," or whether he is in the next moment blown to pieces by a "civilized, scientific" bomb, either *in augmentum gloriae nominis Dei* or for the sake of "the greatest happiness of the greatest number" so unashamedly promised by communism, capitalism, democracy, totalitarianism, and other hollow cults of our time. Even this damage could be compensated by the fact that the storm's fireworks would make the last part of my life highly exciting and free from the boredom of monotonous day-to-day living.

Not being frightened by the storm, neither am I surprised by it: more than thirty years ago I diagnosed its nature correctly and predicted its momentous explosions. Since that time I have repeatedly warned my fellow men of its gathering fury, have urged them to prepare themselves for its blows and, whenever and wherever possible, have tried to prevent and mitigate its devastations. I have taken similar steps for the protection of my own integrity and peace of mind. First, so as not to be a party to the storm-brewing forces of the dying sensate order, I have alienated myself from its hollow values, sham-truths, and highfalutin pretenses. I deliberately became "a stranger" to its glittering vacuities, short-lived "successes," to its hypocrisy, lust for power, and "civilized bestiality."

Second, to guide myself through the chaos of the Sensate *Gotterdammerung* I completed my building of the Integral *Weltanschauung*—an integral system of science, religion, philosophy, sociology, psychology, ethics, politics, economics, and the fine arts. In my mentality and conduct this *Weltanschauung* replaced the tattered remnants of the obsolescent Sensate philosophy.

Unifying into one harmonious whole the universal and perennial values evident in Sensate as well as Ideational *Weltanschauungen,* and being free from the false values of each, the Integral standpoint has served me much more adequately than any other viewpoint. Reuniting into one *summum bonum* the supreme Trinity of Truth, Goodness, and Beauty, wrongly divorced from one another by Sensate mentality—Integralism has given me a firm foundation for maintenance of my integrity and has wisely guided my conduct amidst the bloody debris of the crumbling Sensate civilization. I have no missionary zeal to convert anyone to this Integral "denomination" but I would not be surprised if it proves to be helpful to many who are lost in the mental and moral confusion of our time.

Third, desirous to mitigate the devastations of the deadly storm and to prevent its future recurrence, I began our studies of creative, unselfish love. Together with creative Truth and Beauty these three are the only real powers that can help in this mitigation and prevention.

In these three ways I prepared myself well to meet, undismayed, the deadliest storm now raging in the human world. These steps have insulated me against its worst blows, including death itself.

Unfortunately I cannot say the same about the decadent Sensate part of humanity and its leaders. They seemingly are still not fully aware of the most critical state mankind is in now, nor about the merciless ultimatum given to man by mysterious Providence or capricious chance: "Perish by your own hand from your own folly and beastliness or rise to a higher mental, moral, and social level by the grace of constructive creativity and unselfish love."

So far the Sensate power-elites of the West and the East, and a large portion of humanity have not met this ultimatum squarely. Born and reared in the decadent Sensate atmosphere, they still believe in, live by, and act according to the moribund precepts of this disintegrating sociocultural order. Instead of solving their problems by constructive creativity, they fruitlessly continue to solve them by bombs and missiles. In place of resolving their conflicts by following the precepts of the *Sermon on the Mount* they still try to settle them by mutual extermination, naked force, and fraud. Pursuing their power-policies, these "grave-diggers of man and civilization" have cast to the winds all divine and human laws. Unashamedly they vie now in striking "the first blow" in their tribal wars of murdering untold millions of human beings. No wonder, therefore, that instead of creating a happy millenium these blind leaders and their sheepish followers have led mankind from one catastrophe to another until they have brought the whole human race to the verge of unglorious death. If left unrestrained by the truly creative forces of man, they would certainly terminate man's life and creative mission on this planet.

I am not confident, but I still hope, that man's constructive genius, at the last perilous hour, will be able to prevent the *dies irae* of his doom. If it is averted, I wish better luck to future generations in growing nobler, wiser, and more creative than we are. If they could transcend the main weakness of human nature and could realize fully its highest potentialities, they would undoubtedly create a much finer personal, cultural, and social order in the human universe than have past and present generations. In this sense they would fulfill Nietzsche's dictum: "Contemporary man is a shame and disgrace; man must be overcome and transcended." From the distance separating me from such generations, I salute and welcome these superhuman offsprings of our human race.

With this anguish and hope for the future of man I shall end the story of my own journey by repeating the concluding lines of my *Leaves from a Russian Diary:*

> *Whatever may happen in the future, I know that I have learned three things which will forever remain convictions of my heart as well as of my mind. Life, even the hardest life, is the most beautiful, wonderful, and miraculous treasure in the world. Fulfillment of duty is another beautiful thing, making life happy and giving to the soul the inconquerable force to sustain ideals—this is my second conviction. And my third is that cruelty, hatred, and injustice never can and never will be able to create a mental, moral, or material millenium.*